The Life of
JAMES SHARP
Archbishop of St Andrews

The Life of
JAMES SHARP
Archbishop of St Andrews
1618–1679

A Political Biography

JULIA BUCKROYD

JOHN DONALD PUBLISHERS LTD
EDINBURGH

for my darling B
without whom not

ISBN 0 85976 184 3

Distributed in the United States of America and Canada by Humanities Press Inc., Atlantic Highlands, NJ 07716, USA.

The publishers acknowledge the financial assistance of the Scottish Arts Council in the publication of this volume.

Phototypeset by Quorn Selective Repro, Loughborough.
Printed in Great Britian by Bell & Bain Ltd., Glasgow

Preface

This biography arose out of my investigations into the ecclesiastical policies of the Restoration government of Scotland. Although there is a large amount of writing on Sharp from the presbyterian point of view, it proved impossible to find any rational account of Sharp's motives and intentions or any sympathetic consideration of him at all. I have therefore attempted to fill that gap.

I have been fortunate to be able to make use of manuscripts in the National Library of Scotland, particularly the Yester Papers and the collection of the letters of Sharp and Alexander Burnet. I have also made use of the Lauderdale Papers in the British Museum, and Justiciary Court Records in the Scottish Record Office.

There are only two contemporary accounts of Sharp's life on which any reliance can be placed for biographical information: *A True and Impartial, Account of the Life of the Most Reverend Father in God Dr James Sharp*, 1723, a biography which claims to have been written some years earlier, and which is laudatory in tone; the second account is *The Life of Mr James Sharp, Archbishop of St Andrews* [n.p.], 1678, which abuses Sharp at length. Of the two the first is the more reliable because it attempts to back up its statements with documentary proof.

There are also three other accounts of Sharp's life, all derivative. One is a manuscript in the University Library, St Andrews (MS. DA 770 F2) and is entitled *Accounts of Scottish Bishops*. It contains a brief life of Sharp, written about 1725, which derives from the *True and Impartial Account* and contains little additional factual material, but is concerned to blacken Sharp's character. The third account is an extremely rare work, *The Life and Transactions of J. Sharp*, published in 1786 and available to my knowledge only in the David Hay Fleming Library in St Andrews and the British Museum. It too is concerned to blacken Sharp's character and relies heavily on the *Life* to do so.

In 1839 *The Life and Times of Archbishop Sharp* by Thomas Stephen was published in London. This is the only full-length biography ever written of Sharp. Unfortunately the author's grasp of Scottish history was poor and he was concerned almost exclusively to vindicate Sharp. This he did by relying heavily on the *True and Impartial Account*.

A much more scholarly evaluation was attempted by Osmund Airy, editor of the *Lauderdale Papers*, towards the end of the century. In the introduction to the second volume of the *Lauderdale Papers* of 1885 and in an article in the *Scottish Review* for 1884 he attempted to use the documentary evidence he had unearthed as editor. He was very harshly critical of Sharp and his work gave fresh authority to the interpretation favoured by Wodrow of Sharp as villain.

A thesis for Edinburgh University by A. T. Miller completed in 1946 is the last major piece of work to have been done on Sharp. This provided a comprehensive survey of the published sources, but used little in the way of manuscripts.

Acknowledgements

In preparing this book I have been indebted for assistance to the staff of the National Library of Scotland, the Scottish Record Office and the British Library Manuscripts Department. I owe a particular debt of gratitude to the staff of the David Hay Fleming Library, St Andrews and to Mr R. N. Smart, the Keeper of the Muniments, St Andrews University, and also to the minister and Kirk Session of the parish of Crail for permission to read the transcription of the Kirk Session Records. I have also been helped and encouraged by the interest of the Earl of Lauderdale, Sir Alexander Sharp-Bethune, John Tuckwell of John Donald Publishers, Professor Gordon Rupp, Professor Gordon Donaldson, Professor Ian Cowan and members of the Institute of Historical Research of the University of London.

The jacket illustration, a portrait of James Sharp after Lely, is from a painting in the collection of the Scottish National Portrait Gallery, and is reproduced by kind permission of the National Galleries of Scotland.

Contents

1

Introduction

On Saturday 3 May 1679 James Sharp, Archbishop of St Andrews, Primate of all Scotland and one of his Majesty King Charles II's privy councillors, was brutally murdered. The murder took place as he was travelling home from a meeting of the privy council in Edinburgh to his residence in St Andrews. It happened only two miles from St. Andrews, on Magus Muir, in broad daylight, at about midday.

Sharp had attended a meeting of the council on Thursday 1 May, and on Friday, accompanied by his daughter Isabel, had travelled homewards by coach. They spent Friday night at the home of a friend, Captain Seaton, who lived in the village of Kennoway in Fife, and on Saturday morning set off for St Andrews at about nine or ten o'clock. They had with them a retinue of five servants — a sixth had been sent to pay the archbishop's respects to the Earl of Crawford whose home was nearby. The party was well on the way home and had just passed through the tiny village of Magus when the coachman noticed that they were being pursued by a band of mounted men. Ahead lay a lonely stretch of moor. No good office could be expected from the gang whose galloping horses were rapidly bringing them closer. St Andrews was not far, only two or three miles. Sharp ordered the coachman to whip up the horses and make a run for it. For some time the archbishop's sleek coach horses managed to keep ahead, dragging the coach along the rough highway, but one of the pursuers drew level. As he came alongside the coach he fired into it and then managed to bring the horses to a halt, slashed at the postillion's face with his sword, wounded the leading horse and grabbed the reins.

Sharp was unhurt. One of the bullets had grazed his chest and had been fired at such close range that his clothes had been scorched but Isabel had stopped the fabric from smouldering. As the coach lurched to a halt the other pursuers drew up, nine of them altogether. They opened the door of the coach and forced Sharp out, stabbing him in the kidneys as they did so. Isabel was hustled out of the way with the servants. There could be no doubt what fate was intended for the archbishop and he fell on his knees, begging them to spare his life. He was again struck with a sword, this time above his right eye. To his pleas for mercy his attackers replied that he was but receiving his just deserts for his own cruelty and injustice. Sharp lifted his hands in prayer and as he did so they slashed at his arms and set about him. They hacked at his head with such force that they split his skull, exposing his brain and killing him instantly.

1

A contemporary engraving of the murder of Archbishop James Sharp on the Magus Muir, near St. Andrews.

Isabel and the servants had been obliged to look on while this ghastly scene took place. The servants had done their best to protect their master, but were hopelessly outnumbered. The postillion and the coachman had between them managed to keep up the pace of the coach for half a mile or more. Even when the leader of the attackers had drawn level the postillion had refused to rein in the horses until he was wounded and the coachman had used his whip to try to keep off the pursuers. One of the two mounted servants had tried to use his gun, but both of them were dismounted and disarmed. While the murder took place, Isabel and the servants were guarded by two of the gang. They made no further resistance, although when her father was wounded Isabel screamed so loudly that she was heard in Magus village more than half a mile away.

Once Sharp was dead the assassins did not immediately leave the scene of the crime. First they searched Isabel, the servants and the coach. They were looking for papers and arms, and what they found they took. They may also have taken some valuables. With these spoils they rode off only to come almost immediately upon the servant sent to the Earl of Crawford's house. They forced him to dismount and drove away his horse and then, pausing only to collect their cloaks which had been discarded during the chase, they left the way they had come, 'riding', as one witness observed, 'less hastily than when they had come'.

Isabel and the servants, left alone once more, loaded the battered blood-soaked corpse in to the coach and with their melancholy burden made their way to St Andrews.[1]

The death in this manner of the single most important man in Scotland in 1679 raises profound questions about him and about Restoration Scotland. Who was Sharp? How had he become archbishop in a presbyterian country? What enemies had he made to inspire the hatred which prompted his murder? What was the state of Scotland when such animosities could flourish and be acted out? What was Sharp's role in public life that it had made him the target for assassins' swords and bullets?

These are the issues with which this biography is concerned.

2
Early Years, 1618–1648

James Sharp was murdered on 3 May, 1679; on 17 May he was given a State funeral in St Andrews. The forms of the funeral procession and of the service at Holy Trinity church, followed by the burial in the abbey grounds, were prescribed and recorded by the Lord Lyon, King at Arms, whose responsibility it was to organise such occasions. The order of the funeral procession — something of an art form at this period — was laid down in minute detail, beginning with

> Old men to the number of Sextie in mourning with hoods and Gowns Each bearing a staff on the same the Armes of the Archiepiscopall Sea impaled with those of the defunct and haveing on the Shoulders letters for his name and age[1]

and continuing with horses, footmen, trumpets, magistrates, university professors, ministers, gentlemen and knights, nobility, and a display of the arms of Sharp's family, on to heralds and a macabre display of the coach in which Sharp had been travelling, with the bloodstained gown he had been wearing.

The funeral was that of a great man, the archbishop of St Andrews and a Privy Councillor, and was without question designed to impress. The Precedency Book which records these details records similar funerals provided for the highest-ranking nobility in Scotland. The Duke of Rothes, for example, who died the following year, 1680, was provided with a similar celebration.

What clues do the funeral and other sources give to the nature of Sharp's background? There were four branches of his family whose arms were displayed in the funeral procession, and all of these were lairds. Much of the magnificence, dignity and authority that Sharp could lay claim to was vested in his office of primate and archbishop and what else had fallen to him as a consequence, but his family was not entirely obscure and seems to have been well-established as fairly prosperous gentry.

The incompleteness of the Lord Lyon's records illustrates what is very apparent from any investigation of Sharp's background: little is known about his family or their circumstances. Contemporary records are few, while contemporary biographies are without exception violently partisan and correspondingly untrustworthy.[2]

This obscurity is in itself revealing since it demonstrates how remarkably Sharp had prospered by the exercise of his talents, rather than through the power and influence of his family. However, enough is known with some certainty about his father to place him quite accurately in seventeenth century Scottish society. At the time of James Sharp's birth in 1618, William Sharp his father was sheriff clerk of

Banff.[3] The role of sheriff clerk was that of a professional lawyer in the nationwide system of sheriff courts. The office of sheriff itself was a hereditary jurisdiction, held in this case in 1618 by the earl of Buchan.[4] The sheriff himself would almost certainly not have any legal training and so depended for the day-to-day running of the court on a professional lawyer, the sheriff clerk.

Other details of Sharp's family background are the subject of two contradictory accounts. *The Life of James Sharp*,[5] a very hostile biography, written and published during Sharp's lifetime, suggests that William as a young man was a servant of the Earl of Findlater who 'had him bred in letters' so that he could take care of the Earl's affairs. The *Life* claims that William got a degree, but remained a 'common clerk' until he left the Earl's service to become first a country lawyer, 'a landward Notar', and then, by the influence of Lord Findlater, sheriff clerk of Banff. According to this author, William's father had been a piper, which in seventeenth-century Scotland probably implied an itinerant beggar, and his mother had had to brew beer to support the family.

It is certain, however, in view of other available evidence, that Sharp's family was not so humble. *The True and Impartial Account of the Life of ... James Sharp*,[6] a very adulatory biography frankly written to defend him, gives an account of a rather more prosperous background which is supported better by other sources. In this account William Sharp's father was a merchant in Aberdeen, his grandfather a 'gentleman in Perthshire' and William was sent by his father to university in Aberdeen before he joined the Earl of Findlater's household. The same source asserts that William's maternal grandmother was also from the gentry, the daughter of the laird of Pitcur in Angus. This evidence of membership of the laird class is additionally supported by the undisputed fact that William married Isobel Lesley, the daughter of the laird of Kinninvy. Although this marriage is described by the author of the *Life* as being above William Sharp's station, and by the author of the *True and Impartial Account* as having been arranged with the help of the influence of the Earl of Findlater's wife, there is evidence to establish that when William became sheriff clerk of Banff in 1617 he was recognised as a member of the laird and professional class.

What is also evident from the story is that William had become sheriff clerk of Banff by a combination of talent, hard work, education and patronage. It offers an interesting sidelight on seventeenth-century society in Scotland that this should be so. Perhaps the Scottish Reformation of 1560 is the clearest demonstration that the Scottish political community was not exclusively aristocratic. The century 1560–1660 is one during which the Scottish gentry or middle class assumed a progressively more important role in national life. For a man of talent and education who was also prepared to apply himself, the way could be open to advancement; open that is, if the 'lad o' pairts' could find a patron. The patronage still rested with the landowning hierarchy. So William Sharp owed his advancement in part to the Earl of Findlater, and his security in his post as sheriff clerk to the sheriff, the Earl of Buchan.

James Sharp himself was perfectly willing to acknowledge that his father's relative success had been achieved with the benevolent patronage of the nobility. Thus in 1660, when he himself was in a position to convey favours as archbishop of St Andrews, and thus *ex officio* a member of the aristocracy, he wrote to Lauderdale:

> My father had a special dependence upon the late Earl of Buchan, upon which account I would do any good office within my reach to this earl, his son.[7]

What, then, William Sharp had won for himself and his family was first a theatre for the exercise of his talents and his education; secondly, security within a system. The sheriff clerk was housed in the Castle of Banff and lived there until his death in 1638. It appears moreover that he was succeeded in the post and in the Castle by his youngest son, Robert, until his death in turn in 1675.[8] Thirdly, William had won status within the community. He was a royal servant, a professional man and on the edges of the landowning class. This standing was sufficient for him to become an elder of Banff kirk session.[9]

From all this arose William's confidence in aspirations for his sons: James, born in 1618, William and Robert. If Scottish society was open for the father, then it could also be open for his sons.

The process of advancement began with education. The role of education for children in Scotland in the seventeenth century is to be understood in terms of the Reformation of 1560 and of Protestant theology. One of the bases of reformation theology was a confidence in the capacity of each believer to receive revelation and spiritual nourishment directly — 'the priesthood of all believers'. The agent of this spiritual growth was not, as in pre-Reformation theology, a sacramental system mediated through a priesthood, but the Scriptures, as studied and absorbed by the individual believer, guided and stimulated by the church. This theology was the motivation for the translation and use of the Scriptures in the vernacular. It was also the basis in Scotland for the emphasis on universal literacy.

The reformers in 1560 therefore, in their programme for the Reformation in Scotland, the Book of Discipline, urged the setting up of a school in every parish. This programme took far longer to realise than had been anticipated, but in 1620, as part of that ambition, Banff appointed a schoolmaster. The reformers had recommended, 'seeing that God hath determined that his church here in earth shall be taught not by angels but by men', that 'every several church have a Schoolmaster appointed, such a one as is able, at least, to teach Grammar, and the Latin tongue, if the town be of any reputation'.[10]

When the schoolmaster of Banff was appointed, his remit was more ambitious. His duties were described as follows:

> to teach, bring up and instruct the youth, such as shall be committed to his care and discipline, in the Latin and Greek grammars, [so they shall be] well versed with such authors, both poets and [prose] authors, as accord [with custom] and are used to be taught in any other schools within the burghs of this kingdom. And to such as please, likewise he shall teach the art of music and learn the youth to sing and play, and shall attend, instruct, examine and correct the said youth as becomes [him], and exercise all other points of his calling as becomes a dutiful master to do his disciples.[11]

What was being envisaged in Banff, then, was not a basic literacy, but an education in the classics and an acquaintance with the social graces as well. To have a classical education was to share in the common European cultural frame of reference in the seventeenth century, and to read Latin was to possess the necessary tool to enter the world of learning. Not until the late seventeenth century were textbooks and academic treatises written in anything but Latin. So James Sharp, attending the grammar school at Banff, was being grounded in the basis of all further instruction.

In sending his son to the school in Banff, where James acquitted himself well according to both the author of the *True and Impartial Account*, and that of the *Life*,[12] William Sharp was not only acting on the basis of his own experience that education was the key to advancement, he was also taking advantage of a social and intellectual trend in Scottish society towards an enlargement of the educated middle class. In one way, then, the education of James represented a creative and radical development in Scotland.

At another level, however, it should perhaps be noted that the education offered in Banff took notice whatever of the Renaissance, apart from the mention of Greek. It might then be true to say that James Sharp's basic education was conservative, even medieval. In later life Sharp was always intellectually and theologically on the conservative wing. Perhaps the basis of that attitude was laid in Banff grammar school.

By the same token an attempt to understand the significance of Sharp's family background suggests on the one hand an experience of success and upward mobility, but at the same time may also constitute a benign experience of an essentially conservative culture. True, William Sharp had been successful, but only in the context of aristocratic patronage. His post of sheriff clerk was a reward of merit and an opportunity for the exercise of professional skills, but at the same time it was a post of subordination to an artistocrat in whose hands power remained, and a position as a servant of a royalist and hierarchical regime. In that system power still lay with those who owned land, and landownership remained the theoretical basis of entitlement to participation in the government of the country. William Sharp's talents might therefore be useful, but as a man on the outer fringe of the landowning classes, he, in a traditional understanding of the distribution of power in the political community, participated only by permission of his patrons. Moreover Banff was in a part of the country where these conservative associations and attitudes were particularly strong.[13]

It is certainly true that James Sharp moved a long way from Banff and his family during his life, but its influence is perhaps not to be discounted in the formation of his attitudes. He at least never quite forgot where he came from. In his will he left 1,000 merks to the poor of Banff.[14]

In 1633, at the age of 15, Sharp embarked on the next stage of his education and matriculated as a student at King's College, Aberdeen.[15] The youth of the students had a considerable effect on the life they led. As undergraduates they were members of a society of scholars, but they were junior members. As such it was felt that they ought to be disciplined and restrained by the senior members of the society who stood *in loco parentis.* The life they led therefore was not unlike the regime of a nineteenth-century English boarding school. Each student had his hours of getting up and going to bed fixed. His classes were compulsory and he ate communally with his fellow students. Attendance at chapel was compulsory and a close watch was kept on his behaviour. His red student's gown was designed to make him conspicuous in public and thus bring his misdeeds to light so that they could be punished. A description of a day at King's College about 1600 gives a picture of a way of life which had probably changed little when Sharp first matriculated there thirty years later:

> The students get up at six when a bell rings and read until eight. Then they gather in the chapel for prayers. To prevent absentees the names of all the students are read and each must respond 'present', so that those not there can be listed for later punishment. After prayers the students return to their classes until nine and are then free until ten. A bell rings to bring them back to classes until eleven, and at that point all the students with their teachers gather together so that the students may each be assigned to their rightful place in the class. They spend the time until twelve in discussion and at noon each student asks permission to return home for a meal ... from which they do not return before two. From two until about five they stay in their own classrooms, then when the bell goes all the students and the teachers gather for prayers. Before service there is a roll call as in the morning. After prayers everyone goes home for dinner. At eight they are taught philosophy so they return to the college, and then at nine they go to bed.[16]

Probably there were a good number of opportunities for students to evade at least some of the rigours of such a timetable. Certainly it was frequently found necessary to repeat injunctions concerning the behaviour of the young men. The only real escape, though, was for those members of the nobility who had brought their own tutors with them to university, and were thus regarded as being more his responsibility than that of the university authorities. A young heir to an earldom might spend a few very agreeable years at college if his tutor were sufficiently indulgent, as for example the young Montrose seems to have done at St Andrews.[17] But Sharp was certainly not in that class, and for him life as an undergraduate probably followed the pattern of 1600 fairly closely.

When he matriculated in 1633 Sharp embarked on the traditional four-year arts degree. The set texts for the course were selected classical authors, particularly Aristotle, and the New Testament. These were studied under four headings: Greek, Logic, Moral Philosophy and Natural Philosophy. During Sharp's time at King's there was a tutor, known as a regent, for each of the four subjects. There were periodic examinations during the course, culminating in a final oral examination. This took place in public and consisted of an exposition and defence by the candidate of a proposition taken from the material studied during the course.[18] This form of examination, known as a thesis, must have been a particularly trying event for the student; however, it was an ordeal which Sharp evidently survived, for in 1637 he graduated as a Master of Arts.[19]

These four years were undoubtedly very important for Sharp's development. They can be understood in different ways. First he had earned his degree as a reward for proficiency in certain formal learning exercises. The inspiration for the syllabus was medieval and, like Sharp's earlier grammar school education, it had taken little account of the influence of the Renaissance and the modern world. By European standards it was an old-fashioned programme of study. On the other hand he had gained a qualification which was an essential prerequisite for entry to the professions.

In terms of intellectual formation however, Sharp had been a student in Aberdeen at a time of intense intellectual ferment in Scotland as a whole, and at a time when Aberdeen was very much influenced by the activities of Bishop Forbes and the circle he gathered round him.[20] As bishop of Aberdeen since 1618, Patrick Forbes had addressed himself with zeal to his duties as *ex officio* chancellor of the university, King's College, and its sister college, Marischal College. The result of his reforming zeal had been repairs to the buildings, an end to financial corruption and a general improvement in discipline. Sharp as an undergraduate had doubtless enjoyed the fruits of these improvements.

The more important part of Forbes's reforms, however, had dealt with academic innovations. Forbes was primarily interested in the universities as a training ground for the parish clergy. The Reformation in Scotland as elsewhere had reacted against the ignorance and poverty of the pre-Reformation clergy, by requiring high standards of education for ministers, and endowing them in turn with considerable status within the community. The reformers had hoped for a ministry of graduates; Forbes's vision was to improve the status of theology by making it a postgraduate study. In order to make this possible he instituted chairs of Divinity in both colleges in Aberdeen. Within a few years the calibre of the incumbents of these chairs — John Forbes, the bishop's son, at King's, and Robert Baron at Marischal — had attracted a whole 'galaxy of intellectuals', known to posterity as the Aberdeen Doctors. Their intention had been to revive the medieval notion of the doctorate which had fallen into disuse and disesteem since the reformation. The doctors thus educated would, it was anticipated, provide the church with leaders of the highest calibre.

Bishop Forbes died in 1635, but his influence and the prestige of the circle he had gathered round him were immense. Here was no formal learning exercise. To sit at the feet of the Aberdeen Doctors was to be a witness of and a participant in debate on current ecclesiastical disputes which had immediate political implications.

In the 1630s the long-term implications of the Reformation of 1560 in Scotland had by no means been completely worked out. In particular the relationship between church and state continued to be stormy. After the initial fervour and excitement of the Reformation, the development of the church had been guided, not by Knox, the prime mover of the Scottish Reformation, but by Andrew Melville, his successor. Under Melville's influence the office and function of a bishop had been replaced by a series of committees: the system of presbyterian church government. Melville had seen great value in a system in which no one minister enjoyed greater power because of his office than any other. This theory, the 'parity of ministers', had not however met with the approval of James VI, who saw the political value to the crown of an episcopal system where the king had a hand in the appointment of the bishops. The parity of ministers had also been associated with far-reaching claims by Melville and his associates to power and influence within the state. As a result James had countered the threat of ministerial dominance with the re-introduction of bishops. The appointment of the key figures within the church was thus once more in royal hands. This step had been accompanied by attempts by the king to make the Scottish church more like the English in matters of ecclesiastical ceremony. In 1618 this policy culminated in the introduction of the Five Articles, which required, among other things, kneeling at Communion and observation of the festivals of the Christian year.

These developments, particularly as they affected the form of worship, were not welcome to all Scots. The debate they provoked was intensified by the actions of Charles I who succeeded his father in 1625. Charles was as determined to retain bishops and to impose ritual as his father had been, but far less skilful in achieving his ends. His proclamation requiring use of a Scottish form of the English Prayer Book in 1636 crystallised much of the resentment felt against him among the ministers. Its use in 1637 provided the occasion for a riot in Edinburgh and provoked widespread protest.

It was at this period that Sharp was a student in Aberdeen under the Doctors. In the revolutionary atmosphere now developing in Scotland, their attitudes differed profoundly from those of their brethren of the ministry in Edinburgh. The radicals in the south looked back with nostalgia to the days before James had revived the office of bishop, and saw the king's intervention in church government and worship as a betrayal of the Reformation. Far removed from the centre of events, and in a part of Scotland traditionally strongly royalist and episcopal, the Aberdeen Doctors saw the contemporary issues in a much longer perspective. They were prepared to maintain that bishops were a longstanding and useful institution in the church. They were willing to concede that episcopacy was not a necessary institution in the Christian church of any century, but it was certainly, they felt, a desirable one.

To the radicals' claim that the king had exceeded his authority as 'godly ruler' in introducing bishops and ceremonies, the Doctors replied that the king had no authority over fundamental matters in the church, such as doctrine, but had the right to alter less important matters. The Doctors believed, as the radicals did not, that issues of church government and ceremonial were of secondary importance only. If the king chose to alter them, the Doctors maintained, it was within his power to do so, and it was the duty of the subject to obey.

The debate had more than ecclesiastical implications, of course. In a time of revolution in Scotland, the Doctors were placing themselves on the side of the conservatives and of the king. When in 1638 the National Covenant was drawn up in Edinburgh, the city of Aberdeen, led by the Doctors, refused to support it. The National Covenant constituted a comprehensive indictment of Charles I's government. To royalists and conservatives such as the Doctors, it was unacceptable. Their resistance was intolerable to the radicals in Edinburgh. In November 1638 those who would not sign the Covenant were threatened with punishment, and gradually over the next two years Aberdeen was obliged to give at least token assent to it.

Initially Sharp seems to have identified himself with the Aberdeen Doctors. Both the author of the *Life* and of the *True and Impartial Account* suggest that he remained in Aberdeen until at least 1638. According to the *True and Impartial Account*, he stayed to study theology with Dr Forbes, the bishop's brother, and Dr Baron with whom he was friendly.[21] It looks as though Sharp was embarking on postgraduate study for a doctorate, just as Bishop Forbes had envisaged. In its turn that probably indicates Sharp's ability and promise as a student and future churchman.

Despite this association with the Doctors, both biographers agree that in or about 1638 Sharp went to England with the object of finding a job in the church there. The author of the *True and Impartial Account* alleges that Sharp met 'Dr Sanderson, Dr Hammond and Dr Taylor', and also visited Oxford and Cambridge.[22] Presumably this was a way of conveying that Sharp was well thought of in England and in touch with major theological figures of the day. There is no means of verifying these assertions, but on the face of it they seem unlikely in that none of the three theologians was well known at this point and none of them was at either university.

It is useful nonetheless to consider why Sharp might have left Aberdeen and what he was about during the years until he surfaces as a junior academic, a regent, at St Andrews university in 1642. The massive and general support given to the National Covenant in 1638 and the energy with which the resistance of the Aberdeen Doctors was confronted by the radicals within the church demonstrated very rapidly to what extent the Doctors constituted a conservative minority within Scotland. Up to 1637 it might well have been possible to see them as the authors of one of a number of current theories of relationships between church and state. By 1638 it seems certain that their views were evidently those of a conservative minority and implied a capitulation to the interventions of Charles I in Scottish church and political life. English society and English kingship were both more used to this model than Scottish, so it might not be too surprising that a young disciple of the Doctors should think of making a future in England at a time when the country was not yet in such a ferment over Charles's rule as Scotland. In practical terms it would have been impossible for a protégé of the Doctors to remain studying in Aberdeen when his mentors were known opponents of the Covenant.

If however Sharp did imagine that England would be more congenial, there is no record that he ever obtained any preferment there, and indeed it seems likely that he would have found himself somewhat out of sympathy with English episcopacy about the year 1640. For the preceding fifteen years the church in England had been under continuing pressure from the Archbishop of Canterbury, William Laud, and his supporters, to introduce the doctrines and practices of the Dutch theologian, Arminius. Arminius's aim had been to correct what he felt was an undue stress on the doctrine of predestination in protestant churches. The practical consequence of his views in English worship had been a re-emphasis on the importance of the sacraments, particularly communion, as a means of grace to be reverently used by all Christians. In turn this re-emphasis had brought about the resumption of pre-Reformation practices such as kneeling at Communion and placing the Communion table against the east wall of the church. It was these innovations and others associated with them which had so distressed the Scottish church in the years immediately preceding the drawing up of the Covenant.

Now although Sharp had studied under the Aberdeen Doctors who favoured the acceptance of these rituals and supported an episcopal form of church government, he had not thereby been exposed to Arminian doctrine. The attitude of the Doctors towards the innovations was based on their views on church order, and not on the theological implications. The Doctors, and the vast majority of the Scottish church with them, were not Arminians, but Calvinists. Sharp had far more in common theologically with the Covenanting ministers than with the English Arminians. Although therefore the whole period of Sharp's time in England is obscure and can only on present evidence be the subject of conjecture, his return to Scotland is not unexpected on theological grounds alone.

By early 1642 Sharp was employed at St Andrews university as a regent.[23] The precise date of his arrival there is unknown but his candidature was supported by two impressive referees and was almost certainly made on academic grounds. According to his biographers Sharp was recommended for the post at St Andrews by Alexander Henderson, one of the most prominent of the Covenanting ministers, and was supported also by the Earl of Rothes, likewise a Covenanter of importance and a local nobleman with a strong interest in St Andrews university. The account given by the *True and Impartial Account* is that on his way home from England Sharp met James McGill of Cranston, later Viscount Oxenford, who took him to his home. There he met the Earl of Rothes and through his influence was chosen as a regent for St Leonard's College.[24] The *Life's* version is that Sharp got to know Alexander Henderson who was then in London as Commissioner for the Church of Scotland and from him got a recommendation for a regent's place.[25] In 1641 a Commission had been appointed to visit the university with a view to its reform.[26] In 1642 that body began its work under the leadership of Henderson. It therefore seems most probable that Sharp was appointed on the strength of his academic record as one of those to put the reforms into practice.

In addition, however, it seems most unlikely that Sharp could have been given this post had his reputation been that of a continuing disciple of the Aberdeen Doctors. In order to take up his post as regent, for example, he would have been required to sign the Covenant.[27] It is difficult, but perhaps possible, to trace the process which brought the pupil of Forbes and Baron to become the protégé of Henderson. One strand in that process is the theological common ground in Calvinism which had already been discussed. Another strand also already mentioned is Sharp's ability; the man marked out by the Doctors was clearly also noticed by Henderson. But perhaps the most important element in the process was Sharp's own ambition and appetite for advancement. One way of describing Sharp's time in England would be as the attempt of a man who refused to throw in his lot with the defeated minority in Scotland, but instead tried to find a situation where the views of his teachers and mentors were the views of the ascendant majority. It seems probable that England had proved less congenial than Sharp had hoped, and certainly not a theatre for his advancement. His solution may have been to return to Scotland and put his talents at the disposal of the Covenant party.

The pattern of Sharp's father's life had been to find a mentor who would promote him as an undoubtedly able man. This was the situation which his son James had created for himself with the Aberdeen Doctors. Changes in political and ecclesiastical fashions had however destroyed the power and influence of those first mentors. Exile in England was no solution for a man whose hope was to make a significant contribution to the church in his own country — for why else would he have embarked on graduate work with the Doctors? His solution was to seek other more powerful mentors, Alexander Henderson and the Earl of Rothes, and to ally himself with the men of the future.

This change of direction in Sharp's life has been savagely criticised by his hostile biographers, both at the time and since. The assumption had been made that his motives were entirely unworthy and lacking in principle. But this interpretation is not the only one that can be made. Sharp was certainly a pragmatist and has left no body of theoretical writing on the issues of his day. A benign interpretation of this combination of circumstances might suggest a man who did not enjoy being pushed to any extreme position — as he certainly must have been had he held to his original identification with the Doctors. Ironically one of their gifts to him may have been their own reluctance to identify one particular form of church government or theology as absolutely true for all time. In his developing career in the church, Sharp became the man reluctant to take up any inflexible position. Perhaps that can be understood not so much as base opportunism but more as maintaining an attitude of mind that refrained from absolute judgments. He was to be recognised almost immediately in the church as a reconciler and a negotiator of great talent. It may not be unreasonable to suppose that these qualities were those which earned him his new-found post at St Andrews.

St Andrews was the oldest of the four Scottish universities and consisted by the time of the Reformation of three colleges, St Salvator's, St Leonard's and St Mary's. In 1579 post-Reformation re-organisation had made St Mary's a theological college, while St Salvator's and St Leonard's became arts colleges. It was to St Leonard's college that Sharp was appointed. The post of regent was a junior academic appointment. In the medieval universities the regent had been in charge of a year group throughout its four-year undergraduate career. It had been one of the reforms attempted after the Reformation to assign instead a regent to each of the four subjects: Greek, Logic, Moral Philosophy and Natural Philosophy. This change permitted a degree of academic specialisation and thus helped raise the standard. Sharp had been fortunate enough to spend his time at King's College during the brief period when this reform had been in force there. An attempt to do the same at St Andrews had largely failed so that Sharp was now responsible for taking a year group through its course.

Sharp's duties as regent were partly academic and partly moral. He was required to teach his pupils. There still exist lecture notes taken down by one of his students from logic lectures delivered between 1643 and 1645. The lectures were mainly on Aristotle and perhaps were less than perfectly enthralling since the student enlivened his notebook with sketches of the lecturer. Research on these notes suggests that they were rather a conventional treatment of the subject.[28] Perhaps Sharp had been wise enough to conserve his own notes from Aberdeen.

The moral welfare of the students was also however Sharp's concern. The duties of a regent included expounding 'controversies of religion' to the students on Sunday mornings before public worship. He himself was undoubtedly required to attend daily worship in the university community and in general to behave himself as an exemplar for the youths in his care. St Andrews was a small town and the regents were men of some status in the community. No doubt Sharp's conduct and that of his fellow-regents was the object of local interest and scrutiny.

Sharp does not seem to have escaped being the object of gossip during his time as a regent. The author of the *Life* alleges that he had fathered a child on a local woman in St Andrews and then had summarily murdered the fruit of his fornication. Such a crime was certainly enough to have sent him to the gallows. No evidence survives that any charges were made against him or any investigation carried out. *The True and Impartial Account* dismisses the whole story as the ravings of an unbalanced woman in the town.[29]

Another story retailed by both of Sharp's biographers was of a scuffle or a brawl between him and another regent, Mr John Sinclair.[30] Sinclair is said to have been a fellow-candidate for the regent's job at St Leonard's which Sharp got. He was probably appointed two years later in 1644 and was certainly in office in 1645.[31] It seems probable that relations between the two men might well have been difficult since they had been competitors for the same job. Both biographers give an account of a quarrel between them at the college table in the presence of the other senior masters of the college. According to the author of the *True and Impartial Account* the subject of the argument was church government; he pictures Sharp upholding the arguments of the English episcopal theologians. This fits in well with the author's attempt to show Sharp as a lifelong supporter of episcopacy, but it does not fit in with what else can be ascertained about Sharp's intellectual development to this date. Whatever the subject of the quarrel, both authors assert that Sharp eventually hit Sinclair. According to the *True and Impartial Account* this was the result of the provocation of being flatly contradicted by Sinclair. The result appears to have been a temporary period of disgrace for Sharp, but evidently it was not regarded very seriously since before long he seems to have been restored to favour among the senior academics.

It is hard on the basis of such evidence to have much feeling for what these reports might indicate about Sharp, but the most certain evidence for his generally recognised probity is his advancement to the parish ministry, with the approval of the presbytery of St Andrews, in 1648. One of the results of the Covenanting revolution had been the initiation of reforms within the church. In the 1640s a strenuous effort was made to purge the ministry of men whose way of life left them open to suspicion or blame. Sharp would certainly not have been accepted for the ministry had there been any stain on his character. The reformers' zeal was further reflected in the procedure for examining candidates. In November 1647 the presbytery of St Andrews received the presentation from the Earl of Crawford, patron of the parish of Crail, nominating and presenting James Sharp to be minister at Crail and requiring the presbytery to 'enter him to his trials'. For three months, from November 1647 until January 1648, Sharp was repeatedly summoned before the presbytery to be examined on different aspects of a minister's duties and knowledge. Even though the parish sent representatives to the presbytery to urge him to hurry with the trials because they had been without a minister for several years, the procedure was still lengthy and careful. Among other tasks, Sharp was required to submit an essay on a subject chosen by the presbytery, to preach a sermon suitable for a congregation, and to answer questions arising from the catechism. By the end of January the presbytery were satisfied and arrangements were made for Sharp's formal admission to his parish. The minutes for 27 January read: 'The Presbytery met at Crail for the admission of Mr James Sharp minister there, where Mr James Bruce did preach'.[32]

So Sharp was launched on his career as a churchman. What might that have meant to him? His father's experience had been to achieve success as the servant of the aristocracy. He had power, but it was power in subordination to a continuing social and political system of aristocratic control. The only section of the community that had been able to challenge that control in seventeenth-century Scotland was the church. It had been true before the Reformation, but much more obviously true since. In the late 1630s ministers were involved in political life and policy-making in a way that was unprecedented. If Sharp was looking for a way in which he as a man of obscure and non-noble background could satisfy his ambitions, then in the Scottish society of his day the church was the only route. Moreover the church was the vehicle for all kinds of ideas and concepts that after the seventeenth century became separate and discrete. In the Scotland of the 1630s the church provided the language in which political issues were discussed. There was neither a secular language nor a secular profession through which a man of non-noble background could take part in public policy-making.

What part in all this did religious conviction play for Sharp? His enemies during the Restoration period certainly thought of him as a man who was not at all pious or 'sanctified'. On the other hand there is nowhere any serious suggestion that Sharp's behaviour was other than correct. Most probably, to ask whether Sharp was 'religious' or whether he entered the church in order to attain prominence and success is to set up an apposition that would have been meaningless to Sharp and his contemporaries. The church and religion embraced a vastly greater spectrum of functions and ideas than in subsequent centuries. Also it is very doubtful if unbelief was a concept available to Scots in the 1630s, although no doubt practical atheism flourished. The question whether Sharp was religious or a believer is therefore probably unanswerable. All that can be said is that he was sufficiently religious to satisfy the exacting requirements of his fellow ministers in 1648 and to win their approbation as a coming man during his time as minister of Crail.

Crail in the seventeenth century was a prosperous town. As a royal burgh it was administered by a provost and town council and had the right to send representatives to the Convention of Royal Burghs. It was therefore a place with some civic pride and consciousness. The main activity in the town was the fishing and curing of herring, but its harbour also enabled it to engage in a wider range of shipping and trading activities. In the long term Crail was to decline because of the development of west-coast ports, but in the middle of the century it was still one of the chain of busy ports along the coast of Fife.[33]

Sharp was therefore going to take his place in a thriving community, probably of something less than one thousand inhabitants. Such a figure seems very small now, but in the seventeenth century it placed Crail in the rank of medium-sized communities. Appointment as minister of Crail was therefore no relegation to a backwater. Within the presbytery of St Andrews, Crail had status second only to that of St Andrews itself. None of the other seventeen communities in the presbytery except St Andrews had had a second minister during the early part of the century, as Crail had done.[34] It was therefore a recognition of Sharp's abilities by his brethren that he should be placed in the parish of Crail at his entrance to the ministry. The records of the parish, as well as Sharp's subsequent career, indicate that the confidence of his fellow-ministers was not misplaced.

The parish had been vacant since 1645 when the previous incumbent had died. Sharp's first act was therefore to galvanise it into activity once more. The usual procedure in time of vacancy was for the presbytery to supply a preacher as often as possible and to leave the day-to-day administration of the parish in the hands of the Kirk Session. Inevitably this placed a heavy burden on a few men, which could not always be sustained. In Crail any systematic minuting of church business had apparently been abandoned. Almost as soon as he arrived Sharp organised the revival of the Kirk Session records. These survive today and are the major source of information on Sharp's time in Crail.[35]

The Session consisted initially of about six elders, later increased to nine, with the minister as chairman. In April 1648, at the first meeting with the new minister, the master of the grammar school was appointed Session clerk. The functions of the Session were to administer the finances of the parish; to take care of the maintenance of the church; to provide for those in distress; and most obviously to superintend the behaviour of the parishioners and to punish any lapses. The picture that emerges from the records is of a minister and elders extraordinarily diligent in carrying out these functions. Throughout his time in Crail, except for periods when Sharp was absent in England, a Kirk Session meeting was held about once a fortnight. This was maintained even when Sharp was a member of national committees of the church and was travelling frequently to Stirling and Perth to attend their meetings.

One indication of the new minister's energy was that the question of the maintenance of the church was tackled. During the vacancy the church had evidently not been properly maintained, and almost immediately the heritors were approached about the necessity of repairs. They, particularly Erskine of Cambo, were no more willing than previously to honour their obligations. For the next ten years the repair of the church was a recurring subject of discussion in the Session.

Sharp also seems to have been a frequent preacher. Judging from the cases brought before the Session for failure to attend sermon, he preached twice on Sunday and also during the week. A surviving manuscript indicates that he took his turn also to preach at presbytery meetings.[36] At a time when the vast majority of the parishioners would be unable to read, their instruction on religious matters was the entire responsibility of the minister. In addition Calvinist theology considered that the preaching of the Word formed the chief means of grace for the Christian elect. For these reasons much emphasis had been placed on the minister's duty to preach, ever since the Reformation in Scotland. To preach twice on Sundays, and during the week as well, fulfilled even the most stringent requirements and highest hopes of the General Assembly. Mention of pre-Communion catechising further suggests a minister alive to his duties as instructor and teacher.

The major preoccupation of the Kirk Session was undoubtedly discipline, and in this Sharp seems on the whole to have stood for moderation. There is a suspicion that the parish was urgently in need of reform when Sharp arrived. The lack of records and the need for immediate repair to the church suggest as much. More dramatically, it seems possible that there were brothels in the town. Soon after Sharp arrived the Session recommended to the baillies of the town that they 'take order with loose women who keep houses by themselves'. Certainly the Session acted as if reform of behaviour were its most pressing task. Virtually every meeting was entirely given over to dealing with sexual offences and Sabbath breaking. The rest of the business discussed occupied very little time indeed.

To begin with some punishments were severe. A number of men and women were put in the jougs — an iron collar attached by a chain to a wall in which the culprit was secured for a certain length of time in the manner of the stocks. This was the punishment for persistent fornication or Sabbath breaking. It was not used after June 1649 except occasionally as a threat. The implication may be that by then the parishioners had been reduced to better order (or at least were more circumspect). But another explanation may be the intervention of the Cromwellian government of occupation which forbade ecclesiastical courts to impose civil penalties.[37] The vast majority of punishments consisted of formal rebukes, fines and public repentance, but the Session had the power to banish wrong-doers from the town, as being 'not worthy to live in a Christian society'. Initially there was a wave of such sentences, but again they stop quite soon. When in September 1656 the Session was considering the case of Elspeth Bradford, 'quadrilapse in fornication' and pregnant, banishment was discussed, but 'considering her present condition, near the time of her delivery, the Session conceive they cannot cause her presently remove out of town'. She was ultimately banished six months later.

The general impression given by the records is that Crail was a fairly ordinary parish and that the way in which its Kirk Session operated was fairly standard. There are really no grounds for thinking that Sharp was a particularly harsh minister as some biographers and modern-day anecdotal opinion tries to suggest. The supposition that punishments during Sharp's time were not cruel or excessive is strengthened by evidence of positive concern and compassion. Illegitimate children were baptised, collections were made for sufferers from misfortune in other parts of Scotland, widows' sons were educated or apprenticed, eight poor boys were educated at the Session's expense, payments and gifts of clothes were made to individuals in great need, collections were made for the poor in hard times, and a census was taken of those in need, with a view to helping them.

So far as the Kirk Session records go, therefore, there seems every reason to suppose that Sharp was a more than ordinarily diligent and effective shepherd of his flock. Nevertheless the *Life* was harshly critical of his ministry. He was accused of failure to preach, indifference to poor parishioners, too great an intimacy with the wealthier and more powerful members of the congregation and, especially, harsh treatment of those who had not adopted the General Assembly's political attitudes. Almost certainly these views arose from hostility to Sharp the archbishop rather than being founded upon an immediately contemporary assessment of Sharp the minister.

There seems no evidence to support most of the points made by the *Life*. What of the accusation of harsh treatment of those who had not adopted the General Assembly's political attitudes? In 1647 the Scottish nobility had made one last attempt to save Charles I from his enemies and from himself. In return for a promise that Charles would enforce presbyterian church government in England for a trial period of three years, the nobility promised to restore the king to his throne in England, by force if necessary. Force was necessary, and in 1648 a Scottish army marched into England to rescue the king. This agreement, known as the Engagement, was opposed by the General Assembly who regarded the plan that presbytery should be introduced as an experiment in England for three years as a betrayal. The failure of the expedition and the defeat of the army at Preston by Cromwell gave the church's view great moral authority. Accordingly in December 1648 the General Assembly decreed punishments for those who had supported the Engagement — the Engagers, as they were known.

In February 1649 Crail Kirk Session required supporters of the Engagement to make public acknowledgement of their fault before the congregation and to sign a declaration renouncing the Engagement. Since the Engagement had been a plan devised by the nobility, it is not surprising that its supporters in Crail were five of the most important members of the parish, Lord Balcomie and four lairds. The author of the *Life* alleges that this action over the Engagement was regarded at the time as unduly severe. In view of the continuing good relations that Sharp enjoyed with these men, shortly to be discussed, this allegation seems unlikely. What is almost certainly the case is that Sharp followed the order laid down by the General Assembly for the reception back into the church of repentant Engagers.

That Sharp's exercise of his functions as a minister was regarded as satisfactory by his fellow ministers can be deduced from his election to membership of the standing committee, or Commission, of the General Assembly. His political activities resulted in significant absences from Crail. In 1651 he made frequent journeys to Stirling or Perth to attend its meetings. He was among those members of the committee taken prisoner by Cromwell in 1651 and sent prisoner to

London. He was absent from his parish for the best part of a year. Again in 1657, 1658 and 1660, Sharp was sent by his fellow ministers on diplomatic missions to England and was absent for extended periods during those years.

His absences, and whatever can be alleged about Sharp's behaviour as a minister, seem to have had no adverse effect on his status with his parishioners and fellow ministers, who throughout the thirteen years of his ministry there were consistently anxious to retain him as minister of Crail, despite calls on his services from elsewhere. Almost as soon as Sharp got to Crail there were requests from Edinburgh that he should go and minister there. Such requests were common. If a minister was able, other communities would ask for his transfer to them, often on the grounds that their need was greater and more pressing. If the parishioners were unwilling to lose their minister they were obliged to state their case before the General Assembly or its standing committee. This is what happened in Sharp's case after the request from Edinburgh. In November 1649 representatives of both sides appeared to state their rival claims:

> The said Mr James [Sharp] appearing personally, and the Lord Balcomie and others for the parishioners of Crail, the Baillies and ministers of Edinburgh and diverse others appearing for the town of Edinburgh. The Commission of the General Assembly, having seriously considered the reasons *hinc inde*, for and against the said transportation, and having heard parties at length thereanent, do refuse the desire of the said town of Edinburgh for the said Mr James his transportation.[38]

So eager were Edinburgh to have Sharp that they would not take no for an answer, and renewed their case in 1650. This time they begged the presbytery of St Andrews to release their brother for vital work in the capital city.[39] The presbytery was no more willing than the parishioners to let Sharp go, even though the presbytery of Edinburgh had stressed how useful he could be in the university of Edinburgh. The case was therefore referred to the Synod of Fife. The Synod in turn declined to commit itself. Its members were perhaps unwilling to surrender one of their most promising young members. The whole matter was therefore referred back to the General Assembly. In July 1650 that body was noted as having allowed the transfer,[40] but by then Scotland was a country under siege by Cromwell, and Sharp never took up his post there.

Whatever his ambitions, Sharp had clearly formed close ties with his parish and wished to stay there. The affection was mutual. Lord Balcomie's mission to the Commission of the General Assembly had indicated his regard for his minister. A surviving correspondence between Sharp and the Laird of Wormieston indicates that a warm relationship persisted between them for years.[41] The Laird of Randerston, another of those disciplined for his part in the Engagement, was even more magnanimous; he allowed Sharp to marry his daughter in April 1653. Moreover, Randerston's high opinion of his son-in-law also stood the test of time. In his will he made Sharp a trustee of his possessions in preference to his own son who, rumour had it, was a waster and ne'er do well.[42]

Probably the kernel of truth in all the obviously untrue allegations about Sharp as minister of Crail is that throughout his time there he was involved, and progressively more so, in national church politics and policy-making. Perhaps the more important parishioners were glad that their minister was a figure on the national stage. For others the sense that his interests were not wholly centred on Crail and its parishioners may have created a sense of abandonment, of being second best, especially in a community which had been without a minister at all for an extended period. Perhaps for others it was a matter of envy that James Sharp should move ever closer to the inner circle of policy-makers and be gifted with political skills that were relied upon by the leaders of the church.

3

The Young Politician

In 1649 and 1650, extremely early in his career as a minister, Sharp had been eagerly solicited for a parish in Edinburgh. At an equally early date he was given position and responsibility in local church politics. In April of 1648, the year he was appointed as a minister, he was one of the delegates to the Provincial Synod of Fife at Dunfermline, from the presbytery of St Andrews. There he was appointed as one of five ministers to form a sub-committee to assist in the selection of regents for the colleges of St Andrews University. The following year he made his debut in national church assemblies when he was appointed in June 1650 as one of three commissioners to the General Assembly from the presbytery of St Andrews. At that Assembly he was named as one of the Commission, or standing committee, until the next Assembly.[1]

These appointments indicated that Sharp had won the confidence and esteem of his fellow-ministers. They were also an indication of Sharp's willingness to perform some of the less exciting tasks that fell to a minister who wanted to involve himself in church affairs in a sphere wider than his own parish. The sub-committee to select regents, for example, was the kind of administrative task for which he was certainly better qualified than many of his fellow ministers because of his academic background, but it was hardly a glamorous appointment. Nevertheless in terms of playing a role in policy-making such positions were clearly influential. The appointment to the Commission was particularly important. At this juncture in Scottish life it played a significant part in the running of the country, and Sharp was soon to make a considerable contribution to it.

In 1649 the execution of Charles I had led in England to an experiment in republican government. In Scotland, however, the death of the king had been followed by the proclamation of his son as Charles II. The young king was in exile abroad, but during 1649 and 1650 the Scots used much persuasion to induce him to come to Scotland and attempt to regain his other kingdoms from a Scottish base. Charles himself would have preferred some different means, but Cromwell's successes in Ireland late in 1649 dashed any hope of an expedition from there and made Charles more willing to consider the Scottish proposals. Finally in June 1650 he embarked for Scotland.

The terms on which Charles had been invited to come to Scotland had been negotiated very largely by the radical church party led by the Marquis of Argyll. They had been among the most intransigent opponents of Charles I and were fiercely critical of his son's royalist supporters in Scotland. It was through their influence that James Graham the Marquis of Montrose, the king's most active supporter in Scotland, had been captured and executed, while negotiations with Charles were actually in progress. The king's reluctance to throw in his lot with them was therefore understandable.

The principal requirement of the church party, and the only condition on which they were prepared to support the king, was that he should sign the Covenants. To this demand Charles only belatedly and unwillingly agreed. The implications of such an action on the king's part were very far-reaching. He was being required to condone the past activities of the Covenanting party and thus apparently to betray those like Montrose who had risked all to defy the Covenanters. More than that he was committing himself to recovering England and Ireland on Covenanting terms, the most obvious of which was the imposition of presbyterian church government. He would thus be a monarch not solely advised by his traditional noble supporters but also subject to direction from the ministers.

The practical effect of Charles's taking of the Covenants was that the radical Covenanters, since 1637 a notable influence within Scottish politics, were once again confirmed in their authority. From July 1650 two committees between them ruled Scotland and decided policy in the name of the king. The first was the Committee of Estates, the standing committee of the Parliament of Scotland; the second was the Commission of the General Assembly to which Sharp had been appointed. At this date both committees were dominated by the radicals.[2]

The meetings of the Commission were generally held in Perth or Stirling, both of them about fifty miles from Sharp's parish of Crail. It seems clear that a great deal of his time and energy must have gone into his duties on the Commission. From September 1650 until August 1651 Sharp was present at the Commission on sixty-two days and absent from only seven sessions, and was appointed to more than thirty sub-committees.[3] It is evident from this record that Sharp was valued by his brother-ministers for his political abilities. Again, by the same token, it is clear that he was willing to undertake the commonplace and sometimes tedious tasks that fall to junior members of a committee.

The year of Sharp's service on the Commission was enough to tax the skills of any politician. The presence of the king in Scotland brought to the surface the divisions and hostility among those in power and simultaneously provoked an invasion of Scotland by Cromwell in July 1650, only a month after the king had landed.

The king's signing of the Covenants had been so reluctant that doubt as to his sincerity and motives was immediately aroused in the more theocratic ministers. In August he was therefore requested to purge his household and guard of those attendants not pleasing to the Commission, then required to sign a 'Declaration of the sincerity and reality of his joining in the Cause and Covenant and of his resolutions in the future', the Dunfermline Declaration, and finally he was obliged to keep a day of fast and public humiliation 'that he may give evidence of his real loathing of his former way, and of the sincerity of his owning the Cause of God and the Work of the Reformation'.[4] Meanwhile the Scottish forces were defeated at Dunbar by Cromwell on 3 September. Not only, therefore, was Charles's freedom limited by the ministers, the whole aim and object of submitting to such indignities seemed hopelessly threatened; far from promoting the recapture of England it seemed likely to provoke the extension of Cromwell's power to Scotland.

It was at this juncture that James Sharp, elected to the Commission in July, was first noted as being present, on 13 September 1650. It may be entirely coincidental that Sharp was absent from earlier meetings, or it may be that he felt it was his duty to be present at that particular moment because it was undoubtedly a time of national crisis; but it is also possible that Sharp chose this occasion to make his first appearance for political reasons. It seems likely that Sharp had not wished to be associated with the policies of the Commission carried out in the previous two months. At this point, however, he may have realised, as Cromwell did, that the party of those more sympathetic to the king among both ministers and nobility was about to make a bid for power:

> Surely it's probable the kirk has done their do. I believe their king will be set up upon his own score now; wherein he will find many friends.[5]

It might be said, in connection with Sharp's behaviour towards former Engagers, that he did not wish to be thought too royalist. His timing of his appearance at the Commission suggests that he also wished to avoid the opposite extreme. This early dissociation from the theocratic policies of the radicals was to be typical of his entire career. In this first year as a member of the Commission it seems as though he may have been seeking some way of permitting a more flexible approach to the political problems of Scotland than a clear association with the ideas of either end of the intellectual and theological continuum among ministers would have permitted. It is perhaps in this way that the intellectual legacy of his education in Aberdeen is visible.

The central work for the Commission in 1650/1651 was to hammer out its policy in reference to the major political issues of the day in order to be able to make recommendations to the Committee of Estates and to the Parliament when it was sitting, and thus to influence policy-making. The composition of the Committee of Estates was becoming in general favourable to permitting the king more independence of action than had been envisaged by Argyll and his supporters. The implications of this were a reduction in the power of the ministers and a secularisation of politics with a greater separation between church and state. In order, therefore, for the Commission to have any significant influence on policy-making it was necessary for it to speak with a united voice. In practice this was extremely difficult because of the presence in the Commission of an important group of radical Covenanting ministers. Consequently the year was taken up with a prolonged attempt to prevent an open rupture in the ministry.

Sharp's activities on the Commission during this time can be understood as energetic involvement in the work of attempting to reconcile the disaffected ministers on the one hand, and on the other of presenting church policy to the Committee of Estates and the Parliament.

The issue over which the differences among the ministers were fought out was the defence of Scotland against Cromwell and his invading army. How was the defeat of Dunbar to be explained and what measures should be taken to prevent further losses? The more radical and theocratic of the ministers maintained that the Scottish army had been defeated because of the presence in its ranks of those who had defied the kirk. They referred particularly to those who had without the approval of the kirk taken part in the last abortive attempt to rescue Charles I, the Engagement. That expedition, disastrously officered by the Duke of Hamilton, had been defeated by Cromwell at Preston in 1648, but defeat had not earned the participants the forgiveness of the kirk. Rather, under the leadership of Argyll, the theocrats had used the opportunity to seize political power and to exclude from it all Engagers, by the Act of Classes.

Dunbar had been the first real threat to that regime after two years in power and consequently its defenders made great efforts to shift the blame for that fiasco from themselves. The presence, they maintained, of 'malignant' Engagers in the army on that occasion had been so offensive to God that he had allowed the Scottish forces to be defeated. The solution to the military problem was, in the view of the radicals, to create an army of true believers to whom God would give the victory even in the face of superior forces of the enemy. Such a course of action would also, however, have placed the direction of public affairs once more in theocratic hands.

The unconventional military logic of the theocratic party was by no means new. Over the past twenty years the Covenanters had won victories and celebrated triumphs against such overwhelming odds that their logic had found much support. In the late 1640s, however, the early unanimity of the Covenanting party was dissolving and two opposed parties, those who later became Protesters or Resolutioners, distinguished by the amount of power they were willing to allow the king, were beginning to form. Among the ministers, opposition to the radical and theocratic views of men like James Guthrie and Samuel Rutherford was led by Robert Douglas, Robert Baillie and others. Among the nobility Argyll was increasingly isolated from the large majority who were more sympathetic to the king.

The royalist and secular solution to the military problem was to urge the formation of a large and efficient army which Engagers, having declared their repentance for their former errors, might join. Before long, however, it became evident that this was not a solution agreeable to the radical ministers and their supporters.

On 9 October a Remonstrance was presented to the Commission from the Provincial Synod of Glasgow, meeting at Ayr on 2 October.[6] This document was addressed to the Committe of Estates and was fiercely critical of the Committee's conduct of affairs. The authors angrily asked why the king was being allowed to exercise power without giving any proof that he 'had changed his corrupt principles wherwith he had been educated'. They went on to accuse the Committee of 'exceeding great incorrigibleness' in permitting 'malignants' to be employed in the army and in positions of public trust and accounted for the condition of the country as a punishment for such 'fearfull backslyding'. This document was clearly dynamite in the context of the attempt by the Commission to find some way of retaining the church's influence in public affairs. It was appointed to be considered two days later, and on that day no mention was made of it.

Possibly because of the way this document had been quietly killed off, a much more emphatic version, also addressed to the Committee of Estates, 'From the Gentlemen, Officers and Ministers attending the Western forces', was presented to the Commission by two very assertive and prominent radical ministers, Patrick Gillespie and John Stirling, on 24 October. This time at least a copy of the document was inserted in the minutes. Both documents were presented to the Committee of Estates on 22 October.

There were several difficulties facing the moderates on the Commission in the management of this problem. The first was that the point of view expressed in the Remonstrance was shared by a number of prominent members of the Commission. It could not therefore simply be dismissed. Secondly the Remonstrance addressed issues which the Commission as a whole had already tried to deal with; it therefore constituted an attempt to take over the Commission which, if successful, or even overtly acknowledged, would cause an open rupture in the ministry. Thirdly the Remonstrance urged courses of action which the prevailing secular majority in the Committee of Estates was certainly not prepared to adopt. If the document were adopted as church policy its likely effect would therefore be to deprive the Commission of what power it had to influence events, by creating an unbridgeable gap between Commission and Committee.

The Commission as a whole clearly understood the grave importance of what had taken place and at once drew back from an immediate confrontation among its members. A further meeting was scheduled for three weeks' time and in the meantime a letter was sent out to all the presbyteries soliciting their attendance at that meeting 'becaus the dark condition of the time, and great importance of bussiness, requires counsell and advice more than ordinarie'.[7] Presumably it did not escape the attention of the moderates that a better attended meeting would be likely to ensure a majority for them. It was necessary from the moderates' point of view to defuse the whole issue. Consequently at the Commission's next meeting a sub-committee was appointed to consider the Remonstrance, of which Sharp became a member.[8]

More or less simultaneously the Remonstrance drew a response from the Committee of Estates and Sharp was put on a sub-committee to consider it.[9] Obviously the more moderate members were hoping for a compromise solution which would alienate neither party, and were entrusting Sharp among others with the job of achieving this result. The omens were not particularly promising in that the response from the Committee of Estates was highly critical and came close to calling the Remonstrance treasonable. But again, perhaps because of the contact there had been with the Commission, the Committee recognised the potential danger of allowing a rupture to develop — 'it holds the seeds of a division of ane dangerous consequence'.[10]

Meanwhile the delaying tactics of both Committee and Commission were making the supporters of the Remonstrance restive; a petition was sent from them on 27 November requesting a considered response.[11] On 28 November, 'taking in consideration the Report of the Committee appoynted to consider of the Remonstrance' and 'after long debate thereupon',[12] the Commission announced:

> We doe resolve to forbeare a more particular examination of the said Remonstrance, expecting that at the nixt dyet of the meeting of this Commission these worthie gentlemen, officers, and brethren will give such a declaration and explanation of their intentions and meaning therein as may satisfie both Kirk and State, without any further enquirie or debate thereupon.

This tactical victory was not secured without some losses. Eleven of the thirty-eight ministers present, including James Guthrie and Samuel Rutherford, dissented from the Commission's verdict.[13] From this time these members absented themselves from the Commission's meetings. The danger that these men might provide the nucleus of a faction rivalling the Commission was real, but perhaps more immediately important was the fact that the Remonstrants as they were to be known had not succeeded in taking over the Commission. Their withdrawal left the field of policy-making and negotiation to the moderates. And among these Sharp was now relatively more important, both by virtue of the withdrawal of some very senior ministers among the Remonstrants, notably Samuel Rutherford and Andrew Cant, and in recognition of the experience as a negotiator that he had thus acquired.

Although the Commission was thus somewhat freer to act in relation to the Committee of Estates, it did not give up the attempt to reconcile those ministers who remained dissatisfied with the moderates' conduct of affairs. Sharp took quite a prominent part in this work of negotiation, which continued throughout his year on the Commission.

The most prominent and influential of the Remonstrant ministers began to use their presbyteries to express their dissatisfaction with the Commission's handling of public affairs. In January 1651 Sharp was appointed to a sub-committee to consider a letter of complaint from the Presbytery of Stirling.[14] A few days later the same sub-committee was asked also to consider two letters from the Presbytery of Glasgow, one criticising and one supporting the Commission.[15] A number of meetings took place in an attempt to reconcile these differences of opinion.[16] In February a similar response was made, again Sharp being involved, to ministers in Fife.[17] In March Sharp took part in a further attempt to respond to the increasingly emphatic dissatisfaction of the ministers of Stirling,[18] and in April there were further meetings with the ministers of Glasgow, the Commission

> being desyrous that all differences should be removed, and a good understanding and happie union in judgement might be made betuixt them and their brethren in the Province of Glasgow.[19]

The differences between the two sides in these debates were fundamental and were not resolved very conclusively by these meetings. On the other hand an open rupture among the ministers had been avoided. In the meantime the consideration of the Remonstrance was repeatedly postponed until in July it was referred to the consideration of the General Assembly.[20]

Thus Sharp had been conspicuously identified with that group of ministers seeking to avoid a split in the ministry. Other activities on the Commission show him as also attempting to deal with pressure from the other side, the Committee of Estates. The Western Remonstrance had originally been addressed and presented to the Committee of Estates on 24 October 1650, stating the radicals' position on membership of the army and capacity to hold public office:

> Notwithstanding your solemn engadgment to the Lord to endeavour that all places of power and trust may consist off and be filled with such men as are of known good affection to the Cause of God and a blamelesse and Christian conversation . . . . yet your Lordships . . . have forgotten to walk by the same rule, and have intrusted in eminent places, and doeth still keep in trust, persones both in judicatories and armies which want those qualificationes in the day of your affliction and vowes, when some of your spirits were nearer to God then they have been keeped since that tyme.[21]

The position of the Committee of Estates and Parliament, however, during the autumn of 1650 moved steadily towards a request for the general admission to the army of all capable of bearing arms, and the repeal of the Act of Classes. To this end they repeatedly pushed the Commission to relax the church's strictures against capacity to hold public office or membership of the army. Clearly if the church was to continue to have any political authority some means had to be found of moderating the secular government's desire to employ publicly whomever it chose. Sharp was repeatedly selected as one of those to negotiate with the Parliament and the Committee of Estates on this issue. On 26 November, for example, the Parliament requested a conference with representatives of the Commission to discuss

> the reasones pro and contra quhy men should be admitted or excludit from joyneing with the armie, or acting a part againes the common enemy,[22]

and on 28 November Sharp was appointed a member of the Committee to confer with members of the Parliament.[23] A very crisp response to the Parliament did not, however, omit to mention that persons could be readmitted to public trust if they were prepared to give satisfaction for their former misdemeanours:

> We humblie desire your Lordships . . . to guard for the future against all inclinations of making use of any scandalous, malignant, or disaffected persones for publict trust, or of admitting any to imployment in your counsells or army, except in the way agreed upon by the publict resolutions of Church and State.[24]

This approach had at least some token success. Sharp was appointed a member of a sub-committee directed to enquire into the motivation of prominent Engagers, among them, for example, the Duke of Hamilton, who were seeking to be released from the censures laid upon them.[25] As a result of these procedures lists were given to the Parliament of persons who had satisfied the Commission and who were recommended for employment.[26] It seems very likely that the Commission's eagerness to retain some influence with the Committee of Estates

led to the re-admission to favour with the church over the next few months of
many former Engagers whose 'repentance' was token.

The parliament continued to press the Commission, however. On 10 December
they instructed some of their members to meet with the Commissioners to confer
concerning

> how far incapacities that disables men may be taken aff and men admitted for defence
> of the country to fight aganes the comon enemy.[27]

Again Sharp was one of those appointed to confer on this issue,[28] which returned
very much the same answer as before, but phrased less assertively:

> In this case of so great and evident necessitie, we cannot be against the raising of all
> fensible persones in the land, and permitting them to fight against the enemie for
> defence of the Kingdome ... and, for the capacitie of acting, that the Estates of
> Parliament ought to have, as we hope they will have, speciall care that in this so
> general concurrence of all the people of the Kingdome none be putt in such trust or
> power as may be prejudiciall to the Cause of God.[29]

This response was immediately followed by the readmission to the Church's
favour of large numbers of former Engagers.[30] In January, however, and again in
March the Commissioners pointed out that persons were being employed in the
army who had not satisfied the kirk.[31] By this means they were obviously trying to
ensure that kirk authority was not totally eroded or ignored. The pressure
continued in March with the resumption of the Parliament's sitting and a request
for what amounted to the repeal of the Act of Classes:

> Whether or not it be sinful and unlawful for the more effectual prosecution of the
> public resolutions for the defence of the cause, the king and kingdom, To admit such
> persons to be members of the Committee of Estates who are now debarred from
> public trust.[32]

To this the Commission together drew up a mollifying response delaying a proper
reply until further consideration, by a better attended meeting. Of the few present,
Sharp was predictably one.[33] Finally, early in April the Parliament bluntly asked
for an opinion of the lawfulness of the repeal of the Act of Classes by a General
Assembly.[34] Again Sharp was one of those asked to consider the Parliament's letter
and what response might be made to it.[35] Their answer, predictably, was to delay a
direct response.[36] A further exchange of letters in late April and May again
demanded a response[37] and again Sharp was named as one of those to deal with the
issue, and again an evasive answer was returned urging the Parliament to admit to
public employment only those who had satisfied the kirk according to the forms
laid down.[38] In late May a new committee was convened to consider the Act of
Classes, of which Sharp was again a member.[39] Finally in late May, with many
caveats the Commission tacitly conceded that the limitations imposed by the Act
of Classes could lawfully be removed. Sharp and others were instructed to go to
the Parliament with this decision and to make it clear that the Commission both
feared and deplored the idea that the result might be a total relaxation of all
qualifications for holding office:

The brethren are likewise instructed hereby to labour earnestly with the Parliament that such as have been eminent and constant opposers unto the Cause and Covenant untill of late, and were prime and active instruments in the bloody rebellions within the kingdome, may not be suddenly admitted to judicatories.[40]

On 2 June an act rescinding the Act of Classes was duly passed by the Parliament.[41] Predictably within a matter of days the Commission was complaining that the nominations for the new Committee of Estates including many persons not properly qualified and begged the King and Parliament to revise their lists.[42] Sharp was one of those appointed to present this document to the King and Committee of Estates.[43] No doubt to the relief of the Commission the response from the Committee was left to the consideration of the General Assembly which met on 16 July.[44]

Sharp's work on the Commission has been dealt with at some length because it is the first opportunity to get a reliable idea of his political attitudes and disposition. What is known of his life before 1651 is probably not sufficiently detailed or reliable to enable more than an educated guess as to its likely influence upon him. In the Commission, however, a good deal is known of his position in relation to his fellow ministers. To use the evidence this way assumes that Sharp was revealing something about himself in his work on the Commission. It is certainly true that he could have been a very much less active member. The very regularity of his attendance, in contrast to that of the majority of his fellow members, argues that it was work that he found satisfying. Similarly it was open to him not to be a member of sub-committees. It is not mere chance that he did the work he did.

The amount of work that Sharp did was a function both of his own willingness and of the trust of his fellow members. It has also been indicated where Sharp stood in terms of the theological and political continuum. There are two more conclusions that can perhaps be drawn from this year's work. One is that Sharp was a convinced and relentless negotiator. It seems that he believed completely in the value of discussion. This obviously distinguishes him from the Remonstrants who had walked out of the Commission. It may also be a way of distinguishing him from the Resolutioners for whom a point would also eventually be reached where they were no longer willing to negotiate. Secondly, the work Sharp did on the Commission seems to have been almost entirely reactive. It seems that he and the leading Resolutioners responded to initiatives taken by others, the Remonstrants or the Committee of Estates and the Parliament, rather than taking the initiative themselves. In dealing both with the Remonstrance and the Act of Classes there was obviously a powerful wish among the moderates on the Commission that the problem would simply go away. There is little evidence of the Resolutioners taking hold of affairs themselves. These two factors taken together can, I think, explain the way in which during 1650–1 the Resolutioners were pushed into a major shift of attitude as to the proper response to the Cromwellian invasion. It may also offer clues to the understanding of Sharp's progressive change of attitude over the next decade.

But however carefully and circumspectly the Resolutioners had negotiated with both sides, the summer of 1651 brought all their schemes crashing to the ground.

The General Assembly was unable to maintain unity among its members and by the end of July it was evident that there was schism between Remonstrants (or Protesters as they were now also known) and Resolutioners. Secondly the willingness of the Resolutioners to concede some conditions in order to permit the raising of an army to fight Cromwell did not result in the adequate defence of the country. Cromwell defeated part of the Scottish forces, leaving the way open for a demoralised force to invade England where it was decisively defeated at Worcester. The king escaped from this débâcle to France. Lastly the attempt of the Commission, reconstituted by the General Assembly, with Sharp again as a member, to carry on the work of governing Scotland, whatever the circumstances, with the Committee of Estates, came to an inglorious end when the remnants of both committees were surprised by English forces at Alyth, and taken prisoner on 28 August 1651.[45]

The captives were sent to London and were later joined there by the prisoners from the Scottish army defeated at Worcester. Little by little they were released to return to Scotland on promise of good behaviour. By August 1652 Sharp was back in his parish after rather less than a year's imprisonment.

The period of Sharp's imprisonment is rather an obscure part of his career. No correspondence relating to this period seems to survive. The major clue to what happened is found in the work of the author of the *Life of Mr James Sharp*. He repeats three items of what was no doubt common gossip about Sharp in the 1670s. From this imperfect source, however, it is possible to reconstruct at least something of the significance of Sharp's imprisonment. First of all it alleged that Sharp took 'the Tender'.[46] The Tender was an oath of loyalty to the Cromwellian government. It was required of those from whom it was thought desirable to have some formal statement of intention to live peaceably, but as far as the Scottish prisoners were concerned it seems to have been applied rather arbitrarily. Whether Sharp actually did swear such an oath is impossible to establish with any degree of certainty. When one group of Scottish prisoners, including a minister, were offered liberty on condition they took the Tender, the fact is mentioned.[47] When Sharp was released there was no such mention. This is not conclusive evidence; it only makes it seem rather improbable that he did take it. What is more interesting is the significance of the allegation.

From the vantage point of the 1670s and of his conspicuous support of the government of Charles II, Sharp is being accused of being willing to support any regime and swear any oath that will enable him to achieve his own ends. Similar accusations were made about Sharp's transition from student of the Aberdeen Doctors to regent and signatory of the Covenant at St Andrews. There seems to be a certain amount of wilful distortion in the allegations concerning the Tender, most notably that it was an oath that involved renouncing loyalty to Charles II. The Cromwellian aim was much more modest and pragmatic; the Tender merely involved an undertaking to live peaceably under the regime. Secondly it was an oath which was commonly taken by ministers when required to do so and seems to have incurred no church censure.

Supposing it to be true, then, that Sharp took the Tender, it is worth considering what it does imply. What it illuminates is the attitude of Sharp and his fellow ministers to the more general question of the legitimacy of government. What is demonstrated is the Resolutioners' respect for authority and their fear of anarchy. Years later, on the eve of the Restoration, Robert Douglas, one of the Resolutioner leaders, wrote to Sharp reminding him of their reasons for compliance with the Cromwellians:

> It is true, we have always judged ... that any government is to be preferred to anarchy and confusion, But as to our comparative judgment of diverse forms of government ... we know no man can say we have asserted what is alleged of us that we could wish to be settled in a commonwealth way, and were against the coming in of the king upon any terms.[48]

The author of the *Life* then goes on to say that Sharp fraternised with those who had been responsible for his captivity and his country's defeat. Here again Sharp is being accused of treacherous behaviour; there are more significant implications. In April 1652 Sharp had been allowed out of the Tower of London on bail, on the understanding that he would stay within certain limits in London.[49] This liberty does not appear to have been extended to any other minister. It is extremely likely that Sharp used it to widen the Resolutioners' political contacts in London among the Cromwellians and to get to know the English presbyterians.[50] Throughout his career Sharp had an extraordinary capacity for gaining an entrée and getting himself known. His range of associates was enormous and his name crops up in the most unexpected places. It was this capacity which in the 1650s made him such a valuable negotiator for the Resolutioners. In his activities as prisoner on bail can be seen the beginnings of Sharp's career as agent and diplomat.

Lastly the author of the *Life* points out that Sharp was released from prison rather earlier than his fellow-ministers.[51] Once again he intends to insinuate that this early freedom was obtained in some discreditable way. The accusation is made rather more bluntly by Row, the Protester minister and author of the life of Robert Blair:

> As for Mr James Sharp he was set at liberty shortly after they came to the Tower, having (as was thought) engaged to promote the designs of the Commonwealth.[52]

What it may demonstrate is the value placed on Sharp's presence in Scotland and the efforts made by his brethren to get him released. The presbytery of St Andrews had made it their business to write to General Monck[53] on his behalf and it was probably their intercession which resulted in Sharp being among those Scots released relatively soon. It is, however, also possible that Sharp was released after not too long an imprisonment because of his relative *un*importance. Robert Douglas, the most distinguished of the Resolutioner leaders, was imprisoned for almost another year, while secular leaders such as Lauderdale were not released until the Restoration.[54] In 1651 Sharp was still fairly low in the pecking order.

On 1 July 1652 Sharp was given his freedom and instructed to report to the Cromwellian forces when he arrived in Scotland. By August he was back in his parish[55] and immediately began to pick up the threads of church politics.

In the year of Sharp's absence the antagonism among the ministers had not been resolved. The methods of persuasion used initially during Sharp's time on the Commission had gradually been succeeded by more outspoken statements until by the late summer of 1651 real hostility had developed between what were increasingly two opposed parties within the church. As has been described, the public pronouncements, or resolutions, of the majority royalist party urging the repeal of the Act of Classes and the co-operation of the nation in the military preparations for the campaign which was to end at Worcester, had been met by the protests of the minority theocratic party which had given support to the Remonstrance. Resolutioners and Protesters thus coalesced into rival factions. Matters had not been improved by the Resolutioners' willingness in August 1651 to denounce the Protesters to the English presbyterians as traitors:

> there are among ourselves a few unsatisfied (of whom some have been held in high estimation before this time for their works' sake, and with whom we have dealt with all tenderness in the spirit of meekness for their reclaiming) who, to the great advantage of the common adversary, and the weakening of the hands that were at the work, have obstructed those just and necessary Resolutions, and actively obstructed the use of the lawful and only likely means left of opposition to the prevailing enemy, setting on foot a State separation, which necessarily tends to a Kirk separation.[56]

The confidence of the Resolutioners was, however, much reduced by the capture of the ministers and nobility at Alyth. When that blow was added to by the defeat of the Scottish forces at Worcester and the capitulation of Scotland to Cromwell's army of occupation, the Protesters judged it was time to heal the breach. In November 1652, some three months after Sharp's return home, overtures were made to the Resolutioners. As a result arrangements were made for a unity conference to take place in January 1653. Sharp was appointed as one of the delegates of the Resolutioner party. That attempt at re-union never took place and instead the talks were rescheduled for later in 1653. Again Sharp was one of those chosen to take part.[57] It appears, that although Sharp had been out of the country for a year, confidence in him was strong enough to replace him immediately at the centre of ecclesiastical politics.

At this juncture, however, the Cromwellian occupation forces took a hand in the affair.[58] When Scotland had been defeated and overrun in 1651 the Cromwellians had taken over the administration of the country. The normal institutions of government — the Parliament, the Privy Council, law courts at all levels — had all ceased to meet. Instead the country was administered by a Council composed of English civil servants, representatives of the English occupation forces and a few Scotsmen. Until 1653 that body had allowed church meetings to continue but in July of that year the General Assembly was prevented from meeting.

Of the two parties within the church the Cromwellians preferred the Protesters, especially the wing of the party led by Gillespie. That was because they imagined the Protesters were much more like themselves. In this they were mistaken. Although the Protesters were more critical of Charles II than the Resolutioners, they were not the anti-royalists that the Cromwellians took them to be. Furthermore, although the Cromwellians thought of the Protesters as more like themselves in matters of religion, chiefly because they detected in the Protesters a puritanism and earnestness which pleased them, the theocratic ideas of the Protesters were far removed from the Erastianism of the Independents.

Nevertheless, although Cromwellian preference was based largely on misconceptions, it was sufficiently strong to induce them to take a hand in church affairs in 1653, especially since Royalist unrest that was later to develop into Glencairn's Rising was already evident. Lilburne, the commander-in-chief, was deeply suspicious of the Resolutioners whom he thought able and willing to support the royalist initiatives. The Assembly due to meet that year was really a convention of the Resolutioner party rather than of the whole church. It could be expected to devote itself to criticism of the Cromwellian regime and to renewed controversies on the question of the split in the church. It was therefore not allowed to meet.[59]

The implications of this development for Sharp's career were that once again the leaders of the Resolutioner party among whom he must certainly by now be numbered were thrust into direct negotiation with the civil power.[60] This situation was made even clearer by the disruption of meetings in the late summer and autumn of 1653. The point must have been brought home to Sharp in particular by the forcible interruption of the Synod of Fife, meeting at St Andrews. A party of soldiers disrupted proceedings, but then allowed the meeting to continue while they remained as observers.[61]

In August 1654 the Protesters, or that wing of the party led by Gillespie, used the opportunity of their greater favour with the Cromwellian regime to negotiate a settlement of church affairs which would have rapidly put the whole Scottish church in their power. This agreement, known derisively to contemporaries as 'Gillespie's Charter', submitted the appointment of ministers to regional groups of 'triers' from both the secular and Protester camps. This system gave the Cromwellian regime the influence it wanted in church appointments, but at the price of sacrificing the principles of both presbyterianism and separation of church and state which had been the cornerstone of kirk policy for nearly a century. For these reasons Gillespie's Charter was unacceptable to the 'presbyterian' wing of the Protester party led by Wariston and Guthrie, but even more unacceptable to the Resolutioners.

In October 1654 the provincial Synod of Fife meeting at Kirkcaldy with Sharp as its moderator issued a declaration against Gillespie's Charter.[62] Clearly Sharp as one of a group of leading Resolutioners was taking on the Cromwellian government. Similar statements of opposition were made by the Synod of Lothian and the leadership of the Resolutioners who had formed themselves into a group known to history as 'the Ministers of Edinburgh and some other brethren of the ministry'.[63] For the next six years those men — who included Robert Douglas, James Wood, David Dickson and James Hutcheson — those same men who had formed the leadership of the Commission of the General Assembly after the Protesters had withdrawn in 1650–51, made policy within the Resolutioner party and negotiated with the secular government on behalf of what was probably five-sixths of the ministry of the kirk.[64] Their unwillingness to co-operate, and the aversion of some Protesters also, meant that the Charter was not put into effect.

In any direct confrontation, however, the Cromwellian government was more than a match for the Resolutioners. Their open defiance and the Cromwellians' deep suspicion of their likely support for the royalist rising led to a ban on church assemblies and a renewal in March 1655 of the prohibition against public prayers for the king. As a result the Synod of Fife meeting at Cupar in April 1655 was forced to disperse.[65] Interestingly, however, on that occasion Sharp attempted to negotiate with the officer in charge, Major Davison. He was unsuccessful, but this wish to avoid open confrontation and instead to make terms was typical of Sharp's whole approach to relations with the civil power. It can perhaps be thought of as an aspect of that unwillingness to take up an extreme and doctrinaire position that has already been noted.

There is no doubt that his fellow Resolutioners were aware of Sharp's capacities in this respect. When a unity conference with the Protesters was proposed for the summer of 1655, Robert Baillie, the most eminent of the Resolutioners in Glasgow, was eager that Sharp be included as one of the Resolutioner representatives.

During the summer of 1655 Sharp seems to have been active in persuading James Wood and Robert Douglas, the two most powerful Resolutioner leaders, to offer guarantees of good behaviour in exchange for permission to continue meeting in church assemblies and praying for the king, and then to offer to give up praying for the king presumably in exchange for freedom to meet in church assemblies. Baillie was uneasy about this way of behaving, although he acknowledged that the king had in effect given permission for his subjects to forbear public intercession for him. In September 1655 the Resolutioners agreed to stop public prayer for the king in exchange for remission of penalties on offenders and justified their behaviour by a rather defensive letter to the king.[67]

It could be argued that Sharp's initiative had merely made things easier for the Cromwellians by conceding to them what they might otherwise have effected by force. A more benign interpretation, however, suggests that the willingness to negotiate embodied by Sharp enabled the Resolutioners to win the favour of Lord Broghill who arrived in Scotland in September 1656, and who reversed the Cromwellian policy of favouring the Protesters. Baillie reported that Sharp's intimacy with Broghill had resulted both in his being able to influence appointments as St Andrews University and to get Glencairn released from imprisonment on payment of a heavy security when otherwise he ran the risk of being executed.[68]

Frances Dow points out very clearly how Broghill was not prepared to be owned by either Resolutioner or Protester parties. His aim was strictly the good of the Cromwellian regime and he viewed the kirk and its warring members with some contempt. It is also true, as Dow makes evident, that Glencairn's Rising had obliged the Cromwellians to modify their anti-hierarchical, anti-clerical policies. Nevertheless the Resolutioners could not be disregarded in the formulation of Cromwellian policy as their effective nullifying of Gillespie's Charter had shown, and Sharp's capacity to negotiate almost certainly maintained the influence of the Resolutioners when otherwise they might have been subjected to a continuing persecution and erosion of their influence and authority.[69]

In the winter of 1655–56 Sharp functioned as one of a handful of the most senior Resolutioner ministers in a whole series of negotiations first with the Protester party and then with Broghill. The impossibility of finding a compromise settlement within the church induced both parties to appeal to Broghill in February 1656. His interpretation of this was that a centre party of moderates could be formed. On the Resolutioner side he identified Sharp as one of the six leading men who might be brought to agree to such a compromise. The centre party proved to be no more than an idea of Broghill's, but the spirit of negotiation and compromise with the government with which Sharp was so much identified paid off in August 1656. The Cromwellian government agreed to allow admissions to charges to continue to be the responsibility of presbyteries, provided that the presbytery 'would undertake to certify to the Council the fitness of any minister whom they desired to be admitted to a stipend, and every minister so admitted would voluntarily engage to live peaceably and inoffensively under the government'.[70]

Dow emphasises that the Cromwellians had thus succeeded in eliciting recognition of the secular power even from the Resolutioners. This is certainly true, and demonstrates, just as the Resolutioners' appeals and negotiations had done, a compromise on erastianism. However, it should also be noted that, as Dow points out, Gillespie's Charter and the variations upon it were now a dead letter and the presbyterian system had been restored. In the space of two years, therefore, Cromwellian attitudes to the parties within the church had been entirely reversed. Certainly, as has already been pointed out, this owes a lot to the change in Cromwellian policy following Glencairn's Rising, but it also owes something to the Resolutioners' willingness to allow the talents of a natural negotiator such as Sharp to be exercised.

Not surprisingly the Protesters reacted with outrage, and as Broghill reported with satisfaction, they were about to take the unprecedented step of sending commissioners to London to press their case with Cromwell. The Resolutioners' success, then, was not to be allowed to go unchallenged. Their response to news of the Protester initiative was to commission Sharp to go to London as their representative. This development highlights an aspect of Resolutioner activity that had been visible since the Remonstrance had been presented to the Commission in 1650. Their characteristic way of dealing with things was reactive. They repeatedly found themselves in the position of finding a response to other people's initiatives: the Protesters, the Committee of Estates, the Cromwellian government. Now they were once again responding to a Protester initiative. What is more, that reactive stance put them in a weak position. They were on this occasion, as Broghill triumphantly pointed out, despite being convinced believers in the separation of church and state, putting themselves in the position of competing with the Protesters for the approval of the erastian, secular government:

> I hope, if we manage things well, the two parties of Scotland, viz Remonstrators and public Resolutioners shall both court us, as too long we have courted them.[71]

Sharp departed for London having been fully briefed by his brethren.[72] He was instructed first of all to stress the loyalty of the Resolutioners, to deny the claim of the Protesters to be 'the godly party' and their assertions of the unworthiness of the Resolutioner ministers. In addition he was required to make particular requests that popery should be stamped out; that ecclesiastical government be permitted to function but that no General Assembly be allowed for the present; that admission of ministers be by orderly and required form and that their stipends be paid normally; that rival presbyteries not be recognised. He was further to explain the reasons why attempts at union with the Protesters had failed, and to reiterate that the Resolutioners could make no further concessions in any future attempt at union. With these instructions Sharp was given a letter for Lord Broghill which asked him to give their cause support in London as he had done in Scotland, and commended Sharp to him. He was also given a letter for Simeon Ash, a prominent English Presbyterian, to whom Sharp was similarly recommended.

For the first six months that he was in London Sharp was busy with preliminary matters. In correspondence with the Edinburgh ministers he discussed the Resolutioner attitude to a fast proposed by the Cromwellian government; to the resumption of church courts and ecclesiastical discipline; to the procedure for admitting 'entrant ministers'; and to the abusive scandal being spread by the Protesters. In addition Sharp, assisted by letters from Edinburgh, recommended himself and the Resolutioner cause to Lord Broghill and other Cromwellian soldiers who had been in Scotland, and to the Presbyterian community in London, particularly to three of its ministers, Calamy, Ash and Manton. During this period also a long apology was written by his brethren at home for Sharp's use in London, justifying the Resolutioner position and entitled 'A True Representation of the Rise, Progress and State of the Present Division in the Church of Scotland'.[73] He was thus fairly well prepared with instructions, propaganda and contacts when the time came in February 1657 to present the Resolutioner cause to Cromwell.

Sharp from this time reported the progress of his mission in London to his brethren in Scotland by frequent letters. At the first formal meeting with Cromwell Sharp had come unprepared, not having expected a summons, but he had already had three meetings with Cromwell which had apparently predisposed the Protector in his favour. On this occasion Sharp stressed that the Resolutioners sought no change in church government, but simply a return to the normal system of presbyterian discipline.[74] The Protester party was represented at this meeting by Guthrie, Warriston, Gillespie and others whose right Sharp then challenged to represent the church before Cromwell. This stirred up lengthy responses from the Protesters. The Protector, however, seems to have been reluctant to listen to wrangling over past issues and urged both parties to come to the point:

> The Protector bids us leave that and go to the main business which ought to be driven to an issue at present, and that is whether such men as some of there were, seeking for a reformation, ought not to be heard, so as your church in its present constitution not being in a capacity to reform itself there should be an extraordinary remedy made use of.[75]

In other words, Cromwell wanted to know what opposition there was to permitting the Protesters to put their scheme for purging the church into force. Sharp was astute enough to recognise that to argue on such narrow ground and on such premises would be extremely difficult for him, and so he returned once more to the larger issues. At a later stage Cromwell again attempted to return to this one issue, but Sharp again prevented it. The meeting ended quite inconclusively. Nevertheless Sharp had been able to choose and retain his own ground on which to argue, and despite the Protector's apparent preference for the Protester party, he had been able to forestall a decision in their favour, and had made a favourable impression on a number of those present, including Cromwell. It is not surprising that Sharp allowed himself a gentle pat on the back for his performance.[76]

It is from this first meeting that the phrase Cromwell is supposed to have used, 'Sharp of that ilk', most probably derives.[77] This expression was taken by the author of the *True and Impartial Account* to be a compliment to Sharp — a reference to his quick wits and skill — but it has been used since mostly as an insult to imply evasiveness or equivocation.

Sharp did not remit his efforts to build up a party of supporters in London. The day after the debate he visited Dr Owen, a prominent Independent who was not prepared to declare himself for the Resolutioners but who congratulated Sharp upon his showing the previous day, and he also visited another Independent present at the debate, Mr Caryll. So successful had he been in making contacts that the Protesters complained to Broghill that Sharp had 'prepossessed all the city ministers',[78] and indeed those who had supported the Protesters before the debate now seemed disposed to favour the Resolutioners.

Some days later both parties were again summoned before Cromwell. The Protesters in the person of Guthrie attempted to copy Cromwell's technique of the previous meeting, and before Sharp could speak tried to limit the matter for debate by saying that

> seeing the debate the other day was brought to this point that the government of the church as now exercised could not be for edification and promoting of the work of reformation ... he should be content to speak upon that point now.

Sharp then immediately challenged this prelimitation and the premise:

> I would crave leave to say that I lay at a great disadvantage by the misstating of our contraversy, which is not whether our church be corrupt or not.[79]

He instead posed a number of questions designed once more to widen the debate to the whole field of church affairs since 1650. Then followed a lengthy and acrimonious exchange about the extent of the support for the Protesters and the identity of scandalous ministers. Although Sharp had again prevented the debate from being conducted on ground favourable to the Protesters, he had this time been unable to turn the discussion to the more fundamental causes of disagreement. Cromwell had had enough by now and the meeting was again adjourned.

When the records of these meetings reached Edinburgh, the ministers appear to have felt that little purpose was being served by their continuation, and so they wrote to Broghill asking him to try and get some definitive judgement:

> we cannot but importune your Lordship for some speedy remedy, which as it will not be prejudicial to any interest so it will refresh us more than anything we can enjoy in the world beside.[80]

In March things were no further forward when a petition from James Guthrie was appointed to be discussed. The petition concerned the admission of a Resolutioner minister to Stirling, and Sharp chose this opportunity to distribute the Resolutioner version of events in the form of *A True Representation,* by now printed in London, which seems to have been given a very favourable reception. The consideration of Guthrie's petition provoked widespread irritation at court, and ended as inconclusively as the other meetings had done, not least because the consideration of the case seemed to imply a questioning of the action and authority of the Cromwellian Council in Scotland.[81]

The revelation of the state of church life in Scotland occasioned by the consideration of Guthrie's petition, and the generally unsatisfactory nature of the whole venture of submitting the problems of the Scottish church to Cromwell, were now beginning to be apparent. Gillespie had apparently been distressed by the whole business of the petition and was moved to speak to Sharp:

> 'What' said he 'if I should move the Protector to call us and bid us go home and agree among ourselves'. I [Sharp] said agreement if really intended would be best transacted at home.[82]

On the whole, however, the Resolutioner ministers seemed to have favoured Sharp's remaining in London, and so he continued his policy of making contacts. He had been in touch with the Scottish nobility imprisoned since Worcester and had so predisposed them in favour of the Resolutioners that the Protesters made no headway whatever when they attempted to win them over to their cause,[83] although that is in any case hardly surprising.

Up to this point the two parties had confined themselves to arguing over their differences before Cromwell. In April 1657 the Protesters took advantage of the political situation to introduce an entirely new dimension into the proceedings. The various constitutional devices by which Cromwell had sought to establish stable government during the interregnum were succeeded in the spring of 1657 by The Humble Petition and Advice. This was a plea for the return to a two-chamber Parliament over which Cromwell should rule as a constitutional monarch. The terms of the Petition permitted all those in Scotland to vote who had not positively fought for the king in the Engagement but who 'have lived peaceably, and thereby given testimony of their good affections for the Commonwealth'. The Protesters then drew up an amendment pressing for the 'exclusion from trust' also of all those who had been 'advisers, aiders and abettors of the war 1648 against the Parliament of England' because, they said,

> if these be not excluded, the members from Scotland for the Parliament shall only be of the malignant stamp; and so they being the fountain of all information in relation to Scots affairs in the making of the laws, and being in the magistracy of Scotland,

and so having the executive power of the laws in boroughs and counties, they shall discourage a godly ministry and people and bring in a Malignant ministry and mightily obstruct the work of the Gospel and disaffect the people from the present Supreme Government.[84]

In other words the Protesters maintained that unless effective legislation was passed against the former Engagers, what amounted to a renewal of the Act of Classes, they would use their opportunity to seize power and overturn the Cromwellian government. In fact this was a fairly shrewd political judgment and as such was eventually accepted by Cromwell and the Parliament, but not before Sharp had submitted his objections.[85] After all, the Protesters' view implied that all those former Engagers who had given satisfaction to the Resolutioners were untrustworthy, and that only the anti-Engagers, that is the Protesters and those associated with them, were fit to hold power. It was in effect an attempt to return to the theocratic government of 1648-9. Sharp's amendment was not passed, though in the event the clause was never put into effect.

Sharp had been defeated, if narrowly, and despite his considerable efforts, the business about which he had come was no further forward. Since neither Cromwell nor Broghill was likely to be available in the immediate future he therefore raised, not for the first time, the question of his return to Scotland.[86]

The whole debate between the two parties was, however, reopened with the appointment of a Committee of the Cromwellian council to hear once again what both sides had to say.[87] From the beginning it was obvious to Sharp that the committee was in favour of the Protesters. His technique, therefore, was to prevent the Committee coming to a judgment which he anticipated would be unfavourable to the Resolutioners. His first tactic was to absent himself from their meetings, although he was eventually obliged to appear. His second was to say that he had not anticipated that the affairs of the Scottish church would be tried before a secular court before which he had no authority to appear as a Resolutioner representative. Having eventually appeared as a private minister, he demanded access to certain papers presented by the Protesters, and then stirred up their rage by the submission of papers of his own. By this time he had gained some support in the Committee by private negotiation[88] so that when the Protesters presented their proposals for reform of the church by the setting up of Commissions rather than by use of the ordinary system of presbyterian church courts, Sharp was able to prevent them passing with the assistance of a strongly worded letter from three of the Committee.

The negotiations and tactics dragged on from July to September until the Cromwellian Council had lost interest and patience and it was plain that nothing would be concluded, but both sides were dismissed with exhortations to make up their quarrel. The Protesters left London, and Sharp, after ensuring the goodwill of his large circle of contacts and acquaintances, and appointing an Englishman, Major Beck, to maintain the Resolutioner interest in London, similarly left for Scotland at the end of 1657, after more than a year in the capital.[89]

When Sharp reported on his activities to his colleagues in Edinburgh, he was warmly thanked by the assembled ministers who

D

> do bless the Lord for his faithfulness and do return him hearty thanks for his
> unwearied labours and diligence in his employment.[90]

A letter from Calamy and Ash warmly praised Sharp to the ministers and assured
them that

> Our reverend brother Mr Sharp hath with much prudence courage and
> laboriousness unweariedly attended and managed the trust committed to him, yea (as
> we believe) he hath secured your cause from sundry aspersions which otherwise
> might probably have reproached it, and he hath gained respect in the opinions of
> some in the highest place by his wisdom, and meekness in vindicating it from
> misrepresentations.[91]

These tokens of esteem were entirely in line with indications given to Sharp during
his time in London of the pleasure and satisfaction of the Edinburgh ministers
with his behaviour and with tributes to him by Broghill and others.

But what had Sharp in fact done in London that caused such widespread
satisfaction among his supporters? He had, it is plain, in the two debates and the
series of meetings with the Committee performed the almost entirely negative
function of preventing any decision being made. On all three occasions it had
seemed that any conclusion would be made in favour of the Protesters, and he had
therefore by his tactics prevented the talks developing to a point where a decision
would be inevitable.

This, however, illustrates an aspect of Resolutioner negotiations and Sharp's
part in them which has been noted previously. Sharp's role had been almost
entirely reactive. It was the Protesters and the Cromwellians who had taken the
initiative. Not surprisingly, then, the result had not so much been a victory for the
Resolutioners as a defeat for the Protesters. As Robert Baillie phrased it:

> Mr Sharp, in diverse conferences before the Protector, made them appear so
> unreasonable, that after more than half a year's importunat solicitation, they could
> obtaine nothing at all.[92]

Calamy and Ash at the time and historians since have chosen to interpret
Sharp's actions as a vindication of the Resolutioner cause in the face of a general
predilection for the Protesters. In fact Sharp had simply prolonged a stalemate
within the divided Scottish church while coincidentally opinion in England had
swung somewhat against the Independents and in favour of the Presbyterians.
Sharp had certainly played no part in this latter development although he was to
some extent the beneficiary of it. The religious issues as such had not been the
subject of the negotiations at all among Protesters or Resolutioners.

There is a further aspect, however, to these debates which deserves discussion.
Scotland was an occupied country and all real power lay in the hands of the
Cromwellians. Nevertheless the conflict between the Protesters and Resolutioners
by the mid-1650s begins to look remarkably like a struggle for power within the
Scottish community. While Scotland's natural rulers were in prison, abroad or
lying low, there was a power vacuum in Scottish society. As Dow points out, the
Cromwellians had originally intended to fill this vacuum, not with ministers, but
with representatives of the shires and burghs. The story of the first few years of

Cromwellian occupation is the story of the failure of that policy. The occupation government remained unwilling to return any significant authority to the nobility, but they found themselves negotiating with the ministers as the most powerful representatives of the community. Certainly the manipulation of both parties within the church to the point where they were willing to negotiate with the civil power despite their expressed anti-erastian views was a considerable victory for the Cromwellians. On the other hand, as a great deal of correspondence indicates, the ministers could not simply be ignored, however much such an attitude would have better fitted Cromwellian ideology. In terms of influence within the community the ministers of either party were infinitely more influential than the mavericks such as Swinton, Jaffray, Brodie and others who had actively co-operated with the regime.

The debates in London, then, can be seen not only as a submission to Cromwell of some very particular issues of ecclesiastical politics, and an attempt to get the current secular authority to favour one interpretation of developments within the church over another, but can also be seen as a struggle for political power in the community. Moreover, it seems fairly clear that this was consciously understood, both by Resolutioners and Cromwellians. Sharp retailed a revealing little incident in London to the ministers at home in Edinburgh, which seems to establish this quite clearly. Sir Charles Worsley remarked to Sharp: 'I suppose it cometh to this, these men would get into the saddle and you have no mind to it'. Sharp recorded his response: 'I laughingly said he had taken it up in short'.[93] It cannot then be argued, as presbyterian apologists have often wished to argue, that the ministers during the interregnum were concerned with 'religious' issues and were somehow separate from, and not involved in, the messy business of secular politics. By the mid-1650s it was clear that all parties within the church were prepared to make fundamental compromises in order to retain power in the community.

The immediate sequel to Sharp's return from London was an exchange of papers between Resolutioners and Protesters. The Resolutioners composed *A Declaration of the Brethren* in the form of an overture for peace, but it consisted principally of criticisms of the Protesters.[94] It brought forth in reply, as might have been expected, no overtures of union but an angry rejoinder, *Protesters No Subverters*, which in September the Resolutioners made a reply to.[95] Plainly the struggle would continue.

Cromwell died in September 1658. He was succeeded by his son Richard Cromwell, under whose rule the tenor of interregnum politics continued the general drift to the right that had been going on throughout Cromwell's time in power. This drift was of advantage to the Resolutioners since in general terms it was a move towards presbytery and hierarchy and away from independency and radical republicanism.[96]

In November the Resolutioners began to consider a fresh representation of their case before the government in London. To this date, if Sharp had not exactly triumphed in his mission, at least the English regime had not made any decisive move in favour of the Protesters, and Gillespie's Charter had been completely dropped. The consolidation of this stalemate, if that was the best that could be achieved, was to the Resolutioners' advantage, and worth a further embassy to London. When, however, the Resolutioners heard that Wariston had gone to the Parliament summoned for January 1659 in London as a Scottish member, and that he was to be followed by other Protesters, the possibility of new negotiations became a certainty. Once again the Resolutioners were reacting to the initiatives of others.

Sharp was once again prevailed upon, but apparently with difficulty, to go to London.[97] Several letters were written commending him to allies in London, among them Broghill, Thurloe and the Presbyterians Calamy, Ash and Manton, and in February he was sent on his way with instructions very similar to those he had previously been given, all tending to the reduction as far as possible of Protester power and influence. He proceeded as he had done before, making contacts and assessing who was likely to be sympathetic to his mission, and was introduced to Richard Cromwell, the new Protector, who greatly impressed Sharp. He observed the actions of the Parliament and wrote frequent bulletins to Scotland, but it was obvious that the affairs of the Scottish church no longer commanded the attention they had done on his first visit, and that now far more momentous issues were at stake. The conservative tendencies of Richard's Parliament seemed to the army radicals to threaten the 'Good Old Cause' and to imply the possibility of a return to monarchy or a Protectorate. The army therefore intervened to force the dissolution of Parliament and, in May 1659, Richard Cromwell's abdication. When the Parliament was dissolved in April Sharp was anxious to return home to take care of his parish, and because as a presbyterian he was now being classified as a royalist.

As Sharp had anticipated, the seizure of power by the army brought him under suspicion. He was called before the Council and questioned as to his behaviour, apparently because of a suspicion that he was in collusion with royalist plotters. From the account of his interrogation by the Council it seems clear that he had not been involved in plotting.[98] He was for a while ordered to stay in London but was eventually permitted to return to Scotland at the end of June.[99]

On his return to Edinburgh, Sharp's colleagues declared themselves satisfied with his conduct, but on any sort of objective view he had made much less impact on those in power than on his previous mission. What is more, as the Resolutioners had benefited from political changes earlier, so now the Protesters were benefiting. In these circumstances, as Sharp acknowledged, there was nothing that he could do to alter the course of events. Unfortunately, however, there is little evidence that the Edinburgh ministers understood this. They had accepted the political nature of Sharp's mission but were unable to recognise that circumstances were now altered. While Sharp was sending them descriptions of major political developments which he witnessed as a bystander, and was stressing his ineffectiveness and the uselessness of his remaining in London any longer, his brethren continued to send him assurances that they were convinced of the utility of the mission, and even sent him further minute instructions on issues such as the keeping of a fast and the revenues of vacant parishes. It was this basic failure of the ministers to comprehend Sharp's unwonted insignificance and inability to mould the future in these changed circumstances that was the fundamental reason for the troubles which followed upon his next expedition to England.

4
The Threshold of the Restoration

Sharp arrived back from his visit to the Protector in July 1659. It was nine months or so before he set out on his travels again, and in that period he had some influence on the course of events in Scotland. The political crisis in England proved incapable of resolution. By the middle of 1659 the lines of battle had been drawn. On one side stood the radicals represented by Lambert and his army in England, who were in favour of military government. On the other stood the supporters of parliamentary government and hierarchy. Monck, who was still governor in Scotland, was prepared to side with this second group. During the second half of 1659 it became clear that he would intervene in English affairs with the army of occupation that he commanded in Scotland.

The Resolutioner party among the Scottish ministers was ready to support Monck in this course of action which they anticipated would restore parliamentary government and possibly the king. Certainly the alternative, military radicalism, could not be thought likely to promote Resolutioner interests. On the other hand both Monck and his chief military supporter in England, Sir George Booth, were sympathetic to presbytery. Consequently in the last six months of 1659 the Resolutioners endeavoured to use their influence to make Monck's intervention in politics as effective as possible.

Their major contribution was their co-operation with Monck's efforts to ensure that Scotland would remain calm in his absence.[1] He was after all about to remove from an occupied country the majority of the forces previously thought necessary to keep the peace. It was less than four years since Glencairn's Rising had seriously threatened the Cromwellian hold on the country. True, the policy of the government had been to permit very few Scots to hold arms or to raise any force of armed men. It was hard to see how any real threat could be offered to the regime. Nevertheless even an inconsiderable rising or skirmish would be a grievous embarrassment were it to take place when Monck had left the country. The function of the ministers therefore was to represent Monck as the agent of God in troubled times and thus sway public opinion to his support.

Sharp's contribution to the success of this policy was to compose for Monck's use a 'Declaration of his intentions in marching into England with his army'. The draft of the document still survives in Sharp's handwriting and it is said to have been widely distributed. It was addressed to an English audience and presented to the army, possibly by Sharp himself, as it camped at Coldstream in late December 1659, on the eve of its departure into England.

The Declaration was a plea for a return to civilian government by traditional institutions and an attack on military dictatorship:

> We are confident that all rational and sober Christians and good patriots are sensibly and deeply affected with the sad condition of these nations through the tyrannical usurpations of some whose ambition hath prompted them ... to reduce us unto a chaos of confusion by overturning our governments, laws and liberties.[2]

It went on to ask for the support of the nation for a just and religious cause and excused the intervention of the army in civil matters as a necessary preliminary to the re-establishment of civilian government:

> Our scope and aim in our undertaking and engagements is the recovery of the just liberties and freedom of the people ... by having a free parliament, chosen by the people and protected from violence to settle the civil government.

The Declaration was a masterly piece of propaganda. Its effect in winning support for Monck in England is said to have been decisive.[3] Certainly Monck treated Sharp immediately after this incident with the utmost deference. The principal source of the Declaration's effectiveness was its emotional appeal. Monck's cause had been defined in the words and phrases which had proved so powerful in the civil war: 'just liberties'; 'free parliament'; 'tyrannical usurpation'. At the same time its very imprecision was a boon to Monck. No names were named; he was committed to no definite course of action. It allowed him maximum freedom to achieve his end of the re-establishment of parliament by whatever means he should find appropriate. Furthermore the document had the additional virtue of casting the opposition to Monck in the role of the aggressor. Monck, the Declaration declared, was reluctant, unwilling, to take up arms; only the misdeeds of a destructive clique, it implied, had induced him to defend the right, by force if need be. Additionally, however, it represented the Resolutioners' sense that radical political government, 'the good old cause', was not likely to benefit them, as their experience in the early 1650s had shown, but their enemies, the Protesters.

The satisfaction and gratitude of both Monck and the Resolutioners with Sharp's accomplishment were reflected in requests from both of them that he should once more go to London.[4] What the Resolutioners had in mind was that, with an influential friend like Monck, Sharp should be able to scotch the Protesters once and for all. Accordingly they drew up instructions for Sharp in which he was required to press for the complete restoration of presbyterian church discipline, an end to toleration, and control of vacant stipends and of the admission of ministers.[5] These instructions reveal that the broader implications of Monck's intervention in politics were by no means evident to the ministers. That was hardly surprising since the trend of events remained obscure for some weeks; but this failure in political insight was to persist for some months and eventually was the root cause of the breach between Sharp and his brethren.

A letter from the Resolutioners asking Monck for permission for Sharp to join him in London crossed one from Monck requesting Sharp's presence.[6] His reasons for wanting Sharp were not explained but what he most probably had in mind was that Sharp would provide a useful contact with the Scottish scene through his brethren. Moreover Sharp was a man with some influence among English presbyterians. Monck was entering a political arena from which he had been absent for some time, and in which any allies he could win were welcome. Sharp was a known and trusted political negotiator; his assistance might be worth having.[7]

Sharp arrived in London early in February and almost immediately seemed to enjoy political influence and success which confirmed the value put upon him by Monck and his brethren. His first task was to play a part in the re-admission to parliament of the secluded members. These men, more than a hundred of them, had been expelled from parliament in 1648 by the army when as presbyterians and royalists they had continued negotiations with the king despite the opposition of the army to that course of action. Their readmission in 1660 was thus confirmation of the rising fortunes of presbyterian and royalist opinion.

Sharp's contribution to this development was hardly decisive. He had added his voice to those who had persuaded Monck to readmit them, and he had acted as a messenger between Sir Anthony Ashley Cooper and John Weaver, the pro-presbytery members of the Rump, and Monck, as well as between some of the secluded members and Monck. Nevertheless it was a contribution which indicated that Sharp was close to the centre of political activities and that he enjoyed Monck's confidence. Furthermore the apparent significance of his intervention was heightened by Monck's announcement of his support for moderate presbytery: 'General Monck in a speech declares for presbyterian government not rigid'. Even though Monck's choice of words caused Sharp and his brethren in Edinburgh to whom he relayed it some hesitation, yet his public support for their dearest concerns could not but make them think that all was set fair for a satisfactory settlement in which Sharp would be able to achieve their precise ambitions.[8]

This essentially misleading interpretation of the political scene in London was apparently further ratified by the news a fortnight later that the parliament with the secluded members had given orders for the reprinting of the Solemn League and Covenant, a development greeted with great joy by the Edinburgh ministers.[9]

On any dispassionate observation, however, it could be seen that what Sharp had done towards achieving these happy ends was also very limited in scope. He had arrived in London when negotiations to return the secluded members were already in progress, and had been used by Monck to expedite them. His influence with Monck was by no means to be compared with the City of London's which also desired to see them returned. Parliament's decision on the Solemn League and Covenant and Monck's declaration of support for presbytery were certainly made without reference to Sharp. Furthermore the trend of these developments, satisfactory as it was, needed to be weighed against the rival ambitions of cavaliers and sectaries.

It is clear that Sharp understood some of these implications, but it is certain that his brethren did not. Their unlimited confidence in Sharp's capacity to achieve their desires was increased yet further by his involvement in the release from prison of the Scottish presbyterian nobility: the earls of Lauderdale and Crawford and Lord Sinclair. After the defeat of the Scottish army at Worcester large numbers of Scots had been taken prisoner. Most had been quite rapidly released, like Sharp himself, but the most influential, these three members of the nobility, had been kept in captivity right up to 1660. During the 1650s Sharp and the Resolutioners had kept in touch, and the release of the prisoners had been a matter for discussion at the time when Sharp's latest visit to London had been discussed among the ministers.

On his arrival in London, therefore, Sharp had made it his business to promote the release of these three noblemen. He had discussed the matter with Monck, visited the prisoners at Windsor, and solicited sympathetic MPs. In the first half of March they were duly released.[10] This success, however, had been achieved when the parliament was releasing other prisoners with presbyterian sympathies and when presbyterians were enjoying high favour. No doubt Sharp's intervention had hastened their release but he cannot be given the credit for that achievement.

Sharp's realisation of his own relative unimportance occurred with his attempts to carry out the letter of his instructions and guarantee the future triumph of the Resolutioners over the Protesters. He had discovered that the parliament with the sympathetic secluded members was soon to dissolve in order that elections might be held for another; that no legislation of any significance could be expected from a body so close to the end of its life; and that there was a general disposition to let Scottish matters rest until then. His reaction to his impotence was to ask to be allowed to return home to Scotland. He wrote to Robert Douglas:

> Sir, you will consider what in this juncture is fit to be done, and see that there is no more work for me here, the parliament not being to sit down till the 20 of April, which is to be constitute of members of the 3 nations, and therefore it will be fit to take me off, and return me to my charge. The General hath told me, and I see there is reason for it, that as to my instructions nothing can be done till there be a full House, and again[st] that time it will be advisable whether more be sent here for the interest of our church.[11]

Far from preventing others from coming to London to represent the Resolutioners, as his critics have often alleged, Sharp on this and many other occasions asked to be relieved of a task which he felt was impossible. The ministers in Edinburgh, however, were so pleased with what they saw as Sharp's triumphs so far, and so confident of his abilities, that they urged him to stay in London if Monck thought he should do so. Sharp had certainly made himself useful to Monck so far and Monck, when approached on the subject, was eager for him to stay.[12]

Monck's desire for Sharp's continued presence in London prevented Sharp from answering another call upon his services. On 12 March 1660, Lord Broghill wrote to the Resolutioner ministers in Edinburgh asking them to send an agent, either Sharp or James Wood, to him in Dublin. Broghill had come to an understanding with the Resolutioners during his year in Edinburgh and had given Sharp some help with his missions in London. His commitment to the interregnum had never been more than conditional and temporary, and now that he foresaw that the return of the king was possible he turned to the royalist

Resolutioners for support. It is not clear exactly why he wanted one of them to go to Ireland, but it seems likely he had in mind the co-ordination of the restoration of the king by presbyterian interests.

The Resolutioners were willing to have Sharp go to Ireland, provided that Monck approved of the venture; but Monck did not approve. It is likely that he was suspicious of Broghill and did not want to encourage him in his manoeuvring in Ireland. Furthermore Scotland had so far remained very satisfactorily quiescent and Monck clearly wished to avoid any occasion for restlessness. He therefore discouraged the projected trip and Sharp wrote to Broghill regretting its impossibility.[13]

The real interest of this exchange lies in what it implies about Sharp's reputation. Broghill thought Sharp and Wood capable of helping him in Ireland — in itself a tribute. But when Sharp himself was unable to make the journey, Wood was not sent in his place. Instead Sharp's brother was sent, not as a negotiator, but to bring Broghill up to date with affairs in England and Scotland. The inference that Sharp was the only possible man for the job is yet further evidence of the esteem of his fellow ministers.

As a result of Monck's insistence, for two months, March and April 1660, Sharp became involved in the tangled web of political manoeuvring that preceded the Restoration. He accomplished virtually nothing, not because he did not try or did not have the interests of the Resolutioners at heart, but simply because at a time of major political upheaval he was not important. Those whom he represented could safely be ignored until a more convenient time. At the very beginning of 1660 Monck had needed Resolutioner support and Sharp was capable of assisting him. By March and April events had moved on and Sharp's usefulness to Monck was that of a courier rather than a political ally.

As might have been expected, given that he was going to stay in London, one of Sharp's principal concerns was the activities and fortunes of the Protesters. On previous occasions when Resolutioner and Protester parties had sent representatives to London their suits had been fairly well balanced. No decisive advantage to either party had emerged. Now in 1660 the scales began to tip in the Resolutioners' favour. As it became more obvious that the king would be brought back, so the cause of the Protesters and their allies, the English Independents, faded. This process was hastened by Sharp to the best of his ability.

The first indication that the Protesters realised that their fate was sealed was an approach made to Sharp by Johnston of Wariston, apparently asking him to use his influence with Monck to ensure that no harm came to him. Sharp reported back to Edinburgh:

> Wariston hath been with me, and much in relenting of his late actings, and acknowledgement of his failings; his drift I suppose is that I may speak to the General for him, that he may have a personal protection, payment of his debts, or at least enjoyment of his places, with which I have told him, I cannot meddle.[14]

It was asking a lot to expect the Resolutioners to bail out one of their most relentless opponents the moment things began to go badly for him. Sharp's refusal to get involved was commended by his brethren in Edinburgh.[15]

But that was not the end of Wariston's activities, or of Sharp's dealings with him. Wariston was determined if he possibly could to influence the nature of the coming settlement. During the interval between the dissolution of the one parliament and the sitting of the next Wariston spread so much gossip about the untrustworthiness of the king, as demonstrated by his behaviour in Scotland in 1650 and '51, that he gained great favour with the Independents on the Privy Council. So pleased were they with him that he was given a pension of £600 a year. Just when things had seemed to be going so well for the Resolutioners, the wretched Protesters once again looked like snatching the victory and doing their level best to put difficulties in the way of the king's return.

The only thing that Sharp could do was give Monck his version of the king's behaviour in Scotland and for good measure the Resolutioner view of Wariston and the Protesters. Monck had perhaps never been as keen on Wariston as some members of the Council; his influence was growing while that of the Independents was diminishing; he was therefore prepared to prefer Sharp's attitude to Wariston's. He gave the Resolutioners an assurance that Wariston's pension would be stopped and that none of the Protesters would be given position or places. When Wariston approached Sharp a second time, asking him to use his influence to get him back his post as Clerk Register, it was plain that the battle was over and that the Resolutioners at last had won the day.[16]

Once again, though, as with his earlier successes, Sharp had done what he could to secure the ultimate demise of the Protester party, but he had not initiated their fall. He had merely hastened events down the path that they were already travelling. On all these issues circumstances had combined to work to the advantage of the Resolutioners. They were not to be so lucky in getting their own way on other issues that were decided during this period.

One such issue was the question of Scotland's representation as a nation in the coming settlement. The parliament which had been revived by Monck was the old Long Parliament. It had never had any Scottish representation since it had been summoned long before Cromwell's unification of the parliaments of England and Scotland. Originally Sharp had heard that the parliament which was to succeed the Long Parliament would have Scottish representation, but when the writs finally went out they were for England only. How, then, were Scottish interests to be safeguarded?

The Resolutioner solution to the problem was that the newly released members of the Scottish nobility should be commissioners for the kingdom of Scotland. Such an arrangement would suit their purposes admirably since the noblemen in question all had strong presbyterian sympathies and were certainly thought to be susceptible to direction from the Resolutioner leaders. Sharp had already ensured that they were introduced in the right political quarters and was plainly prepared to exploit whatever influence the noblemen might command in the interests of the Resolutioners.[17]

There were, however, two difficulties in the way of such an arrangement. One was that there were already commissioners for Scotland, elected before Monck left the country. They were still in Scotland and it had been indicated to them by Monck that their presence in London was not desired, but more important than that from the Resolutioner point of view was the fact that they did not represent Resolutioner interests. The most important of them was Glencairn; although a royalist, he represented secular interests, not religious. It was therefore necessary, if the Resolutioners were to secure their ends, to get Monck's permission for a new meeting of the shires and burghs, as the only representative bodies still functioning in Scotland, to elect as commissioners the three members of the nobility now in London. The second difficulty was that it proved impossible to get the necessary warrant for such a meeting from Monck.

Sharp's attempts to get a warrant from Monck were a complete failure. Not only would Monck not provide a warrant but he made it plain that he had no intention of allowing Scotland to be represented in any way at the coming parliament.[18] Although the refusal was diplomatically worded, it signified a total defeat for Sharp as a negotiator. It was an indication of his helplessness in the face of Monck's expressed will.

A second sphere in which Sharp proved equally powerless to influence developments was that of Scotland's independence. The Resolutioners were anxious that the Cromwellian Union should be terminated and Scotland restored as an independent nation. When it was proposed in the English Council that commissioners and judges should be sent to Scotland to carry on the work of the government of occupation, it seemed as though the union was liable to be indefinitely continued. Sharp therefore protested against this development to Monck. The only concession he could win from him was that none of those appointed would be Protesters or their supporters. He was unable to get any assurance that, once appointed, such officials would not be sent. Having failed to make any impression on Monck, Sharp and Lauderdale together made efforts to influence the members of the Council in their favour. They had reckoned without Monck's influence over its members. It made no difference how strongly the two Scots expressed themselves on the subject; the only promise made to them was that the union would be revoked at the next parliament. It was a promise which Sharp realised was virtually worthless. Monck quite frankly told Sharp that the present situation in Scotland suited him very well and would ensure that the nation remained politically dormant.[19] Once again Sharp had met his match.

These questions of national status were important to the Resolutioners, but their real preoccupation was with the form of the ecclesiastical settlement that would accompany any political settlement. Here, as in other matters, Sharp found himself the almost helpless spectator of developments that were far from pleasing to him or to his party. It is also on this issue that he has been accused by G. R. Abernathy of being 'a practitioner of duplicity',[20] and more generally at the time and since of having betrayed the presbyterian cause. Although there seems no evidence to support these charges, and much to confute them, and although psychologically such a course of action seems totally improbable, these accusations need to be considered carefully. There was, of course, no doubt about the settlement that would be satisfactory to the Resolutioners. They hoped for and expected the return of their Covenanted king, Charles II, to establish presbyterian church government in his three kingdoms according to the terms of the Solemn League and Covenant. Despite the unsatisfactory circumstances in which Charles had taken the Covenants, they anticipated that as restored king he would redeem the promises made in the oaths he had sworn. When Sharp was asked point blank in London whether he really thought the king intended to institute presbytery in England and Ireland he replied:

> He did by Covenant and treaty engage to us, by all lawful and peaceable ways to endeavour uniformity in doctrine, discipline, etc. in the three nations.[21]

When Sharp first arrived in London there were threats to presbytery and the Covenant from two sides: the Independents and the Episcopalians. But as the cause of the Independents waned, it became clear that the real challenge would be from episcopacy. First of all the rumour was that moderate episcopacy would be preferred to presbytery — a prospect that Douglas in Edinburgh viewed with disgust: 'We know by experience that moderate episcopacy . . . is the next step into episcopal tyranny'.[22] Soon, however, the increasingly confident cavalier party was bold enough to press its case harder.

A smear campaign against the Presbyterians was initiated. The intention behind it was to demonstrate that Presbyterians, and Scottish presbyterians in particular, were not capable of entire loyalty to the king and that therefore any idea of combining the return of the king with presbyterian church government should be abandoned: 'The buzzing of some is loud enough that *no bishop, no king*'.[23]

The Presbyterians therefore found themselves on the defensive. Very shortly after his arrival Sharp was asked by 'our friends in the City' — that is, the leading presbyterian ministers and their friends — to consider a declaration:

> [they found] it were not amisse that there were published a Declaration from the Nation of Scotland.

The intention of this would be, as Sharp wrote to the Edinburgh ministers, 'to guard against Sectaries upon the one hand, and Cavaleers upon the other'. His own inclination was that the time was not ripe — 'I think it not yet seasonable' — but he asked his brethren to think it over: 'it were fitt you had your thoughts about it in time'.[24]

On this basis Abernathy makes far-reaching accusations against Sharp: that 'the Presbyterian clergy in London sought aid from Scotland in the form of a declaration for Presbyterian government throughout all three kingdoms'. So far as I can see this is not the specific request that was made. Abernathy's conclusion — 'On this point at least Sharp performed a valuable service for the Anglicans by preventing a second Solemn League and Covenant' — seems very much overstated. At another point Abernathy remarks: 'the [London presbyterian] ministers . . . begged Sharp to obtain them a firm alliance with their Scottish brethren. This request Sharp failed to honour'.[25] This does not seem an accurate description of what Sharp was asked to do. What he did attempt, however, was to reassure radical English presbyterians of the king's probity.

Sharp spent some time trying to justify Douglas's sermon at the king's coronation in 1650 in Scotland and the imposition on Charles of the Dunfermline Declaration. Abernathy took this as part of evidence that Sharp was actively in the process of betraying the Presbyterians. He uses a letter written in code to Sir Edward Hyde from Edward Massey, dated 16 March 1660. This letter refers to Sharp's activities as follows:

> I forgott in my former letter to give you an account of what I have been well assured of, that is, that Mr Sharp, a Scots minister, who hath done his majesty all right possible concerning those aspersions, that had passed upon his majesty from Scotland, and satisfyed all reasonable men in the same, and that to his majesty's great advantage, of which I beseech you to inform the king. I doubt not but your lordship will thinke it meete to encouradg him to go on by his majesty's notice of the same.[26]

Abernathy interprets this as Massey notifying Hyde 'that Sharp was working for the king, not the Presbyterians, and should be rewarded'.[27] It seems doubtful whether this interpretation can be justified either as what Sharp was doing, or what Massey thought he was doing. It seems much more probable that Sharp was attempting to defend the Presbyterians against the charge that they were theocrats or necessarily opposed to royal authority. He was, that is to say, maintaining a Resolutioner rather than a Protester position. Massey clearly thought that Sharp's comments were valuable, but the 'aspersions from Scotland' must surely be those of which the king was accused in the Dunfermline Declaration, of corrupt behaviour and treachery. In a letter of 10 March 1660 Sharp describes what sounds very much like the source of Massey's letter:

> I found also that these [the Earl of Manchester, the Lord Wharton and some parliament men] and severall ministers have been possessed with the belief, that the King whilst he was in Scotland did breake to us in all the engagements upon him by the treatie, and was vicious and unclean whyl he was amongst us, and a scorner of ordinances, and discountenancer of honest ministers. I have told them, it was my duty to bear testimony to the truth, that all these were great lyes, and malicious forgeries; whyl he was in Scotland we could not say he did break to us, and so forth with in contradiction to all those false alledgances; and that the honest party of the Nation were well satisfied with him.[28]

Abernathy's interpretation seems to echo the willingness of the royalist enthusiasts at the time to suppose that anyone who supported the king must necessarily have abandoned any and all other priorities and loyalties.

Sharp was also approached by Episcopalians ready to do a deal. In exchange for political support for the return of the king, some Episcopalians were ready to promise concessions to Presbyterians when the Restoration was accomplished. Sharp notified his brethren in Edinburgh of these moves:

> Some of the episcopall party have sent message to me twice or thrice to give them a meeting, which I have refused; and upon this I am reported both here and at Brussels to be a Scottish rigid presbyterian, making it my work to have it settled here. They sent to desire me to move nothing in prejudice of the Church of England, and they would doe nothing to the prejudice of our Church. I bid tell them it was not my imployment to move to the prejudice of any party; and I thought did they really mind the peace of those Churches, they would not start such propositions.[29]

The Resolutioner leadership in Edinburgh was not averse to Sharp presenting the Presbyterian position:

> If it be not offensive to the presbyterians, I see no cause but you might have condescendit to meet with some of the prelaticall party upon their desire.[30]

It is, however, quite clear from these instructions that the Resolutioners did not countenance any kind of compromise with episcopacy.

Sharp's response was to negotiate with the English presbyterians with the idea of presenting a united front and agreed terms. Abernathy's interpretation of the subsequent negotiations is that Sharp and Lauderdale wished to prevent a united presbyterian front especially between Scottish and English presbyterians and instead to work for a compromise with the Anglicans:

> The mission of Lauderdale and Sharp was to prevent any combination or alliance between the Scottish and English Presbyterians. Their strategy was to emphasise the possibility of a compromise between English Presbyterians and Anglicanism, which embraced the calculated loss of the strict Presbyterians.[31]

There seems to be no evidence to support this point of view, which in any case seems to suggest a course of action utterly without motive. What possible reason, in the context of April 1660, could Lauderdale or Sharp have had for such a course of action?

Quite apart from what Sharp might have been doing, however, it was becoming quite clear that the Covenant would not be a condition of the king's return. As far as England, and probably Ireland, was concerned presbytery was unlikely to be enforced. With this realisation came the first flicker of fear for the Resolutioners that perhaps presbytery in Scotland was not after all a forgone conclusion. Sharp remarked dolefully:

> We may look for a settlement upon the grounds of the Covenant ... but I am dubious that this shall be the result of the agitations now on foot.[32]

By 19 April it was known to him that religion would not be mentioned in the treaty that parliament would make with the king, but would instead be 'referred to be settled by a synod'.[33] Douglas was horrified by the very idea: the king and the three nations were in his view irrevocably committed to the implementation of the Solemn League and Covenant. What could there be for a synod to discuss?

The implications of the abandonment of the Covenant were serious for Scotland even if it were assumed that presbytery would continue there. If England were to have episcopal church government, then the very real danger was that it would be extended to Scotland. It had happened under James VI, as Douglas pointed out, and as he well knew there were plenty in Scotland who would gladly enough abandon presbytery and the Covenant, 'feeding themselves with the fancy of episcopacy or moderate episcopacy'.[34]

In the prevailing uncertainty it was alarming to the Resolutioners that the Commissioners previously elected, the men that the ministers had tried to unseat in favour of Lauderdale and Crawford, had taken action. Against all advice from the Edinburgh ministers, from Sharp in London and from Monck, these men were on their way to London. The prospect was appalling to the Resolutioners. They had staked their all on waiting peaceably for the Parliament to restore kirk and nation: 'in quietness we wait for the sitting of the ensuing parliament which will undoubtedly ... take off all force from us and declare that Scotland is a free nation'.[35] Now the realisation of all those hopes was being threatened by Commissioners whose priorities were utterly different.

To these anxieties was added another. It came to Sharp's notice that an embassy from the Scottish nobility had been sent to the king. At first Douglas would not believe that such a thing could be true. He had felt so certain that the Resolutioners were in control of the situation, knew what was going on, and could by their moral authority ensure that no disruptive or divisive action took place. Even though the Commissioners had left for London against the desires and advice of the Resolutioners, Douglas had wrung from Glencairn an undertaking of some sort to prosecute presbyterian interests. But a mission to the king sent without even the knowledge of the Edinburgh ministers gave the lie to all their illusions of power. When Douglas was obliged to admit that indeed Mungo Murray had been sent to the king by the Scottish nobility and without reference to the ministers, he was quite astute enough to realise that such a mission would not operate to the advantage of the Resolutioners: 'I believe that no information that goes that way is for our concernments'.[36]

When the abandonment of the plan to bring the king in on Covenant terms and the activities of the anti-Covenant Commissioners were added to the episcopalian campaign against the Presbyterians and the mission of the nobility to the king, the total was anything but favourable to the Resolutioners' ambitions for a settlement. Douglas's solution to the dilemma was to send Sharp to the king to rescue the Resolutioners' reputation from whatever misrepresentations it had suffered:

> If the General had thought meet to let you step over and give him [the king] information both concerning his [Monck's] and our carriage, it had been, and yet were, to some good purpose .... I do conceive that he [the king] gets bad enough information; I wish he might know who were and are his real friends.

Douglas recognised, however unwillingly, that the enforcement of the Covenant was a lost cause, and entrusted Sharp with the welfare of the Resolutioner interests: 'your great errand', he wrote, 'there [in Breda] will be for this kirk'.[37]

As Douglas had anticipated, it suited Monck very well to send Sharp to Breda with messages to the king, and so with commissions from both parties he sailed from Gravesend on 4 May. Sharp's mission to Breda was to be entirely unproductive as far as securing Resolutioner interests was concerned. Its real importance lies in the assumptions which underlay it. The Resolutioners represented one party among a divided ministry. Furthermore, as they themselves well knew, they did not enjoy the support of all Scotsmen, and certainly not that of all the nobility. They were, that is to say, one interest among others in the Scottish nation. Their own view of themselves, however, was as the party with the best claim to influence the nature of the civil and religious settlement of the country. Moreover that view of their moral right was not tempered by any comprehension of the political realities standing in the way of its realisation. Although Sharp had been faced repeatedly with his incapacity to achieve the ends of his party, neither he nor the Edinburgh ministers appeared to have any doubt that their ambitions for Scotland would be realised with the return of the king. That confidence derived partly from the brethren's rather inflated assessment of what Sharp had accomplished on his trips to London during the 1650s, but also from their political naiveté. In fact Sharp was being assigned a mission impossible from which only bitterness and disillusionment could grow.

Moreover Sharp's journey to Breda was attended by circumstances which ever since have given rise to the suspicion that he betrayed the Resolutioners. On the whole that seems unlikely; nevertheless it is not hard to see how the suspicion developed. In the first place Sharp went on a dual mission: he was agent for Monck as well as for the Resolutioners. The Edinburgh ministers were well aware of that fact; indeed Douglas had assumed that it might well be convenient for Monck to use Sharp as a courier, and Sharp made no secret of it. In a letter to his brethren he explained that Monck wanted him to get the king to 'write a letter to Mr Calamy [the London presbyterian], to be communicated to the presbyterian ministers, showing his resolution to own the godly sober party and to stand for the true protestant religion in the power of it'. In addition Monck wanted Sharp to give the king an account of his recent activities and the state of affairs in Scotland.[38] There is no reason to doubt that Sharp gave an accurate account of Monck's commission to him. The General was not the only one to think that the king would be well advised to make a public statement of his affiliation to protestantism, and his intention to espouse moderation in ecclesiastical matters. Monck, as far as can be judged had the interests of moderate Presbyterians at heart, and was prepared to use the opportunity of his temporary influence with the royal court to safeguard their future. In addition it was reasonable to suppose that Monck would wish the king to be kept informed of his activities, particularly if the message was to be carried by Sharp who had every reason to give a favourable account of Monck's behaviour.

The very fact that Sharp had two commissions, however, one from the Resolutioners and one from Monck, led Osmund Airy, the nineteenth-century editor of the *Lauderdale Papers*, and a ferocious critic of Sharp, to smell a rat. 'It will be clear . . .', said Airy, 'that Sharp was playing the double game. He was supposed by the Resolutioner party to be going to the Hague as their agent. In reality he went as Monk's'.[39] But Airy had not seen the complete version of the correspondence between Sharp and the Edinburgh ministers; in the light of that evidence it seems unnecessary to suppose a conflict of interests between Sharp's two commissions.

There are rather better grounds for wondering, however, whether Sharp was entirely devoted to the Resolutioner cause. One such is his relationship with the Earl of Lauderdale. Lauderdale had first become well known to Sharp when he was still in prison after Worcester and when Sharp was making his first trip to London as Resolutioner agent in 1657. At that time Lauderdale was already interested in forming a royalist alliance between Presbyterians and moderate

E

Episcopalians. Using Sharp as a messenger, he had carried on a correspondence with Baxter, one of the most prominent of English moderate dissenting divines, most likely with the intention of forming some such alliance.[40] In 1660 when the Restoration was plainly imminent, Lauderdale had again been involved with Sharp in the negotiations between Presbyterians and Episcopalians. But in addition he was co-operating at about this time in an attempt to arrange a compromise scheme of moderate episcopacy for England, which it was hoped would have the king's support.[41] In other words Lauderdale had for some time been prepared to consider compromise schemes of church government for England. It is no coincidence that a copy of Bishop Ussher's proposals for moderate episcopacy is among his papers for the pre-Restoration period.[42] Sharp had been closely associated with Lauderdale for some time; to what extent might he have been influenced by Lauderdale's train of thought? If presbytery seemed impossible to attain for Scotland, might he be willing to settle for a promise of moderate episcopacy? Abernathy seized upon Sharp's association with Lauderdale to further his claim that Sharp was 'a practitioner of duplicity'.[43] But as will be described later, Lauderdale was the only member of the Scottish nobility who was willing to defend Scottish presbytery to the king.

It seems likely that eventually in the spring of 1661, a year later, Sharp did settle for this line of reasoning. There is no evidence, however, that he pursued it on his visit to the king at Breda. He and his brethren had reluctantly faced the fact that it was unlikely the Solemn League and Covenant would be implemented, but they had as yet no serious doubts that presbytery in Scotland would continue. The king, they thought, might have been a little misinformed about the attitudes of Resolutioners, but Sharp would put that right and all would be well.

On the other hand Sharp's relationship with the Earl of Glencairn again gives one some reason to hesitate before asserting that he was absolutely single-minded in his devotion to the Resolutioners. Glencairn had been the leader of the major royalist rising in Scotland in the early 1650s. In December 1655 he was captured and imprisoned. There was every reason to suppose that he would be executed, but it seems that he was saved from that fate by Sharp's intervention with the Cromwellians.[44] That action was certain to have created a bond between them, and a sense of obligation to the Resolutioners on Glencairn's part. Thus when he set out for London in April, Douglas had been able to wring from Glencairn an assurance that he would promote their interests.[45] In fact there was very little reason to suppose that Glencairn's own predilections were for presbytery, as Douglas recognised; the relationship between Sharp and Glencairn was therefore bound to be rather complex. On the one hand Glencairn probably wanted to do Sharp a good turn, on the other his affinity was closer to episcopacy.

The implication drawn from this paradox by Gilbert Burnet, author of the *History of his own Times* and no friend to Sharp, was that Glencairn recommended Sharp to the king as the man best able to establish episcopacy in Scotland.[46] It is true that Glencairn did send letters of recommendation of Sharp to both Edward Hyde and the king at Breda. They survive, and describe Sharp as 'no severe presbyterian'.[47] It is possible that this phrase implies something like 'a man who is not firm to presbytery', but it is much more likely that it means 'a man who is not a theocrat, nor a Protester'. The one really important issue in the debate on the survival of presbytery was whether it could co-exist with monarchy: the old issue of 'no bishop, no king'. In his letters Glencairn was probably recommending Sharp as the sort of Presbyterian who was prepared to allow the king effective power.

On the whole therefore the suspicion that Sharp might have betrayed the Resolutioners at Breda and the Hague has no supporting evidence. What is more, there is a great deal of evidence to suggest that he made the best of his opportunities to present his case to the king. In the event he failed to elicit any concrete assurances from Charles about the future of the church in Scotland, but once again it was not because he did not try, but because he was a relatively insignificant figure at a time of crisis.

Sharp had set off for Breda on 4 May. A ship had been provided for him by General Monck's order, but because of adverse winds it was not until the evening of 8 May that he arrived at the court. He spent six days there and during that time had five personal interviews with the king. He had been instructed by Monck to deliver his letters to the king at the first possible opportunity, and so on the evening of the 8th he was ushered into the royal presence by the Marquis of Ormond 'and had a most gracious acceptance'. He delivered the letters and was given an appointment to meet the king the following morning, Wednesday, 9 May, at nine o'clock in the royal bedchamber.[48]

The warmth of Sharp's welcome and his ready access to the king in the next few days are no surprise. In the first place he was bringing up-to-date news of events in London which Charles was certainly very eager to hear. More than that he had met the king before during his time in Scotland in circumstances where Sharp was among those ministers prepared to support the king. That early association between Sharp and the royalist cause had been strengthened by his interrogation by the Council over royalist plots in 1659 and more recently by the letter from London to Hyde which described Sharp as a man who defended the king's reputation against the smears of Protesters and independents.[49] In addition the letter of recommendation that Sharp brought with him from Lauderdale and Glencairn must further have enhanced his status as a man who could be trusted.

The first interview with the king lasted an hour and a half and was taken up 'in giving a full account of General Monck's proceedings and of the activity of these of our nation to improve that opportunity for his Majesty's service'.[50] Sharp took the opportunity to praise the loyalty of the Scottish nobility, but it was not until the second interview that he had a chance to talk of Scottish church affairs. This second meeting also took place on the Wednesday, but in the evening. The king invited Sharp to walk with him in the garden while they talked, surrounded, but perhaps not overheard, by crowds of other supplicants. For nearly two hours the king reminisced about Scotland, asking about ministers he knew and discussing Sharp's activities in London and the doings of the parliament.

At the third meeting, which took place in one of the royal apartments, Charles again talked of events and people in Scotland. On this occasion Sharp seized the opportunity to discuss the Resolutioner-Protester struggle, but was interrupted by the arrival 'of a lord come straight from England' whose news was certainly of more immediate interest to the king. This third meeting was however the last good opportunity that offered at Breda for Sharp to discuss the Scottish church. The court was becoming extremely busy in anticipation of the king's imminent return to England. Although Sharp was given two more audiences, on both occasions the king was interested only in hearing about Monck. His attempts to talk about Scotland were put off by Charles until he should get to England.

From the point of view of promoting the interests of the Resolutioners the trip had not been a great success. It had not been possible to accomplish nearly as much as the Edinburgh ministers had hoped. Indeed no enterprise could possibly have been more pragmatic and opportunist than Charles's restoration. As far as he was concerned, religion was just one more thing to be played by ear and remitted for further attention when he was safely on the throne.

On the other hand Sharp had received an extremely good impression of the king's character and personality. He felt confident that presbytery was fairly safe and commented on the king's apparent goodwill towards Scotland:

> I found his Majesty resolved to restore the kingdom to its former civil liberties, and to preserve the settled government of our church, in both which I was told expressly to move, and had a very gracious satisfying answer.[51]

Nor was Sharp the only one to repose confidence in the king's goodwill. When the court moved from Breda to the Hague, Sharp followed, pausing only to take in a little sightseeing: 'I hastened from Breda by way of Dort, Amsterdam, Harlem and Leyden to take a transient view of those goodly towns, and came the next day after the king, to the Hague'. There he found a deputation of the English presbyterian ministers, similarly impressed with their meetings with the king. Although their suggestions as to how the king might regulate his religious observance more to their satisfaction by abandoning his use of the Prayer Book had been rather brusquely rejected, yet even so they were content to depend on the king's goodwill for the settlement of religion in England and to forgo conditions or guarantees.[52]

At Charles's request Sharp stayed with these men at the Hague until 23 May when the entire court took ship and sailed for England. On 25 May the fleet landed and the king, thronged by ecstatic crowds, began to make his way towards London.

5

From Presbyter to Archbishop

When Sharp arrived back in London he found waiting for him a stack of letters from the Edinburgh ministers. There was a letter for him to present to the king and instructions for him for the trip to Breda. Douglas had anticipated that these instructions would not arrive in time for Sharp to see them before he left for Breda but that they might be useful for reference. In fact the Resolutioners' case was so familiar to Sharp that he noted with some satisfaction that he had on his own initiative and according to earlier instructions brought up many of the issues the ministers mentioned: 'It hath much satisfied me', he wrote to his brethren in Edinburgh, 'that upon perusal of yours at my return I remembered I hit upon some of those [particulars] you touched'. The main points which Sharp had been called upon to raise were the familiar ones of the welfare of the Scottish church, the discountenancing of the Protesters, and the Resolutioners' hopes that the English church would be settled according to the Solemn League and Covenant. The letter to the king conveyed the congratulations and expectations of the Resolutioner ministers. Sharp promised that they would present it as soon as possible.[1]

It was becoming plain, however, from these communications that the Edinburgh ministers had not fully adjusted to Sharp's reports on ecclesiastical affairs, despite their recognition that his concern in Breda should be primarily for the Scottish church rather than for the three covenanted kingdoms. In his absence abroad they had written to their presbyterian contacts in London and elsewhere, voicing their sense 'of the sad consequences of setting up episcopacy and the use of liturgy again', and urging the English presbyterians to make every effort to prevent this happening.[2] Similarly among Sharp's instructions was a petition for him to present to the king in which Charles was urged not to use the service book in his private devotions. More than that, although Sharp had foretold the triumph of episcopacy in England and had pointed out that ministerial interference from Scotland would only harm the Scottish church, yet the Edinburgh ministers persisted in requiring him to urge the matter of the Covenant upon the king.

The basis for this importunity on the part of Sharp's brethren was not only their long-standing commitment to the Covenant and their emotional attachment to a cause for which they had fought so long. They undoubtedly believed that the king was personally well-affected to presbytery and would not betray the oath he had sworn in the Solemn League and Covenant. If therefore presbytery were not implemented in England, it would not, in the view of the Resolutioners, be the king's fault but that of his subjects. Since the ministers were equally pledged to maintain the Covenant it was their duty in the circumstances to urge English presbyterians to urge their case with the king. It was further the duty of the Resolutioners to represent their own desire to see the Covenant implemented, through their agent Sharp. Since they were convinced of the king's goodwill, they were unable to believe that such urgings could possibly be harmful to the cause they supported. This was the line of argument that they presented to their English presbyterian friends:

> We may assure you that you have to do with a moderate prince, who is ready to hearken to sound and wholesome council, whereof we had large experience in that his Majesty was not only content to ratify the religion as it was established amongst us [in 1650] as to the subjects, but did readily condescend to lay aside the service book, and observed the Directory of Worship in his own practice and family all the while it pleased God to continue his Majesty with us. You have now the advantage of humble dealing with a prince long trained in the school of affliction, and preserved therein, and (we trust) fitted thereby to be an eminent instrument in God's right hand for the advancement of his Son's kingdom. And therefore we trust his Majesty will hearken to what humble service God shall put into your hearts for him, that he may be as exemplary in his own practice, and put forth his royal power for a satisfaction of honest men in the matter of religion.[3]

This view of the king was a romantic fiction which had little to do with the objective reality of Charles's persistent reluctance to have anything to do with the Covenant, and his distaste for Scots presbytery. It was perhaps understandable as an expression of a traditional Scottish willingness to honour and think well of the king, but it bore little relationship to Sharp's most recent experience. Even though Sharp had returned from the Hague inclined to think kindly of Charles, yet he had been a witness to the cool reception of the pressures which the English presbyterians had attempted to bring to bear. At the Hague Calamy and his brethren had urged the king to abandon use of the service book until religion was settled by Parliament. Their suggestion had been ignored. It was probably with this incident in mind that Sharp asserted to the Edinburgh ministers: 'For me to press uniformity for discipline and government upon the king and others I find would be a most disgustful employment, and successless'.[4]

Sharp must also have been aware of Chancellor Hyde's aversion to presbytery and perhaps had some idea of the power that Hyde wielded in 1660. Longstanding English antagonisms to the Scots survived in England and he could see only too well what an adverse reaction there would be to anything that looked even faintly like meddling in English church affairs. His response to the ministers' letters was therefore to emphasise with all the vigour at his command that intervening in English church government would do absolutely no good. So strongly did he feel this, that he asked to be replaced in London if the ministers continued to insist on this line of approach: 'If you see cause of application to be made in this critical juncture, you will take me off'.[5]

Indeed it was plain that Sharp had had more than enough of diplomatic activity. He disliked the crowd of Scottish place-seekers now flocking to London, and kept aloof from the manoeuvring that went on among them. He felt increasingly that he could accomplish nothing more and asked to be returned home.[6]

For a time the Edinburgh ministers continued to require Sharp to press their views on the settlement of the English church, but towards the middle of June they began to recognise that if Sharp had made their views known to the king and to the English presbyterians, and they had still taken no notice, then there was nothing more that could be done.[7]

But still nothing had been formally decided about the Scottish church. The king had given assurances that its government would not be altered, but the Resolutioners had had experience of the effects of an English episcopal system on the Scottish church and were nervous about the security of presbytery. Sharp had had difficulty in gaining access to the king to represent these anxieties since, as might be expected, the court was crowded and the king overwhelmed with business as soon as he got to London. He had however presented one of the Edinburgh ministers' letters and eventually on 14 June was summoned by Charles.[8]

Clearly the king had been made aware of the fears and suspicions of the Resolutioners. The interview with Sharp had been designed to reassure them and to put an end to Sharp's mission. He emphasised to Sharp that the kirk was safe and that a General Assembly would be held as soon as the parliament could be summoned for Scotland. He then said that rather than the Resolutioners send more representatives to London, Sharp himself should go back to Edinburgh and give a full report of the situation. He promised that Sharp should have a letter to take with him setting down these assurances in writing.[9]

So Sharp's long mission was nearly over; he would very soon get the necessary permission to leave court and would shortly be back in Edinburgh. While he waited for his official dismissal he reported on the ever-increasing confidence of the extreme episcopalians in London and the sagging morale of the English presbyterians. He also tried to keep the ministers up to date with the rumours about what would happen to Scotland.[10]

On 14 July, exactly a month after the first meeting, Sharp was again summoned by Charles and seized the opportunity to put the Resolutioners' point of view once more. He wrote to Douglas that he had had the chance 'to give a full information to all those particulars you by your former letter did desire'. The king promised the long-awaited letter within a day or two and mentioned that he would see Sharp once more before he left for Scotland.[11]

Shortly thereafter the draft of the king's letter was shown to Sharp and he gave an outline of its contents to the Edinburgh ministers before he brought it with him to Edinburgh. He was delighted to have received such an assurance of the king's goodwill towards the Resolutioners and such a vindication of his own role in the negotiations. Still he could not go until the letter passed the Signet, which in turn depended on the official appointment of Lauderdale as Secretary of State for Scotland. At last it was done and Sharp left London. He arrived in Edinburgh on 31 August 1660, after an absence of some seven months.[12]

On the day after Sharp's arrival in Scotland the Edinburgh ministers convened to hear his report on his negotiations and to receive the king's letter which was addressed to Robert Douglas. Naturally the ministers were pleased with the apparent success of Sharp's mission and were grateful for his efforts on behalf of the Resolutioners' cause:

> [Sharp] delivered the letter to Mr Robert Douglas and made report of his negotiation, for the success whereof the brethren blessed the Lord, and for Mr Sharp's great pains and care therein gave him hearty thanks.[13]

The next step was to arrange a meeting of the presbytery of Edinburgh to whom, according to the king's instructions to Douglas, the royal letter was to be communicated. This was accordingly fixed for the first possible occasion, Monday 3 September.

The letter has since become a focus of controversy.[14] It began with a grateful recognition of the constant loyalty of the Resolutioners and an acknowledgement of Sharp's good services. Later, when the promises made in the letter had been betrayed, disappointed Scots would say that Sharp had penned it himself and thus proposed his own vote of thanks.[15] There is no evidence for this assertion and every reason to think that he deserved an honest tribute.

The letter then went on to assure the Resolutioners that those who had not been as faithful as they to the king's cause — by which the Protesters were obviously to be understood — would be 'discountenanced'. Then came the most important section. The king promised 'to protect and preserve the government of the Church of Scotland as it is settled by law'. This was to be the most contentious section of all. There is no doubt that as matters stood in September 1660 the law had established presbytery,[16] and that the king's letter unequivocally guaranteed that settlement. This was made even more certain by the next part of the letter which gave notice of the king's intention to call a General Assembly and to summon Robert Douglas and some other ministers to consult with him. Finally the ministers were warned not to meddle in civil affairs and were asked for their prayers for the king and his government.

On the face of it therefore the letter was a vindication of Sharp's mission, a demonstration of the goodwill of Charles to the Resolutioners, and a mark of the complete victory of the Resolutioner cause. That is undoubtedly how it was received by the grateful presbytery of Edinburgh who forthwith addressed a tribute of thanks to the king and sent copies of the royal letter to all the other presbyteries in Scotland.[17]

Sharp was also apparently prepared to take the letter at face value. Shortly after his return to Scotland he wrote to Lauderdale telling him how well the letter had been received and how satisfactory the king's assurances were to him:

> I perceive nothing could have more contributed at this juncture for securing and promoting his Majesty's interest in this land among all good people than the sending of that letter.[18]

Sharp clearly shared the Resolutioners' trust in the king. He was not quite so confident about the Scottish nobility and during the next few months made considerable efforts to indicate to his brethren the possible dangers still facing the church from political manoeuvres in London.

The effect of Sharp's return to Edinburgh had been to leave the settlement of ecclesiastical policy in the hands of the politicians in London. The expected summons to Robert Douglas never came. The effect of the letter had been to quieten the suspicions of the Edinburgh ministers and to secure the *status quo* until such times as ecclesiastical policy should be decided in London.

In the long run ecclesiastical policy was to be decided on non-religious and pragmatic grounds by anti-presbyterian politicians. Since Sharp was the only presbyterian minister of any importance who benefited by that change, by being given the archbishopric of St Andrews, the question must be whether the letter that he brought to Scotland was part of a conspiracy against the Resolutioners in which he joined. Was he bribed by the archbishopric?

It seems unlikely. In the first place ecclesiastical policy really had not been decided in the summer of 1660. The discussions which took place in London in December 1660 on the form of church government for Scotland certainly considered the possibility of the continuation of presbytery. Secondly the spirit of anti-clericalism abroad had dictated that Sharp should be sent home to Scotland. It is most unlikely that he had been taken into confidence by the arbiters of policy. Burnet alleged that Sharp had caballed with Middleton to introduce episcopacy.[19] There is no evidence for the assertion, and Sharp's opposition to Middleton's later activities in the spring of 1661 certainly does not suggest an accomplice. On the other hand he was no fool and probably had some idea that episcopacy was in the minds of certain members of the Scottish nobility.

Once the letter had been delivered, Sharp's thoughts turned towards his career. He was still minister of Crail and from time to time during his absence had reminded the Edinburgh ministers of his duties there and his desire to return to the parish. Steps had in fact been taken by the local presbytery to ensure that the parish did not suffer too badly during his absence. During his spell in London, however, a vacancy had occurred in the ranks of the Edinburgh ministers through the death of Mr Law in February 1660. The other ministers had decided that Sharp was the obvious man to fill the post and had proceeded some way to having him transferred from Crail. Sharp himself from the very first was opposed to this idea, and eventually by his earnest requests in letters from London persuaded his brethren to abandon the plan, at least for the time being. On his return to the city, however, the matter was taken up again and he was pressed to agree to a transfer.[20]

There was another possibility that appealed to Sharp much more: to become an academic. He had spent several years as a regent at St Leonard's College before his entry into the parish ministry and was really rather an obvious choice for a senior post. Indeed the prospect had already been mooted a year before when he had been nominated by the Resolutioner Professor of Divinity in St Mary's College for the vacant third master's place there. Samuel Rutherford, the Protester Principal of the College, had however proposed his own candidate instead. The presbytery of St Andrews, whose responsibility it was to fill the place, found itself unable to agree which candidate should be chosen, with the result that in June 1660 the matter had still not been decided and the place was still vacant. The decline of Protester influence had in the interim settled the matter, though, and with Samuel

Rutherford dissenting the presbytery announced its intention of calling Sharp to that place. Clearly nothing could finally be arranged until Sharp returned from England, but when he did he began to incline towards taking the post. He was encouraged further by the request of the Synod of Fife in October 1660 that he should accept it.[21]

As minister of Crail he had attended the meeting of the synod in October. The presbyteries in Fife had deferred their consideration of the king's letter until the synod should meet, and consequently the drawing up of an answer was the chief business of the meeting. It was not accomplished without friction. There were two problems: one was that the old Protester-Resolutioner antagonisms were renewed; the other that the members knew little of what had gone on in England and found it hard to accept Sharp's argument that caution was necessary in framing their reply, in the interests of the welfare of the Scottish church.

Sharp explained to the synod that the Solemn League and Covenant was utterly out of favour in England and that presbyterian church government in Scotland had many enemies at court, even including members of the Scottish nobility. His argument was therefore that the Covenant should be forgotten and the Scots make do with the royal guarantee of presbytery in Scotland, rather than stir up trouble by bewailing what they could not help. The synod should therefore, Sharp maintained, send a reply to the king's letter which could not be construed as offensive, and which would avoid reference to the king's swearing of the Solemn League and Covenant.

This argument was not well received by the Protesters in the synod who wished now to remind the king of his obligations under the Covenant and who thought little of Sharp's achievements in England. The letter was eventually written in the way that Sharp suggested, without mentioning the Covenant or any of the other points at issue between Protester and Resolutioner. But that end was not achieved without difficulty.[22]

Sharp quite obviously believed that if the ministers behaved themselves and refrained from irritating the king by inconvenient reminders of what Charles would rather forget, then the Scottish church would survive with presbyterian government intact. He had supporting evidence for his belief that outspokenness could do no good. A number of Protester ministers were imprisoned by the Committee of Estates in August for composing an address to the king just such as the synod of Fife would have liked to send.[23]

In the first half of November Sharp continued his policy of trying to render the Scottish church acceptable to the king by making moves towards a reconciliation with the Protesters. The Resolutioner attitude to the Protesters was by now rather equivocal. They had for so long made it their chief interest and concern to do down the Protesters that it was hard for them to realise that the struggle was over; they were still quite capable of written attacks on them. On the other hand they had witnessed the recent imprisonment of fellow ministers. Sharp had warned of enemies to the kirk, and it was already obvious to both him and Baillie that the arrest formed a dangerous precedent. For these reasons, then, an initiative towards union was not altogether unexpected.[24] In December, however, this happy and hopeful state of affairs and Sharp's peace of mind were most suddenly and brutally overturned.

Sharp had left London in August after it had been decided to hold a parliament in Edinburgh but before the detail of royal policy in Scotland had been worked out. In the late summer of 1660, however, the king began to turn his mind to Scottish affairs. In August it was decided that the administration of Scotland should, for the time being, rest with a Committee of Estates, and in the same month appointments were made to most of the Scottish offices.[25]

These developments had been followed later in the year by a meeting of the most important of the Scottish nobility, who were all still in London, to discuss the instructions to be given to the Earl of Middleton as Commissioner, that is the king's representative, at the coming parliament. On this occasion Scottish church government was discussed. Although Lauderdale supported a presbyterian system, Middleton and his allies succeeded in persuading the king that episcopacy could be restored without trouble. Middleton was then given complete discretion in the means to be used in effecting this end. This news, or rumour of it, reached Sharp in mid-December.[26]

It was a heavy blow in that it confirmed all Sharp's worst fears. He was not, however, a man to sit down and bewail his fate. He therefore embarked on a series of letters to Lauderdale in London via the Resolutioners' agent, Patrick Drummond, to vindicate himself and to plead for presbytery as a system quite consistent with royal authority. They are undoubtedly impressive letters. The indignation and concern for presbytery that they demonstrate are a strong argument for the integrity of Sharp's behaviour as Resolutioner agent.[27]

There are seven basic themes in this series of letters and they are repeated over and over again. The first is an assertion by Sharp that contrary to any rumour or gossip that might be current, he had not contributed to any attempt to ensure episcopacy in the English church, and conversely that he had no intention of seeking to impose a Scottish presbyterian system in England either. The first accusation is that also made by Abernathy, and in my view inadequately supported by him. It should be noted that in these letters Sharp is protesting his innocence of any such plan to Lauderdale, the man with whom in Abernathy's view he is supposed to have collaborated to this end. It should also be noted that here Sharp is defending himself against precisely opposite accusations: that he plotted to ensure that the Church of England should be either episcopal or presbyterian. This circumstance in itself must cast doubt on the accusations.

A second theme of the correspondence is Sharp's assertion that though he is a Presbyterian, yet he is for the strengthening of the king's prerogative. For this purpose he wanted to see the Protesters subdued. He also wanted a General Assembly to be summoned after the Parliament so that an occasion might be provided on which the Scottish church might demonstrate that the vast majority of Presbyterians were prepared to allow the king effective power and thus demonstrate their loyalty. Similarly he reported the preaching of two sermons before Parliament in which he tried to demonstrate the Resolutioners' willingness to acknowledge royal authority.

A third theme emphatically stated is Sharp's clear understanding that any attempt to introduce episcopacy will not work and will prove counter-productive. He categorically asserts that there is no significant support for episcopacy and that its introduction will cause a great deal of trouble. This is so evidently true to Sharp that in response to charges that he had plotted to bring such an end about he asks what possible benefit he could be thought to gain by collaborating in any such attempt. He has certainly not tried to alter the government of the church of Scotland, and notes ironically that again he is the object of directly contradictory assertions: one that he was supporting high-flying presbytery in the face of the king's legitimate desire for authority, secondly that he was plotting to introduce episcopacy.

As for promoting his own interests, as Sharp points out, he could have found more straightforward ways of doing so. He has, he asserts, neither plotted, nor colluded, nor sought nor received financial reward. Had he wanted a preferment in England he had been offered it. Had he sought preferment in Scotland he would have chosen a more secure route and one more likely to give returns than the job of a bishop in Scotland. Had he sought financial gain he would have gone a better way about it than one which had left him out of pocket and with the promise of a pension that in the current state of the Scottish Exchequer he thought it was unlikely he would ever be paid.

Sharp goes on to say that accusations are being laid at his door that suggest he has superhuman power to influence events and yet it is blindingly obvious that the direction of policies of every kind in Scotland is in the hands of those who have no intention of allowing power to ministers or churchmen of any kind. In the face of such anti-clericalism he is powerless to influence the course of events.

In these circumstances, his last theme goes on, what advantage could be possibly have in betraying the Earl of Lauderdale as he is rumoured to have done? Lauderdale is the man who has throughout been the Resolutioners' only significant noble ally. Sharp has worked closely with him. At this juncture Lauderdale seems the only one willing to defend presbytery. Sharp must be civil to Middleton as King's Commissioner, and he must carry out his duties as royal chaplain, but Lauderdale is the only one he trusts.

But however much Sharp might passionately deny the rumours that were flying about, he was faced in early January with the realities of the political process. The Parliament convened in Edinburgh on New Year's Day 1661. Sharp then began to perform for the first time his duties as King's Chaplain in Scotland. When he had left for Scotland in August 1660 the king had given him this post with a salary of £200 per annum in token of his services. As Sharp himself pointed out when this gift became the object of malicious rumour, the Scottish Exchequer was hardly likely to be able to pay him such a sum in the foreseeable future. The duties of his office were to wait upon the king or his Commissioner in Scotland and to provide him with such religious services as he might require.[28]

When Middleton had arrived in Edinburgh he had summoned Sharp and asked him to say grace at the Commissioner's table daily. This meant that Sharp was obliged to stay in Edinburgh and was daily rubbing shoulders with Middleton and those whom he entertained. On the basis of these contacts he seemed to be optimistic for the church. After all, what he had heard from London had been rumour and notice of intention, whereas Middleton himself had said to Sharp that he had no intention 'to meddle with the church'. He had additional reason for confidence: Middleton's behaviour in the Articles. The Articles was a committee which prepared matter for the approval of Parliament. It was the only place where proper discussion was possible. When a proposal to annul all legislation since 1638 was proposed, Middleton quashed it.[29]

In this more hopeful atmosphere, then, Sharp turned his mind once more to the question of the post in St Andrews University. The Synod of Fife had urged him to accept it. On the heels of that request came a letter from Rothes and Glencairn to the St Andrews Presbytery, supporting the Synod's act and adding their desire that Sharp should be given the post. On 16 January Sharp was officially transferred from minister of Crail to third master in St Mary's College, and at the end of February he was formally admitted as divinity professor.[30]

In the meantime the activities of the Parliament had dispelled any illusion of the security of presbytery. Middleton had been given discretionary powers for the settlement of the Scottish church. It is therefore possible that when he reassured Sharp that he would not meddle with church government he was for the moment undecided what he should do. The subservience of Parliament, however, and its ready agreement to whatever was proposed soon led him to initiate an extravagant programme of legislation, enlarging the royal prerogative, banishing the Protestors from Edinburgh, and rehabilitating the Scottish nobility.

Some of this legislation began to alarm Sharp. In the first place all public officers, including the members of Parliament, had been required to swear an oath of allegiance. Sharp noted that this oath amounted to an oath of supremacy. Now the Resolutioner argument against the Protestors had always been that the king as godly magistrate had a legitimate part to play in the church, which the Protestors had unlawfully usurped. Indeed Sharp had preached on this very theme before the Parliament that same week, and as might have been expected had thus antagonised the Protestors. Nevertheless the Resolutioners were generally not willing to allow that the king was 'only supreme governor of this kingdom, over all persons, and in all causes'. The unease aroused by the form of the oath had induced Middleton to give a formal explanation of it, in which he claimed that the royal supremacy implied was no more than the power traditionally allowed the king to order the external government and policies of the church. Despite this, however, the Resolutioner leaders continued to feel uneasy.[31]

This piece of legislation was followed by others rescinding the legislation of the Convention of Estates of 1643. This was the Convention that had ratified the Solemn League and Covenant. Similarly an Act of 1644, declaring those who had fought with Montrose guilty of treason, was rescinded. Thirdly, an Act was passed which, although it began simply by forbidding Scots to impose the Covenant on

England 'by armes or any seditious way', yet also forbade the renewal of the Covenant without royal permission.[32]

The tenor of this last piece of legislation was hardly reassuring to the Resolutioners. Sharp had at first made little of the Acts, but when he read them began to recognise how far-reaching were their implications:

> By my former I wrote upon information more smoothingly of the late rescissory act in reference to the covenant than now I can do, having yesterday seen the act which to my apprehension doth not only nullify the civil sanction of the former and late covenants [the National Covenant and the Solemn League and Covenant] but doth make void any security we had by law for our religious governments, which, how grevious it is to honest men here, and of what dangerous consequence you may judge. We were promised and expected moderation, but what shall be expected, when such acts pass.[33]

Sharp, however, was never a man to lie down and die in a crisis. He and Douglas composed a letter concerning the recent legislation which they submitted to Middleton and Glencairn who was now Chancellor. They asked that a written addition to the Oath of Allegiance might be passed by Parliament in which it should be explained that the royal supremacy in matters ecclesiastical referred simply to the exercise of the king's legitimate power as godly magistrate, as Middleton had explained verbally. Secondly the ministers asked that since the League and Covenant appeared to be annulled by one of the rescissory acts, the Parliament should declare 'that they intend not to annul or make void the obligation of the oath of God, under which the people lie'.[34] Finally they asked that the Parliament pass an act ratifying the government and laws of the Scottish church.

No direct response was made to this letter but Glencairn and Middleton were apparently sufficiently wary of the ministers to ask them in return to draw up an act for the ratification of the church settlement, and Sharp presented it to them in mid-February. It was a simple enough composition, but effective. The most important section read:

> his majesty with consent of the estates of parliament now convened doth confirm and ratify the true religion professed, received, and practised within this kingdom, in doctrine, worship, discipline, and government, established by general assemblies, approven and ratified by acts of parliament.[35]

However, Sharp was not hopeful that it would be passed by the parliament. There were rumours of a general rescissory act going about and things looked black. At the beginning of March there was definite news that an act to rescind all the legal guarantees in favour of episcopacy had been discussed in the Articles. It had been agreed that the matter should be considered before the rising of Parliament.[36]

Nothing had been lost by petitioning Glencairn and Middleton on the previous occasion, and so the Edinburgh ministers resolved to do the same again. It is a measure of their continuing trust and respect for Sharp that they arranged the meeting for this purpose to be delayed until his return from St Andrews. On this occasion, however, the Commissioner and Chancellor would not even come to a meeting with the six leading Resolutioners. Instead, about the middle of March

Sharp and Douglas met privately with Middleton. They begged that the acts in favour of presbytery might not be rescinded, and that they might be granted their promised General Assembly of which nothing more had been heard. They suggested a compromise — that presbyterian church government might be retained for two or three years so that the Scots might prove their good intentions. Their requests had no effect, despite Middleton's soothing replies. As Sharp said:

> they are not those men who are influenced by ministers, or will be hindered or furthered in their purposes by what ministers offer to them.[37]

Some time in the week before the Act Rescissory was finally passed on 28 March, a letter to Lauderdale and an 'Information' were sent. In the letter sent from Douglas, Dickson and Sharp, Lauderdale was begged most earnestly to prevent the passing of the Act. The ministers warned, as Sharp had done before, that attempts to change the form of church government in Scotland would not be welcome, and they therefore urged Lauderdale to ask the king to allow an Assembly to be held. Until that time they asked that no action should be taken. The Information formally stated the same argument, for presentation to the king.[38]

On 28 March the Act Rescissory was passed, and the same day, the Act Concerning Religion and Church Government. It promised

> to maintaine the true reformed protestant Religion in its purity of doctrine and worship as it was established within this kingdome, during the reign of his Royall father and Grandfather of blessed memorie.[39]

The variety of church government forms within that period rendered the phrase completely meaningless. The Act went on to say that

> as to the Government of the Church his Maiestie will make it his care to satle and secure the same in such a frame as shall be most agreeable to the word of God, most suteable to monarchical Government, and most complying with the publict peace and quyet of the Kingdome.

Again such phrases meant nothing and committed the king to nothing. The only piece of hard information in the whole act was the notice of the king's intention to continue presbyterian courts for the meantime: 'they keeping within bounds and behaving themselffs as said is'.

The continuance of presbytery was the only comfort left to Sharp, and small comfort it was. The rumours and accusations of his complicity in introducing episcopacy into Scotland, first raised in December 1660, by this time were rising to a shrieking crescendo. The passing of the Rescissory Act had caused the redoubling of the chorus, so that now he found himself obliged to justify himself to Lauderdale. He also took the opportunity, however, to suggest that presbytery was not yet lost, and that the situation could still be restored. The only security for presbyterian government now lay with the king. Sharp suggested, therefore, that instead of vying with each other for royal favour by pursuing opposite policies, Lauderdale for presbytery and Middleton for episcopacy, the two of them should agree to do nothing for the moment, and confer together to establish a peaceable settlement for the church. The alternative, and the result of the continuing of the present policies, Sharp warned, could only be a 'dismal storm'.[40]

At this time the most obscure period of Sharp's life begins. To this point it has been argued that Sharp's behaviour had been that of a presbyterian and a man of integrity. He had honestly done his best since 1661 to achieve as much as he could of the Edinburgh ministers' desires for the church settlement. His policy had been to persuade his fellow Resolutioners of the folly of overt protest and action. But it was now clear that this policy had failed. Even though the Scottish church had maintained to a very large extent a posture of stoical calm in a very unsettled situation, yet it had been assaulted by a series of acts which could hardly be interpreted as other than hostile to presbytery. The month of April 1661, after the passing of the Rescissory Act, was a bad one for the church. Everywhere Synods were disrupted when they attempted to discuss recent developments. The antagonism of the nobility to the ministers was becoming more apparent every day. What was Sharp going to do?

He had suggested to Lauderdale that there should be a settlement with Middleton as the preliminary to a compromise settlement for the church. In the middle of April he was appointed by Middleton as the agent of such a compromise and sent to London at the end of the month, possibly on instructions from London, to negotiate there with Hyde and Lauderdale. This time he had no commission from the kirk, but he seems initially to have retained the confidence of Wood, Provost of St Salvator's, and Baillie.[41]

It seems likely that what Sharp had in mind was something along the lines of constant moderators in presbytery. In a letter of late March he had argued that either the church must be completely destroyed by the hostility of parliament and the nobility so that it would be entirely dominated by the civil power, or, as the only alternative, make some concessions to the strong pressure for episcopacy:

> From the difference betwixt us and the Remonstrators . . .; from the differences in judgment among those who oppose them . . .; from the temper of most of the nobility, gentry and burghs of the kingdom; from the irresolution and damp which is upon the spirits of the most of the ministry in Scotland; from the just prejudices which former actings have cast upon the way of the church, from the visible contempt upon all ministers, and the folly and fickleness of too many --- I make this inference --- that we can not hold upon this foundation, but must ere long be subjected either to erastianism of the worst form, or we must fall upon constant commissioners, or Bishops.[42]

There is no evidence to suggest that such a measure was a pleasing prospect to Sharp. To this point everything known about him suggests his satisfaction with presbyterian church government; but he, and the Resolutioners with him, were opportunists. Accordingly, in the conviction that the Resolutioner leaders would see things in the same light, he set out once again to exercise his political skills to achieve the best possible compromise in the unfavourable circumstances.

He arrived in London early in May and reported to Wood that he had spoken to the king on church matters 'in the way I thought most conducing for preventing of grief and prejudice to good men'.[43] It did not take long, however, for Sharp to find himself in very much deeper water than he had bargained for. Although when he went to London the matter of the restoration of episcopacy was still unsettled, certainly at least as far as timing was concerned, yet events in London were daily making it more certain. There the episcopal party were carrying all before them. In Parliament a Rescissory Act had rescinded all legislation since 1641. Sharp commented bitterly: 'the actings of the Parliament of Scotland may be accounted sober in comparison of the parliament here'.[44] He was faced, that is to say, by concrete evidence that things in Scotland could be very much worse, and the church, as he had feared, rendered an erastian cipher.

Secondly, he witnessed the total collapse of the London presbyterian party on whom he had previously so much relied for help and advice. Their concessions of a 'regulated presbytery and commended liturgy' had been ignored, and it was plain that they would be obliged to submit to an episcopal regime of the old sort.

Thirdly, the Scots' great ally, Lauderdale, had been obliged to come to terms with Hyde and the episcopalians. The feud between Middleton and Lauderdale, carried on from pre-Restoration days, had now developed to the point where Middleton was capable of ruining Lauderdale. Middleton had, after all, carried through without disturbance a programme which had virtually destroyed the presbyterian kirk, and had exalted the royal authority to previously unknown levels. Lauderdale in contrast had stood up for presbytery and urged moderation. He was now, therefore, in considerable political danger and no longer able to befriend the Resolutioners.[45]

Lastly, Sharp was no match for the Chancellor, Clarendon, swollen as he was with power and the victory of the episcopal party. He gave Sharp to understand that Rothes, formerly another supporter of the Resolutioners, had changed his tune. The implication of this was plain. Sharp was being pressured to join Middleton's party. In addition, Clarendon finally convinced Sharp, as Middleton had apparently been unable to do, although he had tried, that the king himself was in favour of settling episcopacy. What is more, Hyde let Sharp know that only if episcopacy were established would the English garrisons be removed from Scotland.[46]

In face of the accumulated pressure from all sides Sharp gave in. There were two possibilities: either he could maintain his presbyterian views and retire ignominiously, sacrificing no doubt his post as Royal Chaplain, his position in St Andrews University and any hope of advancement in public life; or he could resign himself to the inevitable, go along with the change and try to ensure that it conformed at least to some extent with the desires of Scots churchmen. He chose the latter course.

Presbyterians and critics since have argued that had Sharp refused to accept the apparent logic of events and rallied support in favour of a presbyterian settlement based on the Solemn League and Covenant, then the Scottish church could have been saved the imposition of episcopacy. This is the same argument that Abernathy makes over Sharp's behaviour in England — that had Sharp rallied the

English presbyterians to an energetic defence of presbytery and the Solemn League and Covenant, and brought Scots influence to bear, then a presbyterian settlement could have been effected. Abernathy himself gives a wealth of evidence to suggest that such an outcome in England was most unlikely, and Sharp at no time had the power or influence to bring about such an end. The same is true in Scotland in 1660. Sharp's influence in the effecting the ecclesiastical settlement that would be to the Resolutioners' taste was simply not of those massive proportions, as a great deal of evidence suggests. The Resolutioners had liked very well Sharp's untiring willingness to negotiate during the Interregnum; the difference between them and Sharp became apparent over an issue that to them was absolute, but to Sharp was not. It has been argued in this book that his major inheritance from the Aberdeen Doctors was a talent for compromise. Eventually for his fellow Resolutioners who had gratefully exploited this capacity for many years it was an inadequate ethic.

Sharp's first task, having made his decision, was to draw up a proclamation to be published by the Scottish parliament before it should rise. The proclamation was composed with Lauderdale's help some time about the middle of May, approved and dated 10th June and read in the Scottish parliament on 18th June. It had two things to say: that the king approved of and confirmed the legislation concerning ecclesiastical affairs formerly carried through by the parliament, and that he wanted to hear no objections to it from the ministers.[47] As far as Sharp was concerned the Proclamation represented his conviction that the Scottish kirk must take what was coming to it, and make the best of it.

The final decision was taken when Middleton returned to London from the Parliament in Edinburgh. Lauderdale and three others urged for proceeding only after a General Assembly or meetings of the Synods had given their views, but his policy of caution was discredited. It was therefore decided that episcopacy should be established. The proclamation was read publicly on 6 September in Edinburgh.

Sharp left London towards the end of August for Scotland. It was now time for him to play his part. The Edinburgh ministers had written to Lauderdale at the beginning of June telling him of their fears for a change in church government, and warning of the opposition likely to follow upon it. They asked therefore that nothing should be done without consultation with leading ministers. The answer to this letter was now composed by Lauderdale and sent down to Scotland for Sharp to deliver. It explained that the king had thought it inappropriate to summon a General Assembly, Synods or ministers to give their advice, because he did not want his authority or that of the Parliament challenged. The king's decision to settle an episcopal system was explained as an inevitable result of the Rescissory Act and the former high-handedness of Presbyterians. The ministers were told in no uncertain terms that their co-operation was expected and that opposition would be construed very harshly. It was, that is to say, a letter which recommended that they accept what they could not alter.[48]

Sharp now attempted to use this letter to force the Resolutioner leaders to face the realities of the situation. He was authorised to offer bishoprics to them and in early September he was hopeful that Baillie, Hutcheson and Wood might all co-operate, although he had failed to bring over Douglas. The effort failed completely. Douglas later boasted that he had dismissed Sharp with a curse.[49] For them there had come a point where pragmatism and realism were no longer significant motivation for their action.

But if the Resolutioner leaders would not 'act the part was expected', others had to be chosen. Sharp could not possibly retreat now. On 15 October he went up to London and there on 15 December was consecrated Archbishop of St Andrews in Westminster Abbey. On the same occasion the bishops of Glasgow, Galloway and Dunblane were also consecrated.

Of these four Sharp and Leighton, who was to be Bishop of Dunblane, had received presbyterial ordination as ministers. It was objected by the English bishops that they must therefore receive episcopal ordination as deacons and priests before they could be consecrated bishops. Sharp objected to this procedure on the grounds that his former ordination was valid, but was overruled.[50] Thus was the transformation of Sharp effected within the year from presbyter to archbishop.

It has been argued throughout this chapter that there was a certain logic in this process: that it grew out of Sharp's longstanding political opinions. An attempt has been made to look on his dilemma with sympathy and understanding, and to analyse his motives for actions all too capable of misinterpretation. There was no such effort made by his contemporaries or by the author of this satire:

December 1661

Judas I am, what ever Court may say
Arch traitour false: for Christ I do betray.
Many base lies, fouls cheats have I devisid,
Ever for these I ought to be despisid.
Satan before this long my heart had fill'd
Serpentine venom therein had instill'd.
Hope have I none, but this alone that I
After some pleasure shall forever die.
Religions coin I clipt soules to deceive,
Perverse Politicks and the best I have.

One letter rests of my Infamous Name
Which may import, who ever paines have tane
Me to describe who Brittains Church have sold
Doth at the least come short an c [hundred] fold.[51]

6

The Highest Seat is the Sliddriest to Sit Upon

After his consecration Sharp remained in London for several months more, and returned to Scotland only in April 1662. In that time certain administrative arrangements were made which indicated that whatever Sharp's intentions in hoping to use his influence to establish a moderate episcopacy, the failure to enlist his brethren as bishops and the far different intentions of the king and Scottish nobility would make moderate episcopacy impossible. From the very first royal proclamation for the restoration of the bishops in August 1661 it had been clear that they would be financially well rewarded.[1] From that it could be deduced that no simple issue of church government was involved, but the restoration of a class of royal servants who should dominate and impress by their secular splendour.

In January 1662 instructions were given to Middleton as Commissioner to the Parliament then intended for March 1662,[2] in which the bishops were required to be restored as a separate Estate of Parliament, to be granted back their power to receive testaments (or wills), to be restored to their 'rights, superiorities, rents, possessions and privileges' as they had been in 1637. In addition the bishops were given authority over the ministers 'in the diocesan and other ecclesiastic meetings' on pain of censure, and restored to their former rights of patronage of churches.[3] The scope of the bishops' control over ministers had already been underlined by a proclamation in December insisting that all entrant ministers must obtain presentation to their parishes from their bishop before taking up their charge. This had put a stop to all planting of kirks with ministers until the bishops should return to take up their duties.[4] In addition all meetings of presbyteries, synods and kirk sessions, which had been allowed to continue till early in January 1662, were then forbidden to meet 'untill they be authorised and ordered by our archbishopes and bishopes upon their entering into the government of their respective seas'.[5]

By no stretch of the imagination could this programme of legislation be seen as the prescription for the 'regulated presbytery', 'presbyterian presbytery', 'constant well qualified presidency', 'constant commissioners, moderators or bishops' of which Sharp had spoken in March 1661.[6] The bishops were being created not to serve the church, but to serve the state. Even if it is true, as has been suggested, that Sharp was responsible for framing these edicts,[7] he was clearly not responsible for their content which could only have been suggested by secular authority.

The measure of the archbishop's necessary allegiance with royal authority and alienation from his former brethren was given on his return to Edinburgh from Court on 8 April 1662. Three of the four newly consecrated bishops had travelled down from London together: Sharp, now Primate and Archbishop of St Andrews, Andrew Fairfoul, Archbishop of Glasgow, and James Hamilton, Bishop of Galloway. The king had already indicated that he required all honour to be shown the bishops,[8] and accordingly they were given a magnificent reception. They were met when they were still some miles from the city at Cockburnspath, Haddington and Musselburgh by members of the nobility 'in great pomp and grandour, with sound of trumpet, and all uther courteseis requisite'.[9] They were then conducted to Edinburgh 'and entered the citie with great pompe'[10] and were treated to a banquet at Holyrood Abbey, the official residence of the King's Commissioner.[11] Such a reception was that usually given to royal servants of the greatest importance. It was repeated a week later when on 15 and 16 April Sharp made a triumphal progress through Fife to St Andrews, accompanied by large numbers of the nobility led by the Earl of Rothes, and he again attended a banquet. The significant feature of his reception on this occasion, however, was the almost complete absence of ministers.[12] The implication was clear. The ministers felt Sharp had deserted them, and they would therefore desert him. From now on he was on his own.

The profound significance of this return was further underlined the next day in St Andrews when Sharp preached in the town church. The sermon was undoubtedly intended as a reasoned piece of self-justification.[13] By the greatest good fortune it is extant, the only one of Sharp's sermons as archbishop known to survive. It deserves careful analysis since it forms Sharp's only major public statement on his metamorphosis from presbyterian minister to archbishop.[14] The text, 1 Corinthians 2 ii, 'I resolved to know nothing amongst you, but Christ, and him crucified', seems to have been intended by Sharp as a plea that his sincerity should be recognised, and it was on this note that the sermon opened. The first assertion he made was that he had not taken up his new office from any personal ambition: 'not out of any ambitious or covetous disposition'.

It would be naive to suppose that Sharp was not ambitious; every step of his career to this point indicates ambition, but it would be equally naive to suppose that ambition would ever blind him to the practical and political implications of his actions. As long before as spring 1661 Sharp had been aware that the office of bishop in Scotland would carry no honour.[15] On the other hand, it is clear he thought the introduction of episcopacy into Scotland could not be avoided. There is good reason to suppose that he hoped to be able to determine the precise nature of the episcopacy. In such a situation to desire and accept the highest office might even be regarded as legitimate ambition.

It is therefore significant that Sharp went on to claim that he had 'undertaken this office out of a desire … to improve any occasion or opportunity God shall put in my hand for the good of the Church and my country'. Nobody knew more than Sharp at this time of the possible and potential dangers facing church and country. His ambition consisted at least to some extent in the desire to be instrumental in avoiding those hazards. It was, that is to say, an ambition not so much for personal aggrandisement as for effective power.

The sermon went on to assert that Sharp had accepted his position 'out of obedience ... to the king's Majesty whom I own to be supreme in all causes Ecclesiastic, and over all persons, and the original of the external exercise of all Church power'. In the early weeks of 1661 the Oath of Allegiance tendered to members of the Parliament had required them to acknowledge the king as supreme in all causes and over all persons. Sharp had then been involved with Douglas in an attempt to have the Commissioner's explanation of this oath, as no more than a recognition of the traditional royal authority to order the external government and policies of the church, put in writing. Sharp's sermon now asserted that he was willing to accept the oath without insisting on written limitations. It was the sort of concession to royal authority that the Aberdeen Doctors would have considered legitimate in that it was an acceptance in good faith of the part the king had to play in the church.

The whole of the rest of the sermon was taken up with a justification of episcopacy. Sharp claimed that he had taken no part in initiating this change of church government. The implication was clear that the form of church government was not for Sharp divinely ordained. He was therefore left with the job of explaining why he had not opposed the change.

He began by asserting that he had never believed that episcopacy was 'contrary to the Word of God, to be unnecessary or useless, much less destructive to the church or prejudicial to the Gospel and to the increase of the knowledge of God'. Indeed, with his intellectual background in the teaching of the Aberdeen Doctors, it is likely that these had been his views, and views shared no doubt by others, on the Scottish church. Such views were not inconsistent either with a belief that in the circumstances of the former times presbytery had been an appropriate system.

But then Sharp went on to say that episcopacy had a long history of acceptance within the church, and he believed as matters stood now was a better method of church government for Scotland: 'that which is most convenient and necessary for Scotland as it stands now stated'. He continued to explain what had brought him to this conclusion: 'the sad disorders and dismal confusion that hath seized on all men and people within the land since that sacred order was unworthily and sinfully cast out'. This was, of course, a familiar royalist view of the period since 1637, but what was remarkable about Sharp's exposition of his case was that he went on to recognise that others might not agree with him in his interpretation of these past events. He had come to the conclusion that history and practical benefits argued that an episcopalian system would be best. Others were free to differ from him. What they were not free to do, he remarked finally, was to translate their disagreement into action. And why not? Because they owed 'their duty and submission to the will and determination of his majesty'. So Sharp returns to the Aberdeen Doctors and their belief that the king was to be obeyed in non-fundamentals such as church government.

As a means to understanding Sharp's mind this sermon is superb. It enables the tracing of the last stages in his slow development over the previous two years. As a piece of practical politics it was a failure, and presaged his ultimate failure over the next two decades till his assassination in 1679. Sharp's correspondence in 1660 with the Resolutioner leaders revealed that he had been able to adapt to changing political circumstances much more readily than they. Depending on bias this capacity for flexibility is pragmatism or lack of principle, desirable or undesirable. In 1660 Sharp's views had prevailed with the leading Resolutioners despite their reluctance, but then his strategies had proved a failure. They had, as he had urged, kept quiet to protect presbytery, and then presbytery had been cynically destroyed. There was therefore on this occasion even less chance that his exhortations to obedience would reconcile them, let alone the leading Protestors, to accepting episcopacy. Sharp's argument reduced to its barest outlines was 'accept episcopacy because you must', but his audience were men who since 1637 had ignored political reality as conventionally computed, and had nevertheless won great victories. They were, that is to say, essentially theologians, whereas Sharp was essentially a politician, and their modes of reasoning did not coincide.[16]

There were many others within the Scottish church who were influenced by the very influences that had worked on Sharp, and who were prepared to accept his reasoning. Indeed, a considerable majority of ministers accepted the episcopalian settlement.[17] Sharp would never have used such arguments, astute politician that he was, if there had not existed a predisposition towards them among his brother ministers. The point was that Sharp was unable to bring over the church leaders of either party, Resolutioner or Protester. This failure ensured his isolation from the men with whom he had formerly co-operated, and with whose help the episcopalian settlement might have survived and prospered. As it was he was forced to rely on more extreme men for his fellow-bishops, and instead of modifying and moderating the nature of the episcopate was instead used and abused by the secular power. It was perhaps an ironic fate for a politician-churchman like Sharp, but it was a dismal one for the Scottish church.

Sharp's first duty, now that he had returned to Scotland, was to see to the consecration of the other bishops. Six were consecrated in Edinburgh on 7 May and a further two in St Andrews on 3 June.[18] Sydserff, the one bishop remaining from 1637, was bishop of Orkney, which left only the Bishopric of Argyll vacant of the fourteen ancient Scottish sees.[19] The first consecration in Edinburgh took place the day before the Parliament sat. Middleton, the Commissioner, was therefore already in the city with a great concourse of those due to attend the Parliament. The opportunity was taken to stage a splendid ceremonial occasion in the church at Holyrood. The archbishops and bishops were decked out in black satin gowns with the lawn sleeves of the surplices showing. The church was carpeted. The ceremonial of the consecration was made formal by use of the Service Book, and in the contemporary view was unacceptably elaborate.

To hold the consecration at such a time and in such a way was, of course, a deliberate piece of propaganda. It demonstrated that the whole power of the establishment was behind the restoration of the bishops, and it was in line with their previous reception into Edinburgh, and their coming reception into Parliament. It was, however, an unfortunate beginning. We have argued that at least in mid-1661 Sharp had had the best intentions in co-operating with the king and the Scottish nobility. Yet every step in that restoration of the episcopate to which he had agreed had been accomplished by pressures and accidents which made it increasingly difficult for him to exert any influence at all on the form the episcopal settlement should take. It is not surprising that he should be seen as a perjured prelate when he took part in forms and ceremonies calculated to be offensive to Scottish churchmen. This was a dilemma from which Sharp never escaped. He had allied himself with the nobility and had been abandoned by his former brethren. The men consecrated at Edinburgh and St Andrews had little of the stature of the former leaders of the church and could offer Sharp little support. Manoeuvred by political events, he increasingly took upon himself the 'prelate' form which he had originally set out to prevent.

The next day, 8 May, the bishops were received back as an Estate of Parliament by the assembled members.[20] No sooner had the members duly convened than the act was passed authorising the bishops' return to Parliament. The earls of Kelly and Wemyss were sent to invite the bishops, who were gathered at Sharp's house in the Nether Bow, to take their places. A procession then formed

> fra the Archbishop of Sant Androis hous with 2 erles, viz the Erle of Kellie and the Earle of Weymis, and the 2 Archebischops in the midst betuix the 2 Erles, besyde much uther companyes of the Provest, bailleis, and counsell of Edinburgh, with barones, gentillmen, and utheris in great number.[21]

When they had taken their places in the Parliament Middleton received them with a speech of welcome. The house then adjourned and processed down the High Street to Holyrood where a banquet had been prepared.[22]

Over the next few months, May to September 1662, the Parliament proceeded to put into law the proclamations and instructions for the restoration of the bishops that have already been discussed. There was however an unnecessarily provocative tone about much of the legislation regarding the bishops, just as the consecration had been carried out in a way calculated to give offence. The act restoring episcopal rights of collation (or confirmation) of presentations to parishes required that ministers admitted to their parishes since 1649 when patronage had been abolished must now seek presentation from the patron and collation from the bishop before 20 September 1662.[23] The act for the preservation of his majesty's person took the opportunity to condemn the covenants out of hand as 'treasonable and seditious',[24] although in the previous session of Parliament in 1661 the government view of the covenants had been well enough ventilated.[25]

When the Parliament rose this provocative tone was continued in the activities of Middleton and the privy council. In late September and early October they made a progress through the west of Scotland,[26] and in Glasgow on 1 October passed an act expelling from parishes those ministers who had not yet submitted to the regulations concerning presentation and collation,[27] thereby removing perhaps two hundred ministers.[28]

Whatever the excesses into which Sharp had been led by his co-operation with the nobility, yet there can be no doubt of one thing: that his ultimate intention was the creation of a united church in Scotland. If the episcopal system could not be satisfactorily imposed and operated, then life would clearly be very difficult for the Primate. At the lowest level, then, of simple self-interest, Sharp must have been anxious that the transformation of church government should take place as smoothly as possible.

To a very large extent the episcopal system had little or no effect on the continuance of the former apparatus of kirk session, presbytery and synod.[29] There was no attempt to re-introduce the contentious Service Book, and so ordinary church services continued as before. There was every reason to suppose that there would be no great difficulty in effecting the new settlement. If, however, deliberate attempts to emphasise the authority of the bishops and the iniquities of the past thirty years were made, the peaceful achievement of a united church was bound to be made more difficult.

Sharp seems to have felt disquiet about these developments as early as June. He expressed the hope that after the latest act referring to the covenants was passed they would be left alone: 'I hope the obligation of them being thus nulled we shall have no more severe proceedings against them'.[30] From the beginning he anticipated difficulty in the matter of presentations, especially in the dioceses of Edinburgh, Glasgow and Galloway, and by November he was remarking that failure to comply with presentation and attend church meetings would result in the voiding of more parishes than had been expected.[31] In particular Sharp was angered by the wholesale eviction of so many of the western ministers by Middleton and the Council.[32] Disruption on this scale would inevitably cause enormous difficulties.

At the diocesan synod, therefore, which met in October, Sharp made an effort once more to commend government by bishops. He stressed that episcopacy and the saying of the doxology and the creed were no innovations. He emphasised the necessity of obedience to the royal will, and preached on the desirability of episcopacy.[33] In November the grave effects of the expulsion of so many ministers began to be evident, and so on the advice of Sharp and Fairfoul an extension of the date for obtaining presentations until February 1663 was allowed.[34]

Middleton's ineptitude with regard to church affairs had arisen from an overweening pride and ambition in the political sphere. During the Parliament of 1662 he had by a process of secret votes tried to establish his political ascendancy by having Lauderdale excluded from the Act of Indemnity. Sharp, as a member of the Committee of the Articles in which this plot had been worked out, had known what was going on. His sympathies in any case were with Lauderdale, and he therefore took as little share as he could in the proceedings, and eventually submitted a blank vote.[35]

In January 1663, when Middleton's downfall seemed certain, the issue was raised of Sharp's going to London,[36] presumably to put another nail in Middleton's coffin,[37] but also to seek advice as to what now could be done for the church settlement. A meeting of the bishops in February had thought it desirable that Sharp should give an account of what had happened, from their point of view.[38]

When Sharp returned in June 1663 it was with permission to be admitted with the Archbishop of Glasgow to the Privy Council; with the appointment of Rothes, the most important man in Fife and Sharp's faithful supporter to this date, as

Chancellor;[39] and with an exhortation to Glencairn to co-operate for the peaceful settlement of the church. It has been argued that throughout 1662 Sharp's fundamentally good intentions for the church had been warped by the overriding power and arrogance of the nobility. He had now been promoted to the inner circle of government with his closest ally as Chancellor, and was hereafter a diligent attender of the Council. It remained to be seen how he would use these advantages.

By the time Sharp returned to Edinburgh in June 1663 there had been a change in the ecclesiastical situation. The extension of the time limit for ministers obtaining presentation and collation had come too late and had failed to achieve its purpose. The result was that something like a third of the parishes in Scotland were without ministers. Many of these vacancies were in the south-west of the country, and there developed in that area during the early months of 1663 a conventicling movement: that is to say, services were held in private houses by the outed ministers.[40]

On the face of it such a movement could be accounted for simply in terms of the people's desire to hear and the ministers' desire to preach the Word. That indeed is the traditional rationalisation of the conventicle church; but there was a great deal more to it than that. In the first place efforts had been made to replace the non-conforming ministers with others more amenable. Much has been said about the insufficiency of those 'curates',[41] and indeed one could hardly expect so many vacancies to be filled at once by experienced ministers. Nevertheless research suggests that they were not so bad as they were painted.[42] But since at least some parishes were planted with these curates the conventiclers were committing a double offence in quitting the legally prescribed services of the church for the unlicensed services of ejected ministers.

The attitude of seventeenth-century government to unlicensed assembly of any kind must also be borne in mind. Any gathering of citizens was likely to be viewed with suspicion in an age before the principle of free association was recognised. Moreover, when such gatherings took place in the south-west of Scotland, from which had come the theocratic opposition to the Engagement of 1648 and then the Remonstrance of 1650, it was not to be supposed that it would be viewed dispassionately. The likely suspicions of the government were given added strength by violent scuffles with the curates which took place in the spring of 1663.[43] As a result steps were taken in March to deal with the situation by using soldiers.[44]

By the time, therefore, that Sharp returned from England and the Parliament was about to sit, in June 1663, the ecclesiastical situation seemed from the government side to have deteriorated badly. Sharp had disapproved of the manner in which Middleton had set about enforcing the law relating to the establishment of episcopacy, but he was convinced it must be enforced. Furthermore, Sharp's attitude to Protesters was well enough known, and most of those involved in the conventicling were of the old Protester party. Even before he had left for London he had entertained suspicions of 'some ministers in the West, Lothian and Fife [who] have as by combination refused to take presentations according to the act of Parliament'.[45] These considerations now influenced his behaviour.

When the Parliament of June 1663 met, Sharp and other bishops performed their traditional and now restored duty of choosing the Lords of the Articles.[46] This body was a Committee of Parliament whose duty it was to discuss, devise and present legislation for the approval of the full house, which tended to be seen merely as a ratifying body. To a very large extent Sharp must have been able on this occasion to select the membership of the committee; Lauderdale was present in the Parliament, Rothes was Commissioner, Glencairn reprieved from disgrace with Middleton was likely to be co-operative. It seems fair to assume that the legislation passed with respect to church affairs was what Sharp wanted, or at least what he would not oppose.[47]

The Act against Separation and Disobedience to Ecclesiastical Authority was the expression of Sharp's desire that the dissident ministers in the west be dealt with firmly. It first of all made public the king's resolve to maintain the newly restored episcopacy.[48] A year before there had been rumours that the king was not fixed in his resolve.[49] This Act was intended to scotch those rumours once and for all. To give the matter extra weight Lauderdale — as former supporter of presbytery — made a speech expressing his entire satisfaction with the episcopal system, and thus removed any hopes that he might lead a presbyterian opposition.[50]

Secondly the act provided for the punishment, as seditious, of those ministers who would not conform with the former legislation restoring bishops, and the fining of those who withdrew from worship in their own parish churches. The precise punishment for those who had not conformed to the law was then framed by a committee of six of the Privy Council, of whom the archbishops were two.[51] In August a proclamation from them ordered that any such minister, or any minister illegally carrying out his functions, should be banished from his own parish and forbidden to reside within twenty miles of a cathedral church or three miles of a royal burgh.[52]

The conclusion to be drawn from this legislation seems quite inescapable. Sharp may have had reservations about the nature of the episcopal settlement in Scotland; he probably had had grave doubts as to the wisdom of the procedure followed in church affairs by the Earl of Middleton; but by late 1663 he had reconciled himself both to the style of the episcopacy and to the rigour with which ecclesiastical ordinances were to be put into effect.[53] Thus in the space of two years he had been transformed from the man who became a bishop to create a moderate episcopate to the man who lent his voice to the establishment of prelacy.

He was influenced by many factors in this transformation, but principally by the failure to bring over the ministry of Scotland in a body to the new establishment; the subsequent unrest among non-conformists who were Sharp's long-time antagonists, the Protesters; and finally the defection of Lauderdale to the prelatic point of view, thus leaving Sharp without a voice at court. The choice of action for him remained the same. He could comply with forces he could not resist, or he could choose not to remain in office. Nevertheless, it should not be thought that from now on Sharp became the pliant tool of the nobility. Rather, it is his attempt to retain some independence for the church that we must now consider.

In 1661 one of the motives for Sharp's willingness to consider some form of episcopacy had been his desire to protect the church from erastian control. The character of the restored bishops as royal servants with a political function had made it clear that the danger of civil control of the church was very real, as had the activities of Middleton. The first demonstration of Sharp's intention to retain some independence for the church, and by implication power in that institution for himself, came over the matter of a National Synod. The Parliament of 1663 had passed an act providing for the setting up of a National Synod[54] which was probably intended to meet in 1664. In 1660 the king had promised a General Assembly should meet the following year, a promise which had given some satisfaction to Sharp and the Resolutioner leaders. Now this act for a National Synod was the king's fulfilment of his promise.[55] The trouble was that the constitution of the Synod would have ensured its total dominance by royal authority, since the agenda of discussion had first to be approved and then ratified by the king. Clearly the meeting of such a body would allow no free discussion of the real problems facing the church, but would simply demonstrate the utter subservience of the ecclesiastical establishment to the secular power. It was presumably for these reasons that Sharp early in January 1664 was heard to speak 'doubtfully of its meeting'.[56]

In October 1663 Rothes brought to Edinburgh a warrant for the meeting of a General Assembly in May 1665.[57] Rothes was to be Commissioner to this Assembly.[58] In March, however, Sharp announced that it would be necessary to delay the meeting until August.[59] The meeting never took place. In 1669 the Act of Supremacy destroyed the only small guarantee of independence for a Synod by abolishing the primate's power of veto. That move was in itself a recognition that the Synod was at all times merely invented as a vehicle of royal control.

The second demonstration of this desire for independence was Sharp's obtaining permission from the king to set up a Church Commission. In December 1663 he made his way to court. When he returned in February he brought the grant with him.[60] The Church Commission in effect took over much of the Privy Council's function in the bringing to punishment of those who offended against the ecclesiastical laws.[61] It had wide-ranging powers of search, arrest and summons and the authority to punish according to the prescription of the relevant laws of parliament and the Privy Council. Its membership was to consist of no less than five persons taken from a list given, of whom at least one was to be a bishop or archbishop. Thus Sharp was now in an even stronger position than he had been in the Privy Council to impose his views on the necessary course of action for the church.

But no sooner had these powers been conferred on Sharp and his independent power in the church been confirmed than an opposition party began to form towards the bishops in the ranks of the nobility. During the early months of 1664 Sharp and Alexander Burnet, Archbishop of Glasgow in succession to Fairfoul who had died in November 1663, became even more convinced of the urgency of suppressing the increasing disaffection to the church by rigorous measures. This rigour demanded the co-operation of the nobility in bringing offenders within their respective spheres of influence to justice. It soon became evident to the archbishops that there was some deliberate foot-dragging in this duty on the part of those members of the nobility who had co-operated in bringing in episcopacy to fulfil their own ends, but were now dissatisfied with the power the bishops commanded.[62]

The response from Sharp and Burnet to this challenge was to begin to build up for themselves a party of supporters amongst the nobility, beginning with Lauderdale and Rothes,[63] and going on to draw in Hamilton,[64] Dumfries and other lesser men such as Traquair, Roslin, Halton, Cochrane and Drumlanrig.[65] They attempted to strengthen their control over these men by appealing for favours for them. Finally, after the death of Glencairn in March and the demise thereby of the last of the important members of Middleton's party, Sharp, with the help of Burnet and the Archbishop of Canterbury, Sheldon,[66] tried to secure for himself the most important secular office in Scotland, Glencairn's former post as Chancellor. In August 1644 he made his way to London to press his candidature[67] and to complain of the lack of co-operation from some of the nobility in the affairs of the church.[68]

The year August 1663 to August 1664 thus marks a further step in Sharp's life from his earlier commitment to the church and its welfare and a further step towards his own supreme elevation in both church and state. Up to this point it has been possible to suppose that his desire for power was impersonal, and directed towards the greater good of the church, but now it was clearly also the ambition of a politician engaged in the pursuit of power for its own sake.

In the event Sharp failed to get the Chancellorship. The decision seems to have been the king's and the reasons for it are not clear. For the meantime the seal was given to Rothes so that the administrative functions of the office could continue, but the post was left vacant.[69] Sharp did not abandon his candidature, and it was being pressed by Rothes and Burnet in 1665.[70]

But even without the Chancellorship Sharp's power in Scotland was now immense and greater than that of any other single individual except Lauderdale who was, of course, in London. The extent of his power was demonstrated in 1665 when he presided at a Convention summoned to provide money for the king's Dutch War.[71] He had in effect become the King's Commissioner in Scotland. This marked the summit of Sharp's power. From now on it was downhill all the way.

To suppose, as has usually been done, that Sharp was disgraced at the end of 1666 because of his severities in the imposing of the ecclesiastical settlement in the church is certainly a mistake. There is no word from Rothes or Lauderdale to suggest that they found any fault with Sharp in this respect. Sharp's mistake was to become so powerful that he could challenge the control by the nobility of Scottish affairs. His disgrace was simply another demonstration of the absolute determination of the Scottish nobility to ensure that never again would they be dominated by ministers. We have already noted that Sharp was aware of opposition to the bishops forming in 1663 and 1664. From mid-1665 he himself acted in such a way as to enlarge that party so that finally he lost the essential support of Lauderdale, and the Pentland Rising was made the pretext for his disgrace.

The first resentment on Lauderdale's part at Sharp's power was demonstrated in May and June 1665, even before Sharp had presided over the Convention. Sharp had heard from Rothes that nominations for vacant bishoprics in Scotland were being directed to Lauderdale. In June 1663 the king had given to Sharp the sole right of recommendation to bishoprics, but if requests were being addressed to Lauderdale it was clear that this privilege was already being eroded. Sharp therefore wrote to Lauderdale to remind him of the king's grant.[72]

Lauderdale took immediate offence at this letter and Sharp was obliged to explain away his original communication.[73] Although Sharp made his point and Lauderdale was obliged then and later[74] to concede Sharp's privilege of nomination, it was not a happy exchange.[75] The subject of recommendations to bishoprics raised the question of clerical privilege. That issue was too reminiscent of the claims to ministerial authority to be welcome to the secular government of the Restoration.

This first major clash was followed very soon thereafter by an acrimonious debate between Sharp and the Earl of Kincardine. Up to this point the laws relating to the church settlement had been applied almost exclusively to common people and to lairds. Although that no doubt indicates that the nobility were in most cases much more sympathetic to the settlement and prepared to comply with the law, it most probably also indicates that rank exempted any non-conformists among them from the operation of the law. The Earl of Kincardine in the Parliament of 1663 had opposed the act punishing non-conformity.[76] In the autumn of 1665 Sharp offended by bringing the same Earl to book for his attendance at an irregularly conducted communion service.[77] The report came to the king and it required all the influence of Lauderdale and Sir Robert Moray to prevent Kincardine's complete ruin.[78] Perhaps Sharp's rigour might have been exonerated had he not chosen to accuse a man who had friends in high places.[79] As it was his action constituted another challenge to the hegemony of the nobility in Scotland. Sir Robert Moray indicated to the Earl clearly enough what he thought of Sharp's boldness:

> If there be no greater restraint than he imagines as to reproving superiors, government and governors must be exposed to the foulest charges anybody can breathe out who satisfies himself with his own conscience and candour.

He expressed the hope that Sharp would redeem his fault by using his influence to get Kincardine 'a good share of the fines',[80] which was indeed what Sharp was then obliged to do.[81] Not only had Sharp offended Kincardine and Sir Robert Moray; he had also found himself on bad terms with Bellenden, the treasurer-depute. In July 1665 a debate had started over the best way to impose the taxation about to be granted by the Convention. Sharp and Rothes had found themselves opposed by Bellenden who agreed with Lauderdale.[82] The matter had eventually been submitted to the king's discretion[83] but plainly Bellenden continued to harbour a grudge. He therefore began a series of letters to Lauderdale in which he complained of Sharp and did what he could to bring him into disrepute.[84] Thus Sharp found himself with yet another enemy among the nobility.

It was therefore a mark of Sharp's fall from grace when in November 1665 the Church Commission was not renewed but allowed to lapse. No change in policy was intended. The Privy Council resumed its jurisdiction and went on with as much rigour as the Commission, but Sharp and the bishops were no longer in control.

In the summer of 1666 Sharp again acted against the interests of the Scottish nobility. In the Parliament of 1662 Middleton had passed the notorious Act of Fines.[85] The act had consisted of an apparently hastily drawn up and arbitrary list of persons excepted from the Act of Indemnity. It was the subject of so much dissatisfaction that payment was prorogued by the king in February 1663 although it was not made public till March of that year. Eventually, however, the first part of the fines was required in July 1664 with the second to be paid in March 1665.[86] Payment was reluctant and so the demand for the fines was repeated in November 1664[87] and October 1665[88] and thereafter.

Undoubtedly these fines had been intended from the first as the means whereby the impoverished royalist nobility might restore their financial situation, and claim the reward they felt was due to them for their loyalty to the king.[89] Sharp, of course, did not stand to gain from any money raised in this way and so was able to recognise the disadvantages of exacting the money. In March 1665 he wrote to Lauderdale: 'As to the business of the fines, I shall presume only to say that from first to last I thought them cursed and unhappy'.[90]

This attitude was hardly likely to make him popular with a nobility desperate for cash.[91] In 1666, however, the fear of unrest in Scotland as a result of the economic suffering caused by the Dutch War,[92] as well as the severities of the ecclesiastical policy,[93] persuaded the king to permit the raising of more troops in Scotland. This had been the desire of the Scottish nobility for some time, since the payment for officers and the control of lesser military appointments could be a worthwhile source of revenue. In July 1666 it was relayed to Scotland that Sharp, who had gone to London in May,[94] had persuaded the king to use the fines to pay for the troops to be raised.[95] So the money on which royalists were counting for their rehabilitation would instead be used for paying a few officers and many ordinary soldiers. Royalists, instead of being able to hope for military appointments as an extra source of revenue, would discover that such appointments were their only hope. This decision caused dismay among the nobility.[96]

By this time, therefore, Sharp had made himself many enemies among the nobility, but these tensions could not harm him while he retained the favour of Lauderdale, and thus royal support and protection. The autumn of 1666 marks the point where Sharp began to lose that essential support.

Since 1662 Sharp had enjoyed the friendship and assistance of Rothes. The connection between the two was of long standing. Rothes' father had helped Sharp gain his first post as regent at St Andrews, and the son had been no less helpful. Rothes' lands were in Fife, and Sharp had enjoyed Rothes' support in putting the ecclesiastical settlement into effect. By 1665 and 1666 Sharp and Rothes between them controlled Scotland.

In September Sharp began to try and detach Rothes from Lauderdale and instead make an alliance with Middleton.[97] Middleton by this time was living in obscurity in England, and his party in Scotland was no longer significant. Sharp's idea presumably was to set up Middleton as a figurehead at court and thus with Rothes have a free hand in running Scotland.

This was not the first time Sharp had challenged Lauderdale's hegemony. In 1664 he had tried to imply that the difficulties of the church in Scotland were Lauderdale's fault, but had been outmanoeuvred and forced to back down.[98] Now again he was seeking to destroy his political support, but this time in Scotland itself.

Rothes was no great politician but he plainly could see that his own best interests lay in supporting Lauderdale, and so rather than join in Sharp's intrigues he revealed what was happening to Lauderdale, who[99] had in any case already been alerted by Bellenden. The truth was that Rothes had none of the ambition for independent political power that moved Sharp.[100] He was content with the existing situation and not prepared to risk his present satisfaction for a gamble. The result was a breach between Sharp and Rothes,[101] and Sharp's isolation in November 1666 in the face of a formidable collection of antagonists, now including Lauderdale.

It was at this stage that there occurred the Pentland Rising. Rothes had gone to court[102] to make his peace with Lauderdale, thus leaving Sharp as acting President of the Privy Council.[103] No sooner had Rothes gone than on 16 November 1666 notice came to the Council of the rising in Dumfries.[104] Until Rothes arrived to take over on 1 December[105] Sharp was responsible for the defence of the country. His conduct during the period, and the Rising itself, were made the pretext for his disgrace.

While the crisis continued Bellenden was writing destructive letters to Lauderdale.[106] In fact, so far as can be told from the Registers of the Privy Council for the period, Sharp did everything necessary with speed and efficiency.[107] Ultimately it was his efficiency that was held against him as yet another demonstration that his power was too great for the comfort of the nobility. Furthermore, the policy of severity towards the non-conformists was a government policy approved by the king and carried through with the support of the nobility. To disgrace Sharp on the grounds that his repressive policies had brought about the Rising was a convenient fiction which disguised the necessity for his fall from political power.[108] A fall it was, however.[109] On 1 February 1667 Sharp made his last appearance at the Council until the beginning of his emergence from disgrace on 4 July.[110]

7

Recovery on Terms, 1667–1669

Sharp was out of favour for much of 1667. In the spring of that year he was dangerously ill,[1] was confined to his diocese in St Andrews,[2] and had little to do with national events. His return to favour was slow and on terms. The price of his rehabilitation was to be his use of his influence over the clergy in the interests of Lauderdale's policies. It has been argued that Sharp's aim between 1662 and 1666 had been to retain for the church, as well as for himself, independence from the erastian interference of the nobility. That policy had brought him in conflict with those in power and had finally deprived him of Lauderdale's support. His rescue from disgrace, it was made plain, would only be at the price of his rendering the church more amenable.

In July Tweeddale estimated that Sharp was sufficiently aware of how close he had come to being expelled from his place to be grateful for offers of Lauderdale's friendship once more.[3] Accordingly Lauderdale made known his willingness for a reconciliation, to which Sharp eagerly responded, fervently reasserting his attachment to Lauderdale's interest.[4] But whatever their mutual professions of good will, it was plain that there had been a fundamental change in the relationship. Lauderdale and his allies were now prepared to use the lever of political disgrace to make Sharp serve their own ends.[5] They were sufficiently cynical to obtain a royal letter to Sharp intimating the king's pleasure with the primate, only in order to attach Sharp to them the more firmly.[6] It was the measure of Sharp's overwhelming desire to stay in office that when such a letter was eventually sent[7] he responded with tremendous gratitude: 'his Majesteyes hand with the diamond seal, was to me as a resurrection from the dead'.[8]

Although Rothes had tried to extricate himself from Sharp's influence, and had done his best by his journey to court in November 1666 and letters since his return to emphasise his dependence on Lauderdale, yet he too was brought to heel. This was done by removing him from his various posts as Commissioner and Treasurer, and instead making him Chancellor.[9] It was done much against Rothes' will,[10] and effectively removed him from power. In his place Tweeddale and Sir Robert Moray became Lauderdale's confidants.[11] During 1667 under their aegis there began that attempt to reconcile non-conformists within the church led by Leighton and known as the Accommodation movement. Although Sharp may well have started out with the intention of promoting moderate episcopacy in the church, since 1662 he had progressively shifted from that ideal. It was not to be expected that he would be favourable towards any movement which made

G

concessions to non-conformists. Nor did it help that the leading spirit of the movement was Leighton with whom Sharp's relations to 1667 had not been particularly cordial.

Sharp's attempts to have his former Resolutioner brethren made his fellow bishops had failed. As a result he had been obliged to consort with men who were certainly not his first choice for his brethren, and with whom his relations were not always satisfactory.

Robert Leighton was a man by no means typical of seventeenth-century Scottish presbyterian ministers.[12] His father was Alexander Leighton, the violently anti-episcopal author of *Zion's Plea*,[13] who suffered imprisonment and mutilation for his puritan assaults on the anglicanism of Archbishop Laud. Robert Leighton himself was sent to be educated at Edinburgh University in 1627. The family had long connections with the lands of Usan near Montrose, and so it was not surprising that the boy should be sent to learn presbyterian doctrine in his father's homeland. Nevertheless Robert Leighton's ties with England were very strong, and it was his preferred country. That was the first difference to mark him from the fiercely proud Scottishness of his fellow-ministers.

After his graduation in 1631 Leighton spent a decade abroad studying and travelling, moving probably in Jansenist circles in France in the days before they had attracted unfavourable attention. This experience of another country, another church and other reading matter marked him off from his Scottish brethren. With very rare exceptions they had little experience of anything but Scotland and the Scottish church, and consequently absorbed themselves in exclusively Scottish disputes and issues with a passion that Leighton could never match.

These differences were already apparent during Leighton's ministry in the parish of Newbattle from 1641 to 1651. Unlike his fellow-ministers he refused to involve himself in contemporary politics or to conform to accepted modes of preaching.[14] Nevertheless he apparently performed his duties as a presbyterian minister, including attendance at church courts, with diligence. He took the Covenants and was friendly with the Earl of Lothian, the patron of Newbattle parish, and one of the leading Covenanting nobility.

In the Resolutioner-Protester debate Leighton was on the Resolutioner side, but was willing to accept from Cromwell the post of Principal of Edinburgh University in 1653. Although the Resolutioners were eager to control the universities, Bailie at least seemed to think the appointment unsatisfactory.[15] Certainly Leighton took no part in carrying on the debate within the church or asserting the Resolutioner cause.

In 1661 Leighton was preferred from the Principalship of Edinburgh to the bishopric of Dunblane. It seems clear that he was nominated by his brother, Elisha, a courtier and ne'er do well, who wanted his brother's advancement in order to share a little reflected glory.[16] It is possible that Leighton was persuaded to accept a bishopric by those same hopes of moderate episcopacy that we have ascribed to Sharp. If so he was cruelly disappointed. His attitude to church government was that of the Aberdeen Doctors in that he simply did not consider it a matter of supreme importance. It seems from what he confided to the Laird of

Brodie[17] that he thought he could as a bishop help to heal the divisions in the church which had so much grieved him while Principal.

From the very beginning, therefore, there were profound differences of background and attitude between Sharp and Leighton. Sharp had for years been employed as a Scot in the defence of presbytery. His life since the late 1640s had been almost entirely a matter of politics. Leighton's nationality was modified by his family background and travels. By experience and temperament he refrained from disputation. Sharp had reluctantly come to episcopacy as a last resort and a political expedient. Leighton saw it as a means to peace. The prognosis for fruitful relations between the two were therefore not good. Between 1661 and 1667 they were further blighted by a series of incidents which revealed an ever wider disparity of attitude between them.

The first such incident occurred over the consecration of the first four bishops in London in December 1661. Neither Sharp nor Leighton had received episcopal ordination and so they were re-ordained before their consecration. As we have seen, the inferred slight on presbyterian orders displeased Sharp although he complied. Leighton, however, far from dissenting, recorded his willingness to agree for the sake of peace in these words: 'though I should be ordained every year I will submit'.[18] There were no re-ordinations of presbyters carried out by Sharp during the Restoration. Clearly he saw such a process as an affront, and to him no doubt Leighton's attitude was spineless and unprincipled.

Immediately after the consecration there was a banquet whose carefree atmosphere distressed Leighton. He was further distressed by Sharp's unwillingness to commit himself to the scheme of moderate episcopacy proposed by Bishop Ussher, until the situation became clearer.[19] Here again was evidence of basic differences of attitude between the two men.

These early differences were soon compounded by a series of demonstrations from Leighton that he had no intention of playing the public role of royal servant that the acceptance of a bishopric in Scotland implied. He absented himself from the ceremonial reception of the bishops into Edinburgh,[20] from the consecration of an additional six bishops which immediately followed,[21] and from the formal reception of the bishops into Parliament.[22] Indeed from this time he seems to have absented himself from all such ceremonies.[23]

In the Parliament of 1662, however, where Leighton had refused to take his place, there occurred the first open clash with Sharp. A number of ministers were required to answer to Parliament for anti-episcopal expressions in their sermons. As a test of loyalty they were required to take the Oath of Allegiance, but would only do so if they could express their own sense of it in writing. The Commissioner in the Parliament of 1661 had expressed verbally the government's sense of the oath, and no reservations had since been allowed in those taking the oath. Leighton, however, now appeared in Parliament to defend the ministers' right to define their sense of the oath.[24] This intervention incensed Sharp, partly because it had taken place without Leighton's giving notice to him, and partly because Sharp now saw taking the oath as a test of obedience and loyalty. Sharp himself had had doubts about the oath, as we have seen, but his recent sermon had shown that he had resolved them to his own satisfaction. He saw refusal to take the oath as punishable defiance.

It must not be forgotten that the ministers in question were Protesters. It is natural to sympathise with Leighton's position, but Sharp had spent more than a decade struggling with the Protesters. He was now in a position to enforce their obedience and submission, and it was not to be expected that he would abandon that opportunity. It was therefore all the more irritating that Leighton, who had taken no part in the former disputes, should set himself up as a champion of those who in Sharp's view had originally caused all the trouble.

There has been a recent tendency to see Leighton as the man who might have saved the Scottish church at the Restoration. In fact his total indifference to matters which had rent the church asunder made him unacceptable to either side. Now as bishop he was alienated from the anti-episcopal ministers, and by his behaviour alienated equally from his fellow-bishops. A measure of that alienation was his omission from the bishops licensed to sit on the Church Commission from 1664. Thus, like Douglas and the other Resolutioners, Leighton had put himself in the position where he could have no effect on a situation which displeased him.

Matters came to a head in 1665 when failure to implement the ecclesiastical settlement in any satisfactory way induced Leighton to complain of Sharp to the king.[25] Leighton was well received by Charles who appeared to be on Leighton's side and criticised Sharp, but this incident for the moment seems to have had no effect. It was characteristic of Charles to agree with supplicants and say what they wanted to hear.[26] Such agreeable manners were by no means always translated into action.

In 1667, however, with Sharp in disgrace and a movement towards compromise and toleration of non-conformists beginning in the English church,[27] the opportunity was taken to put some of Leighton's theories into practice.[28]

Tweeddale and Robert Moray were both supporters of Leighton and sympathetic to the non-conformist plight.[29] On the king's authorisation and under their aegis talks were begun with non-conformists with a view to their conciliation.[30] Sharp was not in favour of these developments[31] but in his vulnerable political situation was obliged to comply.[32] He came to terms with Tweeddale[33] and Moray.[34] He supported the disbanding of the forces and used his influence to dispose the other clergy to agree with him to use 'all courses of lenity and gentilenes at present'.[35]

In the spring of 1668, although the leniency of the preceding year had generally increased disturbances, an indulgence to non-conformists was planned.[36] Even though Sharp had made it plain to Lauderdale that he felt it essential to deal firmly with the increasing conventicles which had now spread to Fife,[37] yet he was obliged to agree to this proposal and to oblige Alexander Burnet, Archbishop of Glasgow, to agree also.[38]

It was at this juncture on 11 July 1668 that an assassination attempt was made on Sharp. He was in Edinburgh with Andrew Honeyman, the bishop of Orkney. Between four and five o'clock that afternoon they were getting into a coach in the

High Street when one among the crowd of poor round the coach to whom Sharp was giving money fired at him with a pistol. The shot missed and instead hit Honeyman in the arm. The would-be assassin immediately took to his heels before the servants and those standing round had recovered sufficiently from the shock to lay hold of him.[39]

Such an outrage in the main street of Edinburgh in full public view demanded exemplary action by the Privy Council. Proclamations were made for the arrest of the offender, and a reward of two thousand merks was offered. The king and Lauderdale had to be informed and a search of Edinburgh was ordered to be made.[40] By 30 July the identity of the man had been established fairly certainly as James Mitchell, *alias* Small, who had been forfeited for his part in the Pentland Rising.[41] The whereabouts of Mitchell could not for the moment be discovered, but a number of women who refused to give information were sentenced to be banished.[42]

As might have been expected, this incident for the moment destroyed the prospects of an indulgence being granted.[43] It had given Sharp the most dreadful fright. A sympathetic letter from Lauderdale[44] drew a reply from Sharp in which he linked those who had taken part in the Pentland Rising with the attempt on himself. He had no doubt that the incident was revolutionary in intention and directed against the stability of church and state.[45] Understandably he was now disposed to be much less co-operative over any plan for bringing in outed ministers.[46] Unfortunately this change in his attitude came too late to win him back the friendship of the Archbishop of Glasgow, formerly his greatest ally, and now because of the Accommodation policy estranged from him.

Alexander Burnet was in his way as untypical of Scottish ministers as Leighton. Burnet's father was minister of Lauder and the son of a laird.[47] During the 1630s and 1640s the elder Burnet suffered for his royalist and episcopal sympathies. These sympathies were passed on to Alexander who graduated from Edinburgh University in 1633 but became chaplain to the Earl of Traquair rather than a parish minister. In 1639 he left Scotland for a living in Kent. During the interregnum he was ejected for his royalism and thereafter was loosely attached to the court of Charles II in exile. At the Restoration he was appointed chaplain to General Rutherford, later Lord Teviot, then governor of Dunkirk. In that capacity he was responsible for the English congregation of Dunkirk. For a brief period from 1660 to 1663 he again had a parish in England before his appointment as bishop of Aberdeen in 1663.

Thus Burnet had been out of Scotland for twenty-four years and had no experience at first hand of the events within the Scottish church in those momentous years. He could not be expected either to understand or to sympathise with the continuing divisions of opinion among the ministers. Furthermore, his personal preference and family tradition was in favour of royalism and episcopacy. That preference was so strong that he had been prepared to live outside Scotland, and even in exile on the continent, rather than endure any alternative. This background hardly betokened a man capable of effecting reconciliation.

Burnet's initial appointment was probably not at Sharp's request,[48] but his translation only months later in January 1664 to the archbishopric of Glasgow on Fairfoul's death must certainly have been with Sharp's approval. Indeed until 1667 the two seem to have enjoyed cordial relations. Burnet, like Sharp, was in favour of rigorous punishment of active non-conformity, and like Sharp he found his efforts to implement the laws frustrated by the nobility. Like Sharp he therefore spent much time writing letters of complaint to Lauderdale and to the Archbishop of Canterbury. In 1665 he had made a journey to London to make his complaints about the backwardness of the nobility to the king, just as Sharp had done in 1664. Like Sharp his opposition to the nobility had made him enemies.

When, however, in 1667 Sharp's desire for political survival obliged him to accept, or at least put up with, the movements towards toleration initiated by Leighton, Burnet would not do the same. This no doubt was the product of two factors: sincerity and stupidity. Burnet was a convinced episcopalian in a way that Sharp was not and never could be. Sharp had been pushed into a corner and had decided that episcopacy was for the moment necessary. Eventually he decided that it was necessary for the support of monarchy anyway. Burnet's choice had been made at an early age, and freely made. On the other hand Burnet was incapable of seeing that his sincerity might damage the very cause for which he acted.

Burnet's opposition to the new trend to leniency and toleration first took the form in July 1667 of opposition to the reduction of the number of troops in Scotland. Sharp, with the rest of the clergy, overrode him.[49] He then objected to the proposals for lenient treatment of non-conformists discussed in the Privy Council. But in this also he was voted down.[50] He then attempted to make a public statement about the danger the church was in.[51] The first such attempt was made in September 1667 at a meeting of the bishops. On this occasion Sharp succeeded in suppressing Burnet's petition.[52] Inevitably these events destroyed much of the goodwill between them.[53]

At this juncture Sharp made a journey to London. He went in August 1668[54] and returned early in November.[55] The effect of this journey was to persuade him, despite the attempt on his life, and despite his reservations, to offer no opposition to the continuation of the policy of moderation.[56] His co-operation was achieved by the renewed assurances from Lauderdale of his continuing favour towards him.[57]

On his return to Scotland, therefore, he immediately put a stop to a second attempt at a public letter to the king from Burnet. This petition had been drawn up the previous month, October 1668, at a synod held at Peebles. It consisted largely of a complaint against the policy of conciliation, and plans had been made to send it to the king without first submitting it to the Privy Council.[58] Sharp vigorously opposed any such bypassing of the ordinary channels of complaint and thus succeeded in putting an end to the whole project.[59]

The following year Sharp's dilemma continued in an even more acute form. In March Tweeddale again raised the issue of an Indulgence.[60] From the beginning steps were taken to ensure that the Indulgence would receive Sharp's consent.[61] Sharp signified to Lauderdale that he would acquiesce in the royal will, but at the same time pointed out his fears that an Indulgence would create a schism in the church by exempting those who accepted it from episcopal discipline and oversight.[62] His fears were increased by the redoubled size and frequency of conventicles that spring.[63]

On 15 July the king's letter declaring the Indulgence was read in the Council.[64] A committee was appointed to consider the letter,[65] and on 20 July Sharp made a set speech to the committee giving his views on the Indulgence.[66] He stressed that he had every intention of obeying the king's expressed will, but at the same time pointed out the dangers of such a course of action. He also took the opportunity in the committee to criticise the wording of the Indulgence and its implications.[67] Tweeddale was displeased with this reluctance on Sharp's part and took him to task about it. Sharp's dilemma was then revealed in his account of the dissatisfactions of some of the bishops and clergy because of the Indulgence.[68] The influence of Tweeddale and royal policy was, however, stronger than the influence of his brethren, and in the Council the letter was duly put into effect.[69]

Now followed the inevitable corollary of Burnet's opposition to the Indulgence. Tweeddale had tried to frighten him into acquiescence as he had frightened Sharp.[70] Burnet was not susceptible to the same pressures.[71] In September 1669 he drew up the third of his complaints: 'The Remonstrance of the Synod of Glasgow'.[72] This document Sharp did not succeed in suppressing before it became public knowledge.[73] When news of it came to court it aroused the fury of the king as well as that of Sir Robert Moray and Lauderdale.[74] The paper was suppressed by order of the Privy Council of 16 October 1669[75] Burnet was removed from the Privy Council and required to resign his archbishopric.[76] Sharp was obliged to co-operate with Lauderdale in effecting this,[77] and Burnet then retired to England. Sharp had thus lost his strongest ally among the bishops, and was now to feel that loss.

For three years Sharp had been made to dance to a merry tune. His political ambitions had led him to seem to support a cause which he did not support, and to antagonise Burnet in the process. His subordination to the nobility was not yet complete, however. The process culminated in Sharp's enforced agreement to the Act of Supremacy.

In October 1669 a parliament was summoned to meet in Edinburgh, to which Lauderdale was appointed royal commissioner. The real business of the Parliament, as the king's letter soon revealed, was to put in train preparations for a union of Scotland and England.[78] The opportunity was also taken, however, to pass a much-enlarged Act of Supremacy. This seems to have been drawn up in August and September 1669 by Lauderdale, Moray and Tweeddale, possibly on Tweeddale's initiative.[79]

The Oath of Allegiance of 1661 had been officially interpreted as allowing the king to determine the external government and policy of the church.[80] In the Act for the Restitution and Re-establishment of the Antient Government of the Church by Archbishops and Bishops of May 1662,[81] the power of the king was more fully outlined to require him to advise with the bishops and clergy in these matters. The effect of the Act of Supremacy of 1669[82] was to allow the king unlimited power and to extend his control to all ecclesiastical meetings and matters to be discussed in them.[83] The Act of Supremacy, therefore, was an act against the bishops.[84] They were no longer required to advise the king, and ecclesiastical meetings specifically authorised by them since the Act of January 1662 were now to meet on royal authority.[85] The late date of the drawing up of this act suggests that it was provoked by the opposition of the bishops to the Indulgence.

There were also wider implications to the Act of particular relevance to Sharp. In 1662 he had regarded episcopal government as an expedient in those particular circumstances — an attitude to church government which had a tradition in the Scottish church. By 1665, however, he had so far changed his views as to argue that episcopal government was *iure divino*.[86] While the Act of Restitution gave the bishops power to advise the king, his supremacy over the external government could be reconciled with the idea of *iure divino* episcopacy. But when the king was given unfettered power over the external government, it was hard to see how the two could be reconciled.[87]

Sharp understood all too well the implications of this act, and as soon as it was shown to him he objected with some justice that a Henrician supremacy was being created in the Scottish church.[88] He therefore tried, probably with the advice and concurrence of his fellow-bishops, by application to Lauderdale to have added to the expressions of the king's power in ordering the external government of the church the phrase 'as it is settled by law'. The effect of this would have been first to ensure that the king did not alter the church government from episcopacy, since episcopacy was settled by law, but more important to retain the qualifications of the royal power expressed in the Act of Restitution. In addition, the primate would have retained his power to veto royal policies in a National Synod, according to the Act of August 1663.[89]

Lauderdale recognised the effect of this addition and would not permit it. Sharp went so far as to preach a sermon before parliament opposing the supremacy. Once again, however, he was prevented from carrying out his views by his greater desire to stay in power. When taken to task for it he made his apologies and thereafter offered little opposition to the act's progress through the Articles and Parliament.[90]

So then, by a strange irony, the man who had originally co-operated with the episcopal settlement to avoid erastian interference in the Scottish church had now co-operated in passing an act which gave the king unlimited power within the church. Sharp had tried to ride the tiger, and the tiger had turned and eaten him up.

8
Lauderdale's Creature, 1669–1679[1]

For four or five years after the passing of the Act of Supremacy Sharp took very little part in national affairs. He had nothing to do with the opposition to Lauderdale in the Parliaments of 1672 or 1673. He made no journeys to London. The era of his political ascendancy was decisively over and there were no more banquets and ceremonial receptions for him. The number of his attendances at the Privy Council diminished severely,[2] and indicated that he no longer formed one of the inner circle of politicians.

The first demonstration of the effects of the Act of Supremacy was the necessity for Sharp to approve of the appointment of Leighton to the archbishopric of Glasgow left vacant by Burnet's resignation. Lauderdale had been planning this change since November 1669,[3] as soon as it became clear that Burnet would be forced out, but it was April 1670 before Leighton could be persuaded to agree.[4] It was a decision which was unlikely to be pleasing to Sharp, but he declared himself determined to acquiesce in the king's will.[5] Matters had changed since 1665 when he pointed out to Lauderdale his right of prior nomination to bishoprics.[6]

The appointment of Leighton indicated that the policy of conciliation was to continue, a policy for which Charles had recently emphasised his support.[7] Despite Sharp's continuing opposition, additional ministers were licensed in 1670 to preach under the terms of the Indulgence of 1669.[8] He was required by royal command to co-operate with Leighton's plans for planting parishes in the west and the Visitation of the diocese of Glasgow.[9] In the summer of 1670 six ministers appointed by Leighton were sent as 'evangelists to the western shires'.[10] Among these was the young Gilbert Burnet who had twice directly confronted Sharp about his activities as bishop.[11] On the second occasion Burnet had gone so far as to compose and circulate in 1666 a paper complaining of the behaviour of the bishops.[12] Sharp had wished to despose him, but was overruled by the other bishops.[13] For a while Burnet had been obliged to retire to obscurity,[14] but by 1670 he was rising to prominence under Leighton's protection.[15] It may be imagined how much Sharp approved of the elevation in this manner of the man who had twice challenged him.[16]

In the autumn and winter of 1670–71 an attempt was made to get non-conformists to agree to a scheme of Leighton's for setting up bishops in presbytery.[17] This was the very same scheme devised originally by Bishop Ussher which Leighton had tried to discuss with Sharp at their consecration in 1661. Sharp was now even less enthusiastic about it than he had been then.[18]

In December 1671 a decision on the best means to fill the vacant bishopric of

Edinburgh was taken without consultation with Sharp or his concurrence, in conformity with a letter from the king. A list of nominations had similarly been drawn up for vacant bishoprics without his knowledge, which included Gilbert Burnet.[19] Although in April 1672 Sharp complained of concessions made to the English non-conformists and again expressed his dissatisfaction with the Indulgence of 1669,[20] yet in September 1672 the Indulgence was extended,[21] despite Sharp's complaints.[22]

For three years, therefore, since the Act of Supremacy was passed, a policy had been deliberately pursued to which it was known Sharp was opposed. Visitations had been made, parishes planted, bishoprics and archbishoprics filled, and general policy decisions made, all without consultation with Sharp and in defiance of his authority as primate. Although in 1668 and 1669 he had equally disapproved of the policies followed, yet at least he had been able to go to London and consult with Lauderdale, and had openly stated his disagreement with the first Indulgence. After 1669, so far had he been stripped of power and influence that he had not even been able to register his protest. He had retained the primacy, but his place had been rendered so insignificant that it was hardly worth the retaining.

He was rescued from this ignominious condition in 1674. By 1672 it was evident that the Accommodation movement had been a failure.[23] Although the two Indulgences had reconciled about a hundred and fifty of the former Resolutioners to the regime, yet it had made virtually no impact on the hardcore Protester opposition.[24] The talks which had been intended to reconcile non-conformists to the idea of a moderate episcopacy were a fiasco.

Such a failure had all along been anticipated by Lauderdale. He was too well-versed in the Resolutioner-Protester struggles to suppose that the Protesters would ever be brought over. His agents of this policy in Scotland, and Leighton's supporters, Tweeddale, Moray and Kincardine, had all gradually recognised the futility of their efforts.[25] In consequence the policies of repression and coercion had continued virtually throughout the period from 1667. The intention had been to bring over those who could be satisfied to the official settlement, and then to crush the remaining irreconcilable minority. This had not, however, been the effect. It had proved impossible to crush conventicling which had indeed increased enormously by 1673. The result of the failure of either leniency or repression led in 1674 to a serious split among the clergy of the established church. Sharp by his well-used political skills succeeded in patching up this rift, and thus regained a measure of favour and influence with Lauderdale at court.

The three petitions attempted by Archbishop Burnet had been directed against the policy of leniency and certainly indicated that there was a body of the conforming clergy who were out of sympathy with that policy.

The apparent trend of the Accommodation movement and the Act of Supremacy had been towards a lessening of the bishops' authority. Thus the suspicion that the king would ultimately agree to abolish episcopacy, alive in 1662, had been resuscitated.[26] It was therefore found necessary to calm the episcopal party and to dash the hopes of the Presbyterians, by repeated assertions of the royal intention to keep up episcopal church government and its authority.[27] These formulae were insufficient to reassure the episcopal clergy. Their dissatisfaction became public in the Synod of Fife in the spring of 1674.[28] They asked Sharp, as moderator of the Synod, to present an address to the Privy Council representing their dissatisfaction with the increase in conventicling:

> finding it hard for them to suffer the people of their charge to be debauched and seduced from the duty they owe to authority and their persons and profession to be reviled and brought into contempt by pitiful insignificant men designedly set about to run this country into confusion, having nothing to commend themselves to the unstable multitude who gad after them but impudency in railing against the king and public settlement, and crying up the covenant and the good old cause which are known to be the ordinary theme of their preachments.

Sharp submitted their petition to Lauderdale and asked for his permission to present it, with a request for assistance to the Privy Council in June.

The petition was not presented as planned, but instead the response from the king was a proclamation against the holding of conventicles and a commission to Sharp and others to take steps once more for their suppression.[29] Archbishop Burnet's petitions had certainly received no such positive response. It was clear that Lauderdale was now alive to the danger of a split in the church.

At about the same time, spring and early summer of 1674, the dissatisfaction of those who had supported Leighton and his movement and had seen it fail, similarly became evident. In May 1673 Leighton had begged to be allowed to resign his see, recognising the hopelessness of the cause he had promoted. He was with difficulty persuaded to continue another year in that office.[30] His intention to resign, however, had already alarmed Ramsay, at this time Bishop of Dunblane and one of Leighton's supporters. He had therefore requested that if Leighton should retire, his place might be filled by one sympathetic to Leighton's ideals.[31] This in itself was a clear enough indication of the antagonisms within the body of conforming clergy.

In May and June 1674, before the act for the suppression of conventicles had been published, Lauderdale was informed of agitation in the presbyteries of Edinburgh and Glasgow to petition the king without reference to the bishops, concerning disorders in the church and to call a National Synod.[32] Motions had then been made in the synods of Glasgow and Edinburgh that a National Synod should be requested. The whole matter had then been raised in the Privy Council where the Duke of Hamilton had urged that the disorders in the church should be reported to the king.[33]

These agitations from either side among the conforming orthodox clergy came at a particularly awkward time for Lauderdale. In the parliament of 1673 he had had to face an organised Scottish opposition headed by the Duke of Hamilton.[34] He had been unable to crush this sign of disaffection and Hamilton with his followers adjourned to court early in 1674 to prosecute their conflict there. At that very time Charles was in political difficulties in England. The prospect of trouble in previously quiescent Scotland was therefore all the more alarming:

> He said that things were ill here [in England], and wee must not, said he, have troublesome busines both in Scotland and here togither.[35]

While Lauderdale was still in Scotland as commissioner, his English enemies were proceeding against him in the Commons,[36] and although Lauderdale was assured of the king's goodwill[37] he was clearly in political danger from two sides.[38]

The association of Hamilton with the malcontents in the church made it more than ever essential that the unrest must be quelled.[39] Sharp was chosen as the man to do the job.[40] He quickly investigated the whole matter,[41] and ultimately three ministers and Bishop Ramsey of Dunblane were suspended.[42] These measures were successful in quelling discontent, and unity was thus restored. Sharp's reward was to be invited to London.

Although Sharp had once again been redeemed from disgrace, yet once again his recovery was on terms. From 1674 his primary political function was to provide Lauderdale with support. His visit to London was exceptionally long and lasted from August 1674 to August 1675. Sharp had been openly threatened on the streets of Edinburgh in June 1674,[43] and such daring was symptomatic of the increasing size, frequency and boldness of conventicles now held in the open air and with armed men present. The length of his stay in London suggests a desire to be relieved from the pressures of such an intractable situation.

His stay also had political purposes. Lauderdale's political troubles continued throughout the period,[44] and Sharp was there to give him what assistance he could. A reconciliation was effected between Lauderdale and the High Church party: Sheldon, Morley and their circle, probably by Sharp's means.[45] Sharp also did what he could to neutralise the influence of Bishop Ramsey, now in London, and ready to stir up trouble with allegations of mismanagement in Scotland.[46]

Meanwhile in Scotland a quite discernible political opposition party had now emerged, led by Hamilton. It was Sharp's job, as Lauderdale's most effective ally in Scotland, to promote Lauderdale's interest and diminish Hamilton's. On his return to Scotland Sharp therefore spent much effort on reconciling Rothes to Lauderdale and weaning him from Hamilton,[47] and on protecting Lauderdale's brother, Charles Maitland of Haltoun, from attacks by Hamilton and 'The Party'.[48]

Alexander Burnet, restored to the archdiocese of Glasgow in September 1674[49] on Leighton's resignation,[50] probably with Sharp's help,[51] was similarly brought in to the circle of active supporters of Lauderdale.[52] The clergy disciplined for their support of a National Synod, including Bishop Ramsey, were induced to submit to Sharp,[53] and thus Hamilton's influence in the church was diminished. In November 1675 Sharp approached Hamilton himself and urged him to abandon his attacks on Lauderdale and his supporters.[54]

Although the Party was not destroyed by these means, Sharp's support was certainly helpful to Lauderdale. It was continued for the rest of Sharp's life. At the convention held in 1678 Sharp supported Lauderdale in face of renewed opposition from Hamilton.[55]

Sharp's political activities in the last few years of his life were not, however, undertaken to the exclusion of his interests in church affairs. After his return to Scotland in 1675 he was for the first time since 1666 once again in virtually unchallenged control of the church. Leighton had gone and had been replaced by Sharp's old ally Alexander Burnet. Gilbert Burnet, Leighton's protégé, had refused a bishopric and thus lost favour and influence. Bishop Ramsay of Dunblane and his three minister collaborators over the movement for the National Synod had been forced to eat humble pie. For the first time since 1666 there was no overt opposition to Sharp among the ranks of the orthodox clergy.

In these circumstances Sharp returned to the attitudes of the early 1660s. Then he had favoured a policy of moderation towards passive non-conformists and of rigour towards the active. By 1675 the two Indulgences had brought back into the church all those who were prepared to be wooed by such methods. Those who still refused to conform were of an increasingly violent and implacable character. Sharp's attitude to them was equally violent and implacable. When the possibility of a further indulgence emerged in 1676 and again in 1677, Sharp was predictably opposed.[56]

There was, however, a fundamental difference in the situation in the mid-1670s from what it had been in the early 1660s. In the '60s the nobility had, as we have seen, for their own ends, stood in the way of the executing of the legislation against non-conformists. By the mid-70s the nobility had divided into two loosely-grouped factions — supporters of Lauderdale and supporters of Hamilton. After 1674 Lauderdale had emphatically rejected the whole movement towards moderation. From that time therefore the supporters among the nobility were prepared to put into force the policies of coercion. Thus from 1675 Sharp's policies of severity could be put into effect. The result was a worsening of the situation in Scotland, and a course of action tending towards the provocation and direct confrontation with the non-conformists.

Sharp was not now among the makers of policy. He was, however, willing to lend his support to the policies of Lauderdale. He was thereby involved in condoning the increasingly high-handed and illegal activities of the regime in the name of the preservation of episcopacy and monarchy. The study of the last years of his life will consist of his part in the three most notorious events of those years: the Kirkton-Carstares case; the James Mitchell affair; and the Highland Host.

James Kirkton had been minister of Mertoun in the presbytery of Earlston until he was outed in 1662.[57] In 1672 he was licensed to preach at Carstairs under the terms of the second Indulgence.[58] In March 1673 Kirkton had not yet taken up residence at Carstairs and was warned by the Privy Council to do so by the first of June.[59] By November 1673 he had still not appeared in Carstairs and was reported to be in England.[60] In June 1674 he was accused of having taken part in a conventicle at Cramond,[61] and, having failed to appear before the Council, was in July declared a rebel and outlaw.[62]

In 1676 Kirkton was in Edinburgh when he was recognised by Captain William Carstares. Carstares was a notorious thug who in May 1765, while a lieutenant, had used the troops under his command to kidnap five men. All five were severely manhandled and taken on board ship while Carstares was apparently paid, and the prisoners destined for transportation to France. When orders came from the Provost of Edinburgh for the prisoners to be put on shore Carstares set about the messengers and destroyed the orders. The Council was then petitioned for help. Carstares was made to pay compensation and restore the goods he had stolen, and was removed from his position as lieutenant.[63] In July 1675, however, he was restored by royal command and on promise of good behaviour returned to his previous place as lieutenant in the same company.[64]

Since Kirkton had been declared a rebel and outlaw, Carstares was duty bound to arrest him and deliver him to the Council. Instead he took Kirkton to his own home and there tried to blackmail him. Kirkton's shouts eventually brought him help and he escaped, leaving Carstares unhurt.[65] Kirkton had no legal redress since he was in any case an outlaw, but Carstares, perhaps in fear of complaint against him to the Council, reported those who had helped Kirkton escape. These men were then fined[66] and required to produce Kirkton himself before the Council,[67] since Kirkton had again been reported as preaching at conventicles.[68]

Carstares was notorious, and the management of this business drew protests from Hamilton and Kincardine.[69] They were, of course, of the opposition party, and therefore likely to protest against the policies and methods of Lauderdale's ruling faction, but their protest had some justification. Hamilton had been present at the Council the previous year when Carstares had been brought before it. He knew what sort of man the Council was dealing with. Furthermore, in order to make the arrest in the first place Carstares should have had a warrant — which was now supplied backdated from the Council.[70] There was some reason for protest against such methods.

Sharp, however, had no such scruples. He wrote to Lauderdale protesting against any opposition being offered to the arrest of Kirkton, and signifying his pleasure that Hamilton and Kincardine had been immediately removed from the Council as a punishment for their opposition.[71] Sharp's point of view was quite clear and uncomplicated. Conventicles were increasing, and with them the threat to monarchy and episcopacy. The ringleaders in the conventicling movement were the ministers who must be restrained. Kirkton was a known outed minister and a rebel and outlaw. To stand on ceremony about the precise legality of his arrest was to foil the whole purpose of the legislation and discourage the very men responsible for putting it into action.[72]

Although Sharp's view is comprehensible and a natural development of his earlier ideas, he was laying himself open to very serious charges by condoning the use of thugs and manipulation of the judicial system. His involvement in this affair was a demonstration that for him the end justified the means, but it signalled his utter bankruptcy as the leader of an independent church, and his subservience to the policies and methods of Lauderdale. Sharp might not have the influence to initiate policy, but his co-operation in carrying it out during these last years is an indication of the distance he had come since 1662.

The second and more notorious incident of this kind was the case of James Mitchell. Mitchell was the man who in 1668 had attempted to assassinate Sharp. Although his identity had very quickly been established, he had managed to evade arrest until February 1674 when he was apparently recognised by Sharp in

Edinburgh.[73] Sharp had then had him arrested by his brother Sir William Sharp.[74] The intention of the Privy Council was to send Mitchell for trial in the Justiciary Court immediately.[75] As a preliminary a Committee of the Council was appointed to examine him. Mitchell confessed to having taken part in the Pentland Rising, and that at the time of the attempted assassination he had been in Edinburgh and had bought a pistol. He did not, however, confess that he had made the attempt on the archbishop until he was promised that his life would be spared. The promise was authorised by Lauderdale and the Council. This confession Mitchell repeated before the full Council, but refused to repeat before the judges of the Justiciary Court, and it was then explained to him that his life would be spared only if we would adhere to his confession and not otherwise. Mitchell still refused to repeat his confession, and in consequence the Privy Council decided to remit him for trial, on the understanding that the promise made by them no longer held.[76]

Later the same month Mitchell was permitted to speak with his lawyers and friends in his prison in the Tolbooth,[77] which suggested that a trial was thought to be imminent, but no such trial took place. Instead Mitchell was kept prisoner. Possibly this imprisonment would have continued indefinitely had not Mitchell attempted to escape in December 1675.[78] That rash act brought him to the Council's attention once more. They were in the same dilemma as had faced them nearly two years before. They obviously did not want to conduct an open trial, perhaps because they feared public reaction, but on the other hand if Mitchell would not make a judicial confession, then legally no action could be taken but to remand him in custody. In January 1675, therefore, the Council decided to try and wring a confession out of him by torture.[79] At this time Sharp was in London and so had nothing to do with the episode. The method was evidently ineffectual, for Mitchell was sent to the Bass Rock, an island prison in the Firth of Forth, there to be kept close prisoner.[80]

In October 1677 the whole issue was reopened when it was decided to bring Mitchell to trial. Sharp has generally been supposed to be the man behind this initiative.[81] It is true that he was at the meeting of the Council at which the decision was taken, and no doubt he condoned it, but October 1677 was a particularly difficult month for Lauderdale's attempted subjugation of the Covenanters. It was the month in which the decision was taken to raise the Highland Host, and Lauderdale may well have thought that to make an example of Mitchell would help to terrify non-conformists into passivity.[82]

The earlier course of dealing with Mitchell without trial had been a great deal more sensible so far as the credit of the Scottish government was concerned, as the conduct of the trial very soon proved.[83] Mitchell was accused of the capital offence of the attempted murder of a Privy Councillor and minister. The defence began on 7 January 1678 by asserting that in fact *attempted* murder was not liable to the death penalty. Mitchell denied having made a confession and it was further asserted that even if he had, since it was not a judicial confession it could not be used in evidence against him. The prosecution countered that Mitchell's act was indeed liable to the death penalty; that even if Mitchell had confessed because he was promised his life, that promise could not stand in law, and that Mitchell's confession was admissible as evidence against him. The defence then replied to the same effect as before. At that point the court adjourned until 9 January.

When the court reassembled the six Commissioners of Justiciary, or judges, gave their opinion that the crime committed was indeed liable to the death penalty, and that Mitchell's confession could not be retracted but must stand. However, they then asserted that any promises made to him at that time were sufficient to secure Mitchell 'as to Life and Limb'.

It has been argued that the whole case had been undertaken with the intention of making an example of Mitchell. But the decision of the Commissioners of Justiciary had now declared that even if Mitchell were found guilty he should not lose his life or be mutilated. This was not at all the intended effect.

The prosecution then produced Mitchell's confession that he had been the person solely responsible for the attempt on Sharp's life, and backed it up with the depositions of various witnesses. When it came to the moment for the cross-examination of those who had promised Mitchell his life if he confessed, they all — Rothes, Hatton, Lauderdale and Sharp — flatly denied that any promise had been sought or given. Sharp alone had the grace to admit that

> he promised at his first taking, that if he [Mitchell] would freelie confess the Fault, and express his Repentance for the same at that tyme, without farder troubling Judicatories therein, his Grace would use his best Indeavour to favour him, or else leave him to Justice.

But Sharp then flatly and explicitly denied that any further promises had been made:

> that he either gave him Assurance, or gave Warrant to any to give it, is a false and malicious Calumny.

Perhaps Sharp was salving his conscience by playing with words. He gave a 'promise' but not an 'assurance'. At any rate he was revealing that some guarantee had been made to Mitchell, and in that he was at least fractionally more honest than his fellow-councillors. At this point in the proceedings Sharp was interrupted by Mitchell's brother-in-law Nicoll Sommerville.[84] Sommerville contradicted Sharp's denial that any promise had been made, and gave instances which seemed to the assembled court to indicate that Sharp was not telling the truth. Sharp then lost his temper and swore that what he said was true. To that Somerville 'cryed out, that upon his salvation what he had affirmed was true'.

Mitchell's defence was obviously very astute, and immediately these denials had been made asked permission to produce the Register of the Council. The entry for 12 March 1674 relating to Mitchell was then read in open court. The implication was very clear. If the report was correct, then the four members of the Council were all perjured men. In the face of such an immense blow to the reputation of the government the Commissioners ruled the extract from the Register to be inadmissible evidence. The house adjourned.

The next day Mitchell was found guilty of a capital crime on his own confession. The promise of life was found not proven. Mitchell was sentenced to be hanged.

His speech at the gibbet, instead of reading, he threw to the crowd since drums prevented his being heard. It contained thanks to the lawyers, and drew careful attention to the perjury of the Privy Councillors.

This was indeed an appalling business for Sharp to be involved in. Not only had he perjured himself, he had been seen to do so. His resolution to support the Lauderdale regime had brought him to the point where he was prepared to involve himself in criminal behaviour in order to maintain his political status and remain in power. It was a dismal indication of his fast-crumbling integrity.

This harsh judgment on Sharp's activities in his last years is further borne out by his co-operation with the punitive campaign by the 'Highland Host'.

In 1677 Lauderdale himself had come to Scotland. In July 1676 a new commission of the Privy Council had been ordered by the king, from which Hamilton and most of his party had been omitted. It was reported to Lauderdale, however, that the party continued to foment unrest. Lauderdale's presence in Scotland was calculated to subdue both the Party and the conventiclers. The effect of his visit was to increase the vigour with which the existing legislation against conventicles and non-conformists was put into effect,[85] and to enact new legislation requiring heritors to exact a bond from their tenants that they would conform to the established religion.[86] Members of the nobility were appointed each in his own shire for the suppression of conventicles to see that legislation was put into effect, disorders reported and penalties exacted.[87] Thus the situation in the early 1660s, when Sharp and the bishops urged an unwilling nobility to implement the laws, had now been reversed. The civil government now took complete control of the means to enforce conformity.

These severe measures at first appeared to be successful,[88] but by late October the situation seemed to Lauderdale to have deteriorated so far as to justify putting in readiness military forces. In September he had asked the king to give orders for the assembly of a force on the coast of northern Ireland under the command of Viscount Granard. In October he ordered highlanders from Perthshire and Argyll to be assembled under the command of the Earl of Argyll, the Marquis of Atholl and the Earl of Caithness. These men were to rendezvous at Stirling. In addition the militia regiments of the area round Edinburgh were ordered to rendezvous at Edinburgh. Finally, arrangements were made for the supply of the troops, and proclamations and other orders were made ready in advance.[89] At the end of January 1678 a force of about eight thousand men was mustered in the west, and throughout February and March a substantial portion of them was quartered in the western shires where non-conformists had been most active.[90]

The initiative for this expedition seems to have come from Lauderdale,[91] and his motives were complex. The whole basis of his function as Secretary of State for Scotland was the maintenance of law and order in Scotland. Charles II was exclusively interested in the governing of his English kingdom. He appears to have disliked Scots and Scotland after his experiences there in 1650 and 1651, and his only concern with his northern kingdom was to be sure that it caused him no disturbance, nor interfered with his plans.

It was Lauderdale's task to promote this state of affairs, and the king was

H

apparently not interested in the means to be used; consequently the nobility had been able to do more or less as they liked throughout the reign. Nevertheless, when disturbances did occur, Lauderdale was obliged to act with authority in order to maintain peace and quiet. Thus in 1667 it had been necessary to disgrace Sharp and Rothes as the scapegoats for the Pentland Rising, although they had not been responsible for it.

Now in 1677 and 1678 Lauderdale was in much greater political difficulty himself. His position had been severely challenged both in England and Scotland by opposition parties. The opposition in Scotland was perfectly well aware of the embarrassment the conventicling movement could cause Lauderdale, and it appears to have deliberately encouraged disorders among the conventiclers.[92] For reasons such as these[93] Lauderdale had been forced to attempt to crush the conventiclers and the opposition once and for all.

By this time, though, Sharp's fortunes were tied irrevocably to those of Lauderdale. Since 1675 at least he had been the chief supporter of Lauderdale in Scotland, and his presence in London in 1674 and 1675 had undoubtedly helped Lauderdale in a time of crisis there. If Lauderdale should fall, Sharp also would fall. Sharp was therefore committed to supporting the Highland Host venture as he had been committed to the proceedings against Mitchell.

It is also true that Sharp was convinced, and had been for many years, that only rigour and severity could deal with the problem of non-conformity. In December 1677, therefore, when arrangements for the expedition were well advanced, Sharp and the bishops drew up a list of suggestions for the conduct of the troops in the west.[94] These suggestions demonstrate that the bishops condoned the principle of the expedition although they were at some pains that those who were innocent and conformists should not suffer. In the event of course the conduct of the troops was predictably arbitrary and illegal. Sharp was ill-pleased by these excesses,[95] but they might well have been anticipated.

The whole expedition was grossly ill-calculated. The Party, instead of being destroyed, hastened to London to give lurid descriptions of the excesses of the soldiery to the king. Reports were received at court of pillaging, rape, and murder. The House of Commons opposition, glad of a cause, began to agitate.[96] The immediate target of all the complaints was of course Lauderdale, and whatever his private reservations, Sharp was then obliged to come to the rescue. Alexander Burnet was despatched to London to ally with Lauderdale's friends, the English high church party, to represent the bishops' sense of the necessity of the expedition and to present a paper, drawn up by Sharp, to that effect.[97]

This move, and the action of other supporters of Lauderdale, proved successful. Although no punishment was meted out to the Party, and the expedition was ordered to be terminated by the end of 1678, Lauderdale suffered no serious effects, and retained the king's favour.[98] Sharp's political future was thus once again secured, but at the expense of his public support and co-operation for a policy that was open to the gravest reservations on human and legal grounds.

This identification with an increasingly brutal and arbitrary regime lasted until Sharp's death the following spring. He appears to have been unmoved by the excesses of the years 1677 and 1678 with which he had identified himself, and in late 1678 was urging that more severity be used towards the non-conformists.

9

The Murder

Sharp had come a very long way since his gradual acceptance of the idea that an episcopal regime would be restored in Scotland. It was a long time since he had co-operated with an episcopal regime in an attempt to modify it. His persistent inclination to weather the ups and downs of political negotiation had in the end become merely a determination to stay in office. The Resolutioner fear of public disorder had been one of Sharp's motivations for supporting a regime which would give no countenance to the Protesters, disturbers as they saw it of order and good government. Ironically his own dogged support for Lauderdale in the end had created just that situation of divided government and public disorder which he had feared. Moreover Sharp's identification with the Restoration regime had once more identified episcopal church government with arbitrary royal intervention in Scottish affairs. To this day the episcopal church in Scotland has not recovered from this association with England. James Sharp, the man who proudly identified himself as a Scot and a presbyter, and who more than any other had struggled to extricate Scotland from the Cromwellian Union, had become identified as an agent of English, episcopal, political interests. By this strange process he had become the enemy of Scottish presbytery and government by the rule of law, a man increasingly identified with outdated ideas of royal power.

It was not, therefore, so very surprising that when in May 1679 the opportunity offered itself to nine young men of the conventicling party to assassinate Sharp, they should take that opportunity. Nor was it surprising that they should see Sharp as a persecutor and perjured prelate. The non-conformists then, and their many sympathisers since, thought that Sharp got what he deserved.

Who were these nine men? How had they come to commit this murder, and what did they intend by it? Two in the party were lairds: David Hackstone of Rathillet and John Balfour of Kinloch; six were the sons of tenant farmers: James Russell in Kettle, George Fleming in Balbuthie, Alexander and Andrew Henderson in Kilbrachmont, William Dingwall in Caddam and George Balfour in Gilston; and one was a weaver, Andrew Guillan, of Balmerinoch.[1] All but the last named were local men whose lands lay in the area where the murder took place. Andrew Guillan had been put out of Dundee for refusing to attend the services held by the episcopal incumbent there.[2]

These nine men were part of a much larger group who had been meeting together in the north-east of Fife for some weeks.[3] Although they had connections with the conventicle church, they seem to have been more like a group of vigilantes meeting without ministers who together were formulating plans for dealing with what had become something like a military occupation of Fife.[4] Troops had been moved into the county because it was one of the areas where conventicling was at its most active. Although the troops had no licence for illegal behaviour, they seem to have used the opportunity for widespread 'robbery and oppression'. It was this behaviour which the conspirators wished to punish, since they saw no possibility of legal redress.[5] Accordingly at a meeting on 8 April 1679 it was decided that action should be taken against William Carmichael, sheriff depute of Fife, who had been involved with much of the persecution.[6] It seems most likely that the intention was not to kill, but to threaten, probably beat up, and terrify Carmichael as much as possible,[7] in the hope that they would get rid of him personally and frighten those whose behaviour had been similar.[8] With the same aim of spreading fear among those responsible for the oppression the conspirators arranged to leave a notice in Cupar. It was posted there on the door of the school by Rathillet in the night of Wednesday 30 April and was found on the following morning.[9]

The message was addressed to 'the Magistrates and Inhabitants of the Town of Cupar in Fife'[10] and threatened 'all that shall any ways be concerned in this villainous Robbery and Oppression' with punishment without fail at the hands of a resolute force. The paper mentions the names of Captain Carnegie, William Carmichael and Sharp, but they were not specially threatened, and indeed the paper was careful not to name any particular targets for its revenge.

It was decided that Carmichael should be dealt with on Saturday 3 May, and so on the preceding evening, Friday 2 May, thirteen men gathered on Magus Muir. One of these dropped out and went home, and the remaining twelve went to spend the night in a barn belonging to a tenant farmer, Robert Black, in Baldinny. One man was sent to enquire about Carmichael's movements and came back with the information that he was to spend the day hunting at Tarvethill, near Cupar.[11] The twelve therefore set out early in the morning to look for him. However, Carmichael had been warned by a shepherd that some men had been looking for him, and so with great prudence he went back to Cupar.[12] Having failed to find Carmichael, three men had already left the group to go home[13] when a boy from Baldinny appeared, sent by Robert Black's wife,[14] who seems to have known and approved of the whole enterprise.[15] He came with the message that Archbishop Sharp's coach was between the village of Ceres and Blebo Hole.[16]

This development was completely unexpected and provoked among the nine a fierce dispute which amounted to a discussion of the philosophical justification which a convenanter could present for committing murder. These nine men had ventured out to manhandle a rough and merciless soldier. They were now faced with the prospect of killing — for that was what they agreed must be done[17] — an archbishop and a privy councillor, when merely to attack a privy councillor was a capital offence, and the sanctity of the priesthood was still an accepted convention. Accordingly, although their venture had begun not as a religious mission but in the desire for revenge on one who had misused his secular authority and flaunted legal restraints, they now began to see themselves as instruments of divine justice. God had delivered Sharp, whom they saw as the man ultimately responsible for their sufferings,[18] into their hands; was it not therefore clear that their duty was to destroy him?[19] The background to this discussion had long been familiar to convenanters from the works of Sir James Stewart of Goodtrees, *Naphtali* and *Ius Populi Vindicatum*:[20] all authority comes from God, but where it is used to oppress the people of God it is no longer authority but blasphemy; the people of God, then, not only have the right, but also the duty, to destroy such blasphemers. Here surely was a clear call to duty, as well as an opportunity to strike a blow for their cause despite the escape of their original victim.

One man of the nine was still not content to proceed: Hackstone of Rathillet, the presumed leader.[21] Hackstone had had occasion to have dealings with Sharp before this date. He had been appointed to farm the revenues of a piece of land which Sharp had inherited and whose profits he had been slow to hand over. It was said that he had used them to buy arms for the conventiclers in Fife,[22] but whether or not that was the case, the bishop's chamberlain had finally become tired of waiting for payment, foreclosed on Hackstone and when he was unable to pay had him imprisoned, apparently without the archbishop's knowledge.[23] Whether Hackstone felt aggrieved about this treatment is unknown,[24] but he realised that knowledge of his case was common and that his participation in the killing of Sharp would be put down to the desire for revenge. He wished to make the religious motives of his associates perfectly clear by taking no part in the action.[25] He was, however, prepared to stay with the other eight since he felt their task was set by God and quite justifiable.[26]

The command of the party therefore went to the other laird, Balfour of Kinloch.[27] The nine of them set out after the archbishop's coach, Hackstone keeping himself at a distance from the rest of the party when they drew near their objective. There have been suggestions that Sharp was their intended victim all along, and that his death had been plotted for some time,[28] but the very ineptitude of their attack, when combined with the wealth of information concerning their proposed assault on Carmichael, makes that suggestion unconvincing. The obvious way to attack Sharp would have been to lie in wait for his coach and ambush it, but instead here were eight men careering after the vehicle, galloping through the village of Magus and attracting a great deal of attention from the inhabitants,[29] very nearly losing their prey because the coachman saw them while he still had time to whip up the horses and make a run for it.

It seems likely that the attackers' original intention had been to ride up to the coach, pour in shot and ride off again, leaving the archbishop dead before anyone had time to recognise them or form any very accurate description.[30] When however they had such difficulty drawing level with the coach, and those shots that were fired failed to kill the archbishop,[31] they had no choice but to stop. That in turn gave them the opportunity to speak to the archbishop and explain their motives as well as to remove papers and arms from the coach. It also gave the witnesses the perfect opportunity to identify them.[32] The whole incident bore the marks of an ill-considered plan thought up on the spur of the moment.

This aspect of the situation evidently did not occur to the murderers, or if it did, did not concern them. They returned by the same route riding, as one witness observed, 'less hastily than when they had come'.[33]

The nine made their way together to the home of James Anderson, a tenant farmer in Tewchets, near Largo, a distance of about twelve miles. Anderson was not at home but his servant, Thomas Cow, was there when they arrived between two and three on the afternoon of the 3rd. He later testified that the men had taken possession of the barn, posted sentries and allowed no one to come or go.[34] They stayed in the barn until about seven o'clock that night, occupied in prayer and thanksgiving for the success of their venture, taking refreshment, and resting themselves and their horses.[35] During the afternoon James Anderson came home. He may have been a supporter of the conventicle church, since he appears to have made no effort to make them leave his property when he heard from his servant what had happened, or to notify the authorities when they had gone. The servant had been able to identify two of the party, and that perhaps was enough for Anderson to realise that they were friends. When the party finally left, they came to speak with Anderson who shook them all by the hand and at the same time took note of each one's name and appearance so that on 31 May he was able to give a very complete and accurate description of all nine to the Committee for Public Affairs,[36] having probably decided in the interval that the risks he ran by concealing his involvement were too great.

When the murderers left Tewchets they split up. Their movements after that point are uncertain and the information given by Russell contradicts the evidence of the depositions. What probably happened is that most of them returned briefly to their homes before making their way to the long-heralded rising in the west.[37]

Meanwhile news of the murder was spreading like wildfire throughout the country. On the very day that the murder was committed Captain Dobie, William Carmichael's assistant, had been out scouring the countryside for suspicious characters and had shot a young man called Andrew Aytoun of Inchdairnie.

He arrested him and his companion, Henry Southall, and brought them both back to Cupar for investigation by Carmichael. Aytoun had in his possession three letters about which neither he nor Southall would say anything at all. Aytoun was mortally wounded but both he and Southall were interrogated several times on Saturday.[38] They knew or would say nothing about the murder.

In the interval the news had reached the privy council who found the occasion sufficiently important to convene a meeting, which was especially well attended, on Sunday 4 May.[39] At that meeting Thomas Carruthers, the footman riding on the coach, gave his account of what had happened, which account later formed the basis of *A Clear Discovery*. The privy council also heard the testimony of James Bowie, one of the servants of Sir William Sharp, the archbishop's son. Bowie had been present when the body was taken out of the coach in St Andrews, a scene which he described vividly.[40] Having heard the testimony of these two men, the council then set about the business of dealing with the situation. The first task was to inform the king and the Duke of Lauderdale in London of what had happened. The duty of the privy council was to maintain law and order in Scotland; the murder of one of the most important royal officials in the land in broad daylight hardly suggested that the performance of their duties had been exemplary, and so much of the letter to the king concentrated on justifying their previous actions and policies towards the Covenanters. They also impressed upon Charles the serious nature of what had happened by reminding him of the implications of an attack on a royal servant:

> we may certainly conclude those of that profession will be unsatiable till by crimes and cruelties they do all that in them lies to force your Majesty from your royal government.

News of the arrest of Inchdairnie and his companion had been brought from Fife that morning by the Justice General and the Laird of Lundy. That information, together with a copy of the notice posted in Cupar on the night of 30 April, was included in the letter to Lauderdale. In addition a proclamation was drawn up for publication at the mercat crosses of Edinburgh and the burghs of Fife and Kinross to be read in the parish kirks of those two counties on Sunday 11 May, and sent for approval to London. This document outlined what had happened in vivid terms, warned that this was but the prelude to widespread lawlessness and therefore ordered the arrest of suspicious persons and the assembling of the people of Fife on prescribed days at the centre ordained for the presbytery in which they lived: St Andrews on the 13th; Cupar on the 16th; Kircaldy on the 20th and Dunfermline on the 23rd. In these places all persons were to be examined by the sheriff deputes of Fife and clear themselves of suspicion. Finally the proclamation offered an indemnity to any of the murderers who turned king's evidence and a reward of 10,000 merks for information leading to the arrest of those responsible for the murder.

Meanwhile in Fife there was also much activity. On the night of the 3rd, the day of the murder, there occurred a very strange little episode. Abraham Smith, the coachman who had been driving the bishop's coach, and William Wallace, one of the two mounted servants, both of whom had attempted to put up some resistance to the attackers, seem to have gone together with a Mr Leslie to Mortoun on the night of the murder. Mortoun was a house which belonged to Rathillet's sister. Someone must have given the men information, for in that house were sleeping Rathillet and Balfour. Perhaps their attack was too noisy because both men got away, but only just; Abraham Smith grappled with Rathillet but failed to hold him. In the house were found the pistol earlier taken from Wallace and the cloak which Rathillet had worn. In the stable were two of the horses that had been ridden by the murderers.[41] Why such a small party went on such a dangerous mission; why the sheriff depute was not asked for aid; why Hackstone and Balfour stayed so close to the scene of the crime, are all questions to which there are no immediate answers. What the episode did ensure was that Hackstone and Rathillet then left the area, and that the initial excellent opportunity for arresting them was lost.

Baillie Carmichael had made a poor start to his investigations with the arrest of the unfortunate Inchdairnie who later died of his wounds, and Henry Southall who was not ordered to be released until 18 December 1679.[42] However, he made up for that mistake by his activity in interrogating witnesses that week on the 4th, the 7th and the 8th. There were probably more depositions made then than are now extant, but even from the limited number now available it is clear that the story told by Carruthers the footman to the privy council had already been substantially corroborated and the names of nine men had been put forward as suspects — although in fact only six of them were involved in the murder.[43]

That same week in Edinburgh the privy council met again, on the 8th, to consider the matter of the murder and take further action.[44] A second letter was sent to Lauderdale recording the arrangements made to search for suspects throughout Fife and for conducting a house-to-house search of Edinburgh. Detailed instructions were issued concerning the manner in which the search of Edinburgh was to be carried out, a testimony to the council's desire to redeem their reputation as the guardians of law and order, as well as to their hope of finding the murderers. More detailed instructions than those in the proclamation of the 4th were then drawn up to be sent to the sheriff deputes of Fife concerning the procedure to be adopted for examining the inhabitants when they appeared to clear themselves at the four designated centres.

So far everybody concerned had done extremely well in responding to what after all was a particularly violent and appalling crime. Within only four days of the murder comprehensive instructions had been issued to the authorities in Fife; a search had been conducted through the largest city in the kingdom; and information had been collected which indicated an outline of what had happened and a list of possible suspects. The privy council's diligence was therefore suitably rewarded when on the 14th there was read at their meeting a letter from the king,[45] which expressed the king's horror at the murder and his conviction that the crime was part of a previously laid plot hatched by a much larger group of men, but also his support for the council's efforts to find those responsible. It must have been with a sigh of relief when they did not have to endure the king's displeasure or a whirlwind visit from Lauderdale that the council wrote back to Charles thanking him for his letter and pledging their services for the finding and punishing of the murderers.

On the following day, however, 15 May,[46] the council learned of the first hitch in the arrangements. They discovered that the original proclamation of the 4th ordaining the gathering of the inhabitants of Fife had not been sent to Fife by the post quickly enough to ensure it was published in the churches on Sunday 11 May. The next date for publication could not be earlier than Sunday 18 May, and so the dates for assembling in each presbytery would have to be changed to the 20th for St Andrews, the 23rd for Cupar, the 27th for Kirkcaldy and the 30th for Dunfermline, all a full week later than had been planned. Thus at the earliest it would now be seventeen days since the murder before any large-scale investigation could be carried out. The foot post, Robert Anderson, was therefore summoned before the council to answer for his failure to take the proclamation, and being unable to advance a 'reasonable excuse', was ordered to be scourged and banished from Edinburgh.

The following Saturday 17 May saw the funeral of the archbishop held in St Andrews. The day of the murder was long past and the body had long since been examined by doctors on the orders of the privy council. Why, then, the delay in burying the archbishop? The answer very soon became apparent. The Lord Lyon had organised the most lavish and large-scale obsequies that could possibly be devised, even in an age of grandiose funerals.[47] The order for a procession was laid down which must have involved the participation of several hundred people: first were to come sixty old men in mourning, one for each year of Sharp's life; then banners and standards, horses and trumpets; after them magistrates and members of the University of St Andrews, ministers and doctors, followed by judges and royal officers. Then came the coffin all decorated, and behind it the bishops, nobility, friends and relations. A detachment of soldiers lined the route from the ruined cathedral of St Andrews where the procession formed to the door of Holy Trinity parish church where the funeral was to take place, and for further dramatic effect the very coach in which Sharp had been riding on the fateful day, and his bloodstained gown, were paraded in the procession. Undoubtedly this magnificent occasion was designed to impress upon the watchers the dignity and power of the government and its forces. Sharp might be dead, but it was not to be concluded therefore that his assassins had brought down the ruling authority within Scotland. The privy council was demonstrating in no uncertain terms that it had both the will and power to resist the murderers and their like. It had meant a delay of two weeks, but it was, when it occurred, an undeniably impressive occasion.

Once the coffin and the dignitaries had been received into the decorated church, the sermon was preached to the assembled company by John Paterson, Bishop of Edinburgh. Why he was chosen is something of a mystery when the Archbishop of Glasgow, Alexander Burnet, Sharp's successor at St Andrews, was the obvious candidate and present at the funeral. It is even stranger that the sermon was not published — for no trace of it can be found — when this would be a very obvious opportunity to publish the government point of view on the whole matter of Sharp's murder. Not even a manuscript copy is known to reveal what was said.

After the service the body was buried, apparently in the grounds of the cathedral. Sir William Sharp later erected a massive marble monument in Holy Trinity Church which is still to be seen,[48] and presumably the body was then transferred to its permanent place in the church.

After the funeral there was nothing much more that could be done in the case until the people of Fife were examined. There was therefore a lull in activity until the end of the month when more information began to emerge. The most important witnesses seem to have been sent to Edinburgh for the privy council to deal with, and it was therefore in that city that James Anderson in Tewchetts and his servant Thomas Cow were examined on 31 May.[49] From their information the council was able to compile a firm list of the nine suspects. Meanwhile in Fife the inhabitants in Magus were questioned and were able to corroborate details of the story.[50]

The privy council should therefore at the end of May have been in an extremely good position to proceed to find the murderers, since it had all the relevant information at its disposal. Instead, however, it was immediately distracted by business of even more importance: the knowledge of the defeat of Claverhouse by a force of rebels at Loudoun Hill, information which reached the privy council on 3 June,[51] exactly one month after the murder. From that point the council was continuously occupied with the details of the military situation, so that it was 20 September, three and a half months later, before the list of murderers was published in a proclamation.[52] By that time, when none of those involved had yet been arrested, all prospect of a reasoned reconstruction of the event and the movements of the murderers had virtually disappeared and the only hope of their being brought to justice lay in the possibility of their being apprehended on chance information or for other reasons.

The question was not however allowed to disappear entirely from the council's view. On 20 June there was read to them a letter from Charles giving them a gentle reminder:

> we must likewise put you in mind that all care and diligence be used for discovering the murderers of the late Archbishop of St Andrews.

This letter also informed them that there would be no possibility of pardon for the murderers — an indication of how dreadful the king thought the crime.[53] On 24 June the council replied, pledging their best efforts 'for discovering and apprehending of the sacrilegious murderers of the late archbishop'.[54]

But just how secondary the murder had become was revealed by a proclamation of 26 June prohibiting the lieges from harbouring rebels and naming a large number including all nine of those mentioned by James Anderson in his deposition given in Edinburgh on 31 May; yet nothing was said in the proclamation to indicate that they were suspected of murder.[55] At that moment their character as rebels was clearly more important.

The king, however, continued to attach great importance to the investigation. On 26 July, clearly having taken into account the total failure of the council to arrest suspects, he wrote to Edinburgh ordering nine of the recently arrested rebels who were known to have associated with the murderers, and who had thereby exempted themselves from royal indemnity, to be executed and hanged in chains on the site of Sharp's murder.[56] Then on 13 August the council, in obedience to the king's demands for further action, began to institute proceedings for forfeiture of the landed men involved in the murder.[57] On 14 August a proclamation reminded all Scots of the reward for taking prisoner, or discovering, any of the murderers, and to assist their efforts ordered those murderers who were in the rebellion, who were still not named, to be hanged in effigy throughout Scotland for their more rapid identification. Special prizes were offered on this occasion for the arrest, dead or alive, of Hackstone or Balfour.[58]

Then the king decreed that the issue of the murder was to be used as a political test, and a means of distinguishing between the prisoners captured in the rebellion. On 26 August a letter from Charles was read to the privy council, requiring them to proceed against those who refused to acknowledge the murder of the archbishop to be a murder.[59] Finally on 19 September, the danger of rebellion now being over, General Dalziel was ordered to arrest the murderers,[60] and on the following day a proclamation was issued which at long last named the nine responsible.[61]

But had these four and a half months of investigations produced absolutely no result? Well, not quite no result, but certainly very little, so far as can be learned from those documents that survive. The unfortunate Inchdairnie, of course, had died, and his companion was kept in prison until December 1679.[62] Two men had been arrested in Perth on 6 May, presumably in a general round-up of those taken to be suspicious characters. One was a merchant who had just arrived in Perth, and the other a periwig maker from Strathmiglo. They seem to have been entirely innocent, but orders for their release were not given until 15 July 1679.[63] A certain Mr Robert Steel, a man 'lately come from England', was interrogated about his doings in the west and what he knew of the murder, but without firm result.[64] Equally haphazard investigations continued after September. Alexander Hamilton, prisoner in the Tolbooth of Edinburgh, found it necessary to write to Lauderdale on 30 September 1679 protesting vehemently that he had nothing whatever to do with the murder.[65] As late as May 1680 a man was questioned in Newcastle because he had been heard drunkenly boasting that he had been one of those who had killed the archbishop.[66]

Bearing in mind the relative efficiency of at least the initial stages of the investigation, and the nature of Scottish communities where a stranger could not fail to be noticed, the conclusion seems inescapable: the murderers had been protected and hidden. Furthermore they had been sheltered even though penalties had been prescribed for assisting them, and rewards for discovering them. To the privy council the murder was an act of political rebellion motivated by religious bigotry, but to the extreme Covenanters it was a heavy blow struck against their enemies in a civil war. On such a basis as that one can understand that they might receive protection.

The murderers did not, however, in the end escape scot free. In July 1680 David Hackstone of Rathillet was picked up after the defeat of the Covenanting side in a skirmish with government forces at Airds Moss. From the very first his fate as a prisoner was sealed. He had been involved in armed rebellion, had renounced the king's authority in the Queensferry Declaration and had been one of the murderers of the archbishop. He was therefore incapable of pardon. Even if he had chosen to plead that he took no part in the murder, he would still have been an accessory to the crime and therefore liable to the same punishment.

In the event Hackstone utterly refused to have anything to do with the conventions of his trial. On 24 July he was brought to Edinburgh. The council were aware that he was coming and made special arrangements for his reception by the magistrates of Edinburgh.[67] He was seated on a barebacked horse facing the tail, with his hands and feet tied — a posture designed to prevent his entering the city like a conqueror, and much like the treatment meted out to Montrose in a similar situation thirty years before. On the same day he was interrogated by the privy council.[68] Rathillet was not prepared to answer any questions of fact as to his precise actions and movements. In particular he had nothing to say about the part he had played in the murder of the archbishop, although the council later found out by torturing a fellow prisoner that Hackstone claimed to have been at the murder but to have taken no part in it.[69] Instead Hackstone wished to use the occasion of his examination by the council to expound his religious and political views, and was indeed given the opportunity to do so, with a forbearance that seems remarkable. What the interrogation demonstrated quite clearly, however, was that Hackstone was not prepared to make a confession, and his bearing quite explicitly indicated that torture would not wring one out of him. On 29 July he was brought before the Lords Justice Clerk and Commissioners of Justiciary but with precisely the same result. He denied the authority of the king and his officers, refused to answer questions about the murder and again stated his political and religious convictions.[70]

There was therefore no alternative left to the council but to remit Hackstone for trial before the Judiciary Court. It is a tribute to the sophistication and respect for law of seventeenth-century Scotland that this was done for a man who had renounced the authority of the law and done his best to overturn contemporary society. Revolutionaries are not always able to benefit from such enlightened behaviour. The trial was conducted properly[71] with a well-prepared indictment backed up by sworn evidence from witnesses, although according to contemporary judicial practice he was allowed no defence. A large number of depositions were produced proving, as well as the other charges, that Hackstone had been present at the murder of the archbishop. He was therefore condemned to death.

In the privy council's view Hackstone was guilty of an abominable crime in the murder of the archbishop. Objectively it must be conceded that the murder was brutal, and the privy councillors could not, by the very nature of the office and responsibilities, be expected to understand or sympathise with the philosophy behind it. It was Hackstone's misfortune that although he was the one of the nine whose motives were probably the purest, he should have been caught. He was sentenced on a recommendation made by the privy council on 29 July, the day before the trial, but after the second interrogation, to a painful execution. His hands were to be cut off and he was then hanged till he was dead, when his body was dismembered and sent to be exhibited in various places round the country. Fortunately at least hanging, drawing and quartering was not the Scottish way of doing things.

The only other of the nine murderers who was executed was Andrew Guillan, the weaver in Balmerinoch.[72] How he came to be arrested is unknown, but he was apparently picked up in July 1683. On 10 July he confessed before seven of the privy council that 'he was present and in company and concurring with the rest when the archbishop was killed'. Having made such a confession, his trial on the twelfth was a mere formality since no proof needed to be produced. He was accordingly condemned to the same death as Hackstone.

It is possible of course that Guillan was tortured into confession, but it seems doubtful. Torture was an accepted instrument of justice in Scotland at the time, particularly when dealing with the non-noble, and therefore frequently noted in the accounts of proceedings. There is no mention of it in the case of Guillan. He may also have suffered a change of heart, but in that case the opportunity to have him publicly denounce his former allies and their ways would surely not have been overlooked. There is no trace of any such denunciation in what is reported of his speech. The psychology of his confession therefore remains obscure.

One other man was tried and condemned for crimes which included complicity in the murder of the archbishop: Balfour of Kinloch. He, perhaps the least idealistic of the murderers, a man whose reputation is not good, was tried in the Justiciary Court in his absence,[73] but so far as is known, despite being forfeit and declared fugitive and outlaw, he was never caught.

William Dingwall was shot at Drumclog in June 1679 and buried at Strathaven.[74] So far as is known the remaining five were neither caught nor tried for their part in the murder.

10

Conclusion

Sharp was the last in the long line of Scottish medieval 'political' bishops which included Cardinal Beaton and Archbishop Spottiswood. Had his background been different, he might well have been one of the generation of ambitious young ministers who tied their fortunes to the Covenants, but his family, his home in the north-east and his education under the Aberdeen Doctors ensured that the Covenants would never be of fundamental importance to him. Though he was intelligent and fully capable of surviving in a university atmosphere, he was no academic. Though he retained an affection and concern for the welfare of the Scottish universities and made it his business to promote their interests, yet the theological debates of the seventeenth century cast no spell on him. Similarly although he won respect from his parishioners as a minister to such an extent that they would not part with him, and though he was offered one of the influential Edinburgh charges, his own preferences were not for the parish ministry.

Above all else Sharp was a politician. His father's obscurity and lowly social status ensured that in seventeenth-century Scotland, dominated by the nobility who held a monopoly of secular power, there was no opportunity for him. As a promising young man the only means of advancement open to him was the church. Nor does that imply a cynical determination to use the ministry as a means to his own ends. For a university graduate without resources the church was the obvious and virtually the only sphere for the exercise of his talents. Nor does the choice of the ministry for these reasons imply any deficiency in Sharp's religious observances or personal morality. In seventeenth-century Scotland men were religious. A few rare spirits were also good, or even saintly, and Sharp was not among them, but his personal conduct and observance were always such as to satisfy the exacting standards of his contemporaries. To say that Sharp was a politician, therefore, does not imply any inadequacy in him. Rather it distinguishes him from those of his contemporaries who were theologians.

As a politician Sharp dealt in everyday realities. His talents were for negotiation, compromise and diplomacy. His life was an endless series of committee meetings in which he sought to modify attitudes, to exact concessions or to clarify issues. It took only a very short time before these talents were recognised by Sharp's brethren and they were glad to employ them. For his part Sharp combined abilities of a high order with rare diligence, so that by 1650 he was one of the inner circle of policy makers within the church. When the split in the church came, the Resolutioners were more than glad to have Sharp employ his talents on their behalf.

There could be no doubt of which side Sharp would be on in the contest within the church. The Protesters were a party of those who had defied the ordinary logic of numbers and common sense and yet had triumphed over apparently enormous odds in the 1630s and '40s. Sharp, like Cromwell, believed in God but kept his powder dry. Moreover, his early dissociation from the Covenant and his background of royalist sympathies drew him naturally to those whose religious zeal was modified by their sense of duty to the king.

A decade of controversy with the Protesters marked Sharp for life. He was never able to forget their willingness to abandon the majority principle on which presbytery was based, their readiness to desert the king, their preparedness to overturn all in their determination that their minority views should prevail. Sharp, then, was not only a politician but a party politician. His antagonism to the Protesters continued throughout the Restoration and was one of the root causes of his progressively more rigorous attitude to non-conformists. Not only was Sharp a party politician, however; he was also a conservative. Like many another in seventeenth-century Scotland he was alarmed by the revolutionary implications of the attitudes of some among the ministers. He was a supporter of kings and nobles and of the long-established social order. Hence when the Restoration came Sharp pledged himself to it body and soul rather than contemplate a return to Cromwellian occupation, an exiled king and a disinherited nobility. For him there was no alternative but to submit to the Stuart monarchy, whatever its inadequacies, since the alternative was unthinkable.

Here again was a potent source of his intolerance of non-conformity. Non-conformists and their sympathisers, whether episcopal like Leighton and Ramsay, or noble like Hamilton, offered a challenge to established government. Sharp therefore ranged himself on the side of monarchy, even when it involved him in the support of Lauderdale and the illegal repressive policies of the late 1670s.

That association, however, was also the product of Sharp's political ambitions. From very early in his career he came to the notice of his fellow ministers and the secular government. For the decade before the Restoration his career had made very rapid strides. By 1660 he was one of the leading Scottish churchmen and had a realistic expectation of very senior status. When his position was threatened by developments outside his control he compromised rather than simply abandon his whole career. Until the Pentland Rising that compromise paid well. Sharp became the most important man in Scotland in both the secular and ecclesiastical government. Hence his fall when it came in 1667 was all the further.

From that time until his death twelve years later his efforts to regain his former power and influence involved him in a series of ever more fundamental concessions. By 1678 he was prepared to commit perjury and condone the use of an army of occupation against his own countrymen. Not only did he fail to retrieve his influence by such damaging concessions to Lauderdale; in the process he lost his own integrity.

Contemporaries and historians since have generally ascribed far more power to Sharp after 1666 than he enjoyed. They have also ante-dated his corruption. Their judgments have therefore been particularly severe. Although those judgments cannot be reversed, yet perhaps at least we can understand something more of the motivations for Sharp's actions and the dismal process of events which brought him at last to his death on Magus Muir.

Bibliography

1. *Unpublished Primary Material*
Bodleian Library Rawlinson Ms C 179.
Bodleian Library Clarendon Ms Vol. 72.
BL Add. Mss 23113, 23115, 23116, 23117, 23119, 23127, 35125.
Edinburgh Episcopal Theological College Ms 1789.
EUL Collection of Mss of the Murder of Archbishop Sharp EUL Ms Dc 1. 16.
GUL Ms Gen. 210.
Minutes of the Kirk Session of the Parish of Crail.
NLS Ms 159, 'The Life of James Sharp, Archbishop of St Andrews and Primate
    of Scotland. Wrote at the desire of General Melvill by Robert Crawford, A.M.'.
NLS Mss 546, 573, 597, 2512, 3136, 3420, 3922, 5049, 5050, 7003, 7023, 7024.
NLS Adv. Ms 5.2.8, 5.2.10.
NLS Wodrow Mss Folio LXV, Folio XXXI, Quarto LXIII.
Precedency Book Ms Court of the Lord Lyon, Edinburgh, 1679.
St Andrews University Library Accounts of Scottish Bishops, Ms DA 770 F2.
St Andrews University Muniments SL 110. R. 9, SL 705/1. 147.
SRO Depositions of the Witnesses of the Murder Ms Small Papers, Justiciary
    Court Records 30 July 1680.
SRO Trial of Hackstone of Rathillet, 30 July 1680 Ms Justiciary Court Records,
    Books of Adjournal.
SRO Trial of Balfour of Kinloch, 2 April 1683 Ms Justiciary Court Records,
    Books of Adjournal.
SRO Trial of Andrew Guillan, 12 July 1683 Ms Justiciary Court Records, Books
    of Adjournal.
SRO PA 11/12–13 Minutes of the Committee of Estates, August–December 1660.

2. *Unpublished Secondary Material*
McNeill, P. G. B., 'The Jurisdiction of the Scottish Privy Council 1532–1708',
    Glasgow Ph.D., 1961.
Marshall, R. K., 'The House of Hamilton', Edinburgh Ph.D., 1970.
Miller, A. T., 'The Life of James Sharp Archbishop of St Andrews', Edinburgh
    Ph.D., 1946.
Yould, M., 'Lauderdale's Ecclesiastical Policy 1669–1679', unpublished essay.

3. *Published Primary Sources*
Accompt of the manner of the death of Mr J. Sharp from two persons who were present.
    Printed in James Russell, *Account of the Murder of Archbishop Sharp*, ed. C. K.
    Sharpe. Edinburgh, 1819.

Acts of the Parliaments of Scotland.

Anderson, P. J., ed. *Officers and Graduates of the University and King's College, Aberdeen, 1485–1860.* Aberdeen, 1893.

--------. *Roll of Alumni in Arts of the University and King's College.* Aberdeen, 1900.

Baillie, Robert, *Letters and Journals.* 3 vols., ed. D. Laing. Edinburgh, 1822.

Baxter, Charles, ed. *Selections from the Minutes of the Synod of Fife.* Edinburgh, 1837.

Burnet, Gilbert. *History of his own Times,* ed. Osmond Airy. 2 vols. Oxford, 1897, 1900.

Calendar of State Papers (Domestic Series).

Caveat for the Whigs. London, 1710.

Clarendon, Edward Earl of. *Calendar of the Clarendon State Papers. II 1649–1654,* ed. W. D. Macray. Oxford, 1869.

--------. *III 1655–1657,* ed. W. D. Macray. Oxford, 1876.

--------. *IV 1657–1660,* ed. F. J. Routledge. Oxford, 1932.

--------. *The History of the Rebellion and Civil Wars in Scotland.* 6 vols., ed. W. Dunn Macray. Oxford, 1888.

A clear discovery of the malicious falshoods contained in a Paper Printed at London, Intituled a True Relation of what is Discovered concerning the Murther of the Archbishop of St Andrews, And of what appears to have been the Occasion Thereof. As also a faithful but brief Narrative of the said Execrable Murther. Edinburgh, 1679.

A Complete Collection of State Trials, II. 2nd. ed. London, 1730.

A Coppie of the Maner of the death of Mr James Sharp, late Archprelate of St Anderous, who departed his life on Saturday, Maij the 3 day 1679, betuext 12 and ane a clock in efternoon; with the particular words on aither syd, and actiones that past at that tyme and place thereof faithfullie and trewlie related by ane impartiall pen. Printed in Robert Wodrow, *History of the Sufferings of the Church of Scotland,* ed. R. Burns. 4 vols. Glasgow, 1828–30.

Dickinson, W. C. and G. Donaldson, eds. *A Source Book of Scottish History,* 3 vols. 2nd. ed. Edinburgh, 1961.

Fanatical Moderation; or, Unparalell'd Villany Display'd. Being a Faithful Narrative of the Barbarous Murther committed upon the most Reverend Father in God, Dr James Sharp. [London], 1680.

Fasti Ecclesiae Scoticanae, ed. Hew Scott, revised edition. Edinburgh, 1925.

Firth, C. H., ed. *Scotland and the Protectorate.* Edinburgh, 1899.

Gardiner, S. R., ed. *Charles II and Scotland 1650.* Edinburgh, 1894.

Historical Manuscripts Commission. Third Report.

Kinloch, G. R., ed. *Selections from the Minutes of the Presbyteries of St Andrews and Cupar.* Edinburgh, 1837.

Kirkton, James. *The Secret and True History of the Church of Scotland from the Restoration to the Year 1678,* ed. C. K. Sharpe. Edinburgh, 1817.

Lamont, John. *Diary of Mr John Lamont of Newton,* ed. G. R. Kinloch. Edinburgh, 1830.

Lauder, John of Fountainhall. *Historical Notices.* 2 vols. Edinburgh, 1848.

Lauderdale, John Duke of. *Lauderdale Papers*, ed. Osmund Airy. 3 vols. London, 1884–5.

Leighton, Alexander. *An Appeal to Parliament or Zion's Plea against Prelacy.* Holland, 1628.

The Life and Continuation of the Life of Edward Earl of Clarendon. 3 vols. Oxford, 1761.

The Life of Mr James Sharp, From his Birth to his Instalment in the Archbishopric of St Andrews . . . With an Appendix Containing an Account of Some of Mr Sharp's Actions, During the Time of his being Archbishop: And the Manner and Circumstances of his Death, by one of the Persons concern'd in it. [n.p.] 1719. First printed without appendix, 1678.

The Life and Transactions of J. Sharp. Edinburgh, 1786.

Mackenzie, Sir George of Rosehaugh. *Memoirs of the Affairs of Scotland*, ed. T. Thomson. Edinburgh, 1821.

Miscellany I. Scottish History Society. Edinburgh, 1893.

Miscellany II. Scottish History Society. Edinburgh, 1904.

Mitchell, A. G. and J. Christie, eds. *Records of the Commissions of the General Assemblies.* 3 vols. Edinburgh, 1892, 1896, 1909.

Nicoll, John. *A Diary of Public Transactions and other occurrences chiefly in Scotland. From January 1650 to June 1667*, ed. David Laing. Edinburgh, 1836.

Peterkin, Alex., ed. *Records of the Kirk of Scotland.* Edinburgh, 1838.

Registers of the Privy Council of Scotland, third series.

Row, William, ed. *The Life of Robert Blair . . . containing his autobiography from 1593 to 1636 with supplement . . . to 1680, by his son in law, Mr William Row*, ed. Thomas M'Crie. Edinburgh, 1848.

Russell, James. *Account of the Murder of Archbishop Sharp*, ed. C. K. Sharpe. Edinburgh, 1819.

Stephen, Wm., ed. *Register of the Consultations of the Ministers of Edinburgh and some other Brethren of the Ministry.* 2 vols. Edinburgh, 1921, 1930.

Stewart, Sir James of Goodtrees. *Ius Populi Vindicatum.* Rotterdam [?], 1669.

––––––––. *Naphtali, or the Wrestlings of the Church of Scotland.* 1667.

Thurloe, John. *A Collection of the State Papers of John Thurloe*, ed. Thomas Birch. 7 vols. London, 1742.

A True Account of the Horrid Murther Committed upon his Grace the late Lord Arch-Bishop of St Andrews, Primate and Metropolitan of all Scotland and one of his Majesties most Honourable Privy Council of that Kingdom. With a detection of the Lyes published in a later Scandalous Relation of that Murther and of the Pretended Occasion thereof. London, 1679.

A True and Impartial Account of the Life of the Most Reverend Father in God, Dr James Sharp, Archbishop of St Andrews. 1723.

A True Relation of what is Discovered concerning the Murther of the Archbishop of St Andrews, And of what appears to have been the occasion thereof [London, 1679].

Turner, James. *Memoirs of his own Life and Times.* Edinburgh, 1829.

4. *Published Secondary Material*

Abernathy, G. R. 'The English Presbyterians and the Stuart Restoration, 1648–1663', *Transactions of the American Philosophical Society*, n.s. 55, ii, 1965, 15–37.

[Airy, Osmund]. 'Unpublished notices of James Sharp, Archbishop of St Andrews', *Scottish Review* IV, July 1884, 1–30.

Bosher, R. S. *The Making of the Restoration Settlement*. London, 1951.

Buckroyd, J. M. 'The Dismissal of Archbishop Alexander Burnet 1669', *RSCHS* XVIII, 1973, 149–35.

--------. *Church and State in Scotland 1660–1681*. Edinburgh, 1980.

--------. 'Anti-Clericalism in Scotland during the Restoration', in *Church, Politics and Society, Scotland 1408–1929*, ed. N. Macdougall. Edinburgh, 1983.

--------. 'Bridging the Gap: Scotland 1659–1660', *SHR* forthcoming.

Bulloch, J. M. *History of the University of Aberdeen 1495–1895*. London, 1895.

Butler, D. *The Life and Letters of Robert Leighton*. London, 1903.

Cant, R. G. *The University of St Andrews*, new ed. Edinburgh, 1970.

Cowan, I. B. *The Scottish Covenanters 1660–1688*. London, 1976.

Cramond, W., ed. *The Annals of Banff*. 2 vols. Aberdeen, 1891–3.

Davies, Godfrey. *Restoration of Charles II*. London, 1955.

------- and P. Hardacre. 'The Restoration of the Scottish Episcopacy 1660–1661', *Journal of British Studies*, I, ii, 32–51.

Donaldson, Gordon. *Scotland: James V to James VII*. Edinburgh, 1965.

--------. 'Aberdeen University and the Reformation', *Northern Scotland* I, ii, 1973, 129–42.

--------. 'Scotland's Conservative North in the Sixteenth and Seventeenth Centuries' in *Transactions of the Royal Historical Society*, 5th series, xvi, 65–79.

Dow, F. D. *Cromwellian Scotland 1651–1660*. Edinburgh, 1979.

Elder, J. R. *The Highland Host of 1678*. Glasgow, 1914.

Foster, W. R. *Bishop and Presbytery*. London, 1958.

Henderson, G. D. *The Burning Bush*. Edinburgh, 1957.

Knox, E. A. *Robert Leighton, Archbishop of Glasgow*. London, 1930.

Lamb, J. A. 'Archbishop Alexander Burnet 1614–1684', *RSCHS* XI, 1951–3, 133–48.

Lenman, Bruce. *An Economic History of Modern Scotland 1660–1976*. Hamden Ct, 1977.

Lynch, K. M. *Roger Boyle, First Earl of Orrery*. Knoxville, Tennessee, 1965.

Notes on the Evolution of the Arts Curriculum in the Universities of Aberdeen. Prepared for the General Council by its Clerk. Aberdeen University Press, 1908.

Ogilvie, J. D. 'A Bibliography of the Resolution-Protester Controversy 1650–1659', *Edinburgh Bibliographical Society Publications* XIV, 1928–30, 59–74.

Packer, J. W. *The Transformation of Anglicanism 1643–1660 with special reference to Henry Hammond*. Manchester, 1969.

Powicke, F. J. 'Eleven Letters of John, Second Earl of Lauderdale (and First Duke) 1616–1682, to the Rev. Richard Baxter, 1615–1691', *Bulletin of the John Rylands Library* VII, 1922–3, 73–105.

--------. *A Life of the Reverend Richard Baxter, 1615–1691.* London, 1924.

Rait, R. S. *The Universities of Aberdeen.* Aberdeen, 1895.

Robertson, A. *The Life of Sir Robert Murray.* London, 1922.

The Sheriff Court. HMSO, 1967.

Smout, T. C. *Scottish Trade on the Eve of Union.* Edinburgh, 1963.

Snow, W. G. S. *The Times, Life and Thought of Patrick Forbes, Bishop of Aberdeen, 1618–1635.* London, 1952.

Stephen, Thomas. *The Life and Times of Archbishop Sharp.* London, 1839.

Stevenson, David. *Revolution and Counter-Revolution in Scotland 1644–1651.* London, 1977.

--------. *The Scottish Revolution.* London, 1973.

Walker, Patrick. *Life of Cargill.* Falkirk, 1792.

Wodrow, Robert. *The Sufferings of the Church of Scotland from the Restoration to the Revolution.* ed. R. Burns. 4 vols. Glasgow, 1829–30.

Appendix
Accounts of the Murder

At a distance of nearly three hundred years after Sharp's murder it is very hard to discover exactly what happened on that memorable day, not least because it was followed by the writing of at least eight differing and independent accounts of the event. First in the field, and perhaps strangest of all, was *A True Relation of what is Discovered concerning the Murther of the Archbishop of St Andrews, And of what appears to have been the occasion thereof*, a pamphlet published without indication of date, place or publisher, but apparently in London very shortly after the event. This account was written by somebody opposed to the episcopal establishment in the Scottish church, but also opposed to the murder. It attempts to prove that the deed was done by someone with a grievance against Sharp on personal grounds and that therefore it was not a political murder. One imagines that the author must have been a moderate presbyterian who perhaps foresaw what consequences were likely to flow from such an act and who was anxious to play down the importance of what had happened. His attempt was totally unsuccessful, for there then appeared three accounts stating in no uncertain terms the government view that this was political murder which deserved, and would be met with, harsh retribution.

Probably the first of the three was *A True Account of the Horrid Murther Committed upon his Grace the late Lord Arch-Bishop of St Andrews, Primate and Metropolitan of all Scotland and one of his Majesties most Honourable Privy Council of that Kingdom. With a detection of the Lyes published in a later Scandalous Relation of that Murther and of the Pretended Occasion thereof*. This piece was published by royal authority in London in 1679 and roughly condemned the murderers for stirring up rebellion, gave an account of the murder which emphasised the pitiless brutality of the assassins and the dignity and piety of the archbishop's behaviour and finished up with a point-by-point review of the earlier pamphlet to show that the murder was not committed for reasons of personal enmity but was the direct outcome of religious bigotry. The similar Scottish work was even more systematic in its denunciation of the first pamphlet. Entitled *A clear discovery of the malicious falshoods contained in a Paper Printed at London, Intituled a True Relation of what is Discovered concerning the Murther of the Archbishop of St Andrews, And of what appears to have been the Occasion Thereof. As also a faithful but brief Narrative of the said Execrable Murther*, it was published in Edinburgh by order of the Privy Council in 1679. So eager was that author to refute the earlier pamphlet, *A True Relation*, that he reprinted that work in its entirety, and systematically presented his case against every paragraph; offered an account of the murder which represents Sharp as a saintly figure and his murderers as 'Presbyterian zealots' and 'bigot fanatics'; then finally presented a letter which explained the nature of the relationship between Sharp and the two men who had been represented as his enemies, and asserted that there was no feud between them. Finally on the government side, there appeared a pamphlet early in 1680 supposedly written by an Edinburgh advocate, and entitled *Fanatical Moderation; or Unparalell'd Villany Display'd. Being a Faithful Narrative of the Barbarous Murther committed upon the most Reverend Father in God, Dr James Sharp*. It was printed most probably in London. This account had only one aim: to show the dignity, piety and compassion of Sharp as he died and the barbarity of his attackers. The author had certainly read the account of the murder in *A True Discovery*, but he also produces original material.

Publishing was at this time fairly closely controlled by the government, and so it was hardly to be expected that any accounts of the murder giving the point of view of those who had committed the crime would be published. Nevertheless, four accounts were written from this point of view at the time and have been printed since. Probably the first account to be written was *A Coppie of the Maner of the death of Mr James Sharp, late Archprelate of St Anderous, who departed his life on Saturday, Maij the 3 day 1679, betuext 12 and ane a clock in efternoon; with the particular words on aither syd, and actiones that past at that tyme and place thereof faithfullie and trewlie related by an impartiall pen*. This is printed in Wodrow, *Sufferings*, III, 49. The account given is very full and seems to have been written either by someone who took part or by someone in very close contact with the murderers. It seems to have been composed only days after the event and so has a strong claim as one of the more reliable descriptions of what took place. It was followed by an account written between 1680 and 1683 and printed in 1719 as part of *The Life of Mr James Sharp, From his Birth to his Instalment in the Archbishopric of St Andrews . . . . With an Appendix Containing an Account of Some of Mr Sharp's Actions, During the Time of his being Archbishop: And the Manner and Circumstances of his Death, by one of the Persons concern'd in it*. This account is a little suspect because a number of details that might have been expected to tally with generally accepted accounts, for example the number of assassins who took part in the venture, disagree with every other account. A third account, *Accompt of the manner of the death of Mr. J. Sharp from two persons who were present*, seems to have been written after 1683 but only shortly after, probably. Lastly, the most famous *Account of the Murder of Archbishop Sharp* was written by James Russell some time after 1683. These last two accounts are published as an appendix to Kirkton, *History*. Russell's account gives a great deal of circumstantial detail, and has generally been preferred to all others in pro-Covenanting secondary writing: for example the account by Robert Wodrow is very largely a rewriting of Russell.

All four of the Covenanting accounts share a common aim. They attempt to justify the murder in terms of the political philosophy of the Covenanters, and they present a uniformly unflattering picture of the conduct of Sharp at the time of the murder.

These eight accounts represent the sum of what has previously been known about the murder of the Archbishop, and so far as I have been able to discover, all other accounts are either direct reprints of one of them, as for example the *Caveat for the Whigs*, printed in London in 1710, which reprints in its entirety and without acknowledgment the account in *Fanatical Moderation*; or they are an amalgam of different accounts, like *A True and Impartial Account of the Life of the Most Reverend Father in God Dr James Sharp, Archbishop of St Andrews*, which was published in 1723, and derived its version of the murder from the three pro-government accounts.

The *Registers of the Privy Council* provide a running commentary on the progress of the investigation, and some additional details are provided by a collection of manuscripts in Edinburgh University Library: MS. Dc 1.16. A small collection of papers relating to the murder in the Episcopal Chest in the Edinburgh Episcopal Theological College is reprinted in T. Stephen, *Life and Times of Archbishop Sharp*.

I have, however, been fortunate enough to find an additional source of considerable importance, in the shape of a number of depositions of the witnesses of the murder, now to be found in Edinburgh University Library and the Scottish Record Office. These are itemised in the Bibliography. They have not, as far as I am aware, been used in any attempt to elucidate the details of the murder, but they provide corroboration of some disputed points and some additional information. The deponents were simple people from the locality who without intending it became witnesses of the circumstances of the murder. Their accounts of what happened are no more to be accepted uncritically than the eight mutually irreconcilable accounts described above, but they do hold out the promise of the means of discriminating between the variations. It seems doubtful whether all disputed points will ever be resolved, but on the basis of the above information we can construct with some degree of accuracy an outline of what took place.

Abbreviations

APS	*Acts of the Parliaments of Scotland*
BL	British Library
CSPD	*Calendar of State Papers (Domestic Series)*
EUL	Edinburgh University Library
GUL	Glasgow University Library
HMC	Historical Manuscripts Commission
NLI	National Library of Ireland
NLS	National Library of Scotland
RPC	*Records of the Privy Council*
RSCHS	*Records of the Scottish Church History Society*
SHR	*Scottish Historical Review*
SHS	Scottish History Society
SRO	Scottish Record Office

Notes

Chapter 1

1. The sources for the information on which this section is based are described in the Appendix.

Chapter 2

1. Court of the Lord Lyon, Edinburgh. Precedency Book 1679, ff. 100–101. There is some debate about Sharp's age. He was born in May 1618 and died May 1679. It is probable that Sharp was almost exactly 61 when he was murdered (Rev. J. F. S. Gordon, *Scotichronicon*, II (1867), 4 gives 'sixty-one old men'). I am indebted to Sir Alexander Sharp-Bethune for drawing this to my attention.

2. I am indebted to Sir Alexander Sharp Bethune for helpful discussions on Sharp's family background.

3. *The Annals of Banff*, 2 vols., ed. W. Cramond (Aberdeen, 1891-3), II, 329, n. *The Annals* attempts *passim* to sort out some of the details of Sharp's birth and parentage.

4. *Ibid.*, I, 12.

5. *The Life of Mr James Sharp, Archbishop of St Andrews*, [n.p.]., 1678, 9–11; *Annals of Banff*, II, 333 n. *Banff*, II, 333 n.

6. *A True and Impartial Account of the Life of the Most Reverend Father in God, Dr James Sharp*, 1723, 25–6; *Annals of Banff* II, 332 n.

7. Sharp to Lauderdale [22 October 1660], NLS ms 2512 f 4.

8. *Annals of Banff*, I, 13; II, 333 n; A. T. Miller, The life of James Sharp, arbishop of St Andrews, Edinburgh Ph.D., 1946. The property was apparently purchased by the family in the next generation.

9. *Annals of Banff*, II, 23.

10. *A Source Book of Scottish History*. 3 vols., ed. W. C. Dickinson and G. Donaldson, 2nd ed., Edinburgh, 1961, II, 176.

11. *Annals of Banff*, II, 167.

12. *True and Impartial Account*, 27; *Life*, 12.

13. Gordon Donaldson, 'Scotland's Conservative North in the Sixteenth and Seventeenth Centuries', in *Transactions of the Royal Historical Society*, 5th series, xvi, 65–79.

14. *Annals of Banff*, II, 57, 60, 62-3, 76-7.

15. *Rolls of Alumni in Arts of the University and King's College*, ed. P. J. Anderson (Aberdeen, 1900), 12.

16. *Notes on the Evolution of the Arts Curriculum in the Universities of Aberdeen*. Prepared for the General Council by its clerk (Aberdeen, 1908), 3, my translation.

17. R. G. Cant, *The University of St Andrews*, new ed. (Edinburgh, 1970), 64.

18. *Notes on the Evolution of the Arts Curriculum*, 18.

19. *Officers and Graduates of the University and King's College, Aberdeen, 1485-1860*, ed. P. J. Anderson (Aberdeen, 1893), 187.

20. For what follows on Forbes and the Aberdeen Doctors see: W. G. S. Snow, *The Times, Life and Thought of Patrick Forbes, Bishop of Aberdeen 1618-1635* (London, 1952); P. J. Anderson, *Studies in the History and Development of the University of Aberdeen* (Aberdeen, 1906); G. D. Henderson, *The Burning Bush* (Edinburgh, 1957), Chapter V, 'The Aberdeen Doctors'.

21. *True and Impartial Account*, 27-9; *Life*, 13.

22. *True and Impartial Account*, 28.

23. I am indebted to Mr Robert Smart, archivist at St Andrews University, for the

discovery of the document which indicates this: St Andrews University Muniments SL 705/1. 147.

24. *True and Impartial Account*, 29–30.

25. *Life*, 13–14.

26 For this and what follows on the University of St Andrews see Cant, *University of St Andrews*, 27.

27. *An Abridgement of the Acts of the General Assembly 1560–1830*, ed. A. Peterkin (Edinburgh, 1831), 102.

28. I am indebted to Christine King, whose researches on dictates included these lecture notes, and who has helped me understand the significance of them.

29. *Life*, 18–23; *True and Impartial Account*, Appendix to the Preface Number 1.

30. *Life*, 16–17; *True and Impartial Account*, 31.

31. St Andrews University Muniments SL 110. R. 9; *Life*, 15.

32. *Selections from the Minutes of the Presbyteries of St Andrews and Cupar*, ed. G. R. Kinloch (Edinburgh, 1837), 37–8.

33. Bruce Lenman, *An Economic History of Modern Scotland 1660–1976* (Hamden Ct., 1977), 33–43.

34. *Fasti Ecclesiae Scoticanae*, ed. Hew Scott, revised ed. (Edinburgh, 1925); *Minutes of the Presbyteries of St Andrews and Cupar, passim*.

35. I am indebted to the minister and Kirk Session of Crail for permitting me to read the records, in the transcription made for them.

36. NLS Adv. ms 5.2.10. f 18 ff.

37. F. D. Dow, *Cromwellian Scotland 1651–1660* (Edinburgh, 1979), 36– 39.

38. *Records of the Commissions of the General Assemblies*, 3 vols., ed. A. F. Mitchell and J. Christie (Edinburgh, 1892, 1896, 1909), II, 78–80.

39. NLS Wodrow Folio LXV f274, 276–8.

40. *Diary of Mr John Lamont of Newton*, ed. G. R. Kinloch (Edinbrugh, 1830), 14, 21–2.

41. HMC 5th Report, 625.

42. *Diary of Mr John Lamont*, 54, 119.

Chapter 3

1. *Selections from the Minutes of the Synod of Fife*, ed. Charles Baxter (Edinburgh, 1837), 155, 166; *Diary of John Lamont*, 3–4, 19; *Records of Commissions* III, 4.

2. For the background to this chapter see David Stevenson, *Revolution and Counter Revolution in Scotland 1644–1651* (London, 1977), Chapters 4 and 5.

3. *Records of Commissions* III, *passim*. The index does not give a complete list of mentions of Sharp.

4. *Ibid.*, III, 10, 18, 26, 28–9, 32–40, 41–2, 43, 46, 49.

5. Quoted in Gordon Donaldson, *James V to James VII* (Edinburgh, 1957), 341.

6. Stevenson, *Revolution and Counter-Revolution*, 187–9; *Records of Commissions* III, 73, text 557–62 and n; 94–107.

7. *Records of Commissions*, III, 106–8.

8. *Ibid.*, III, 111, 112.

9. *Ibid.*, III, 123–5.

10. *Ibid.*, III, 124–5.

11. *Ibid.*, III, 126–7.

12. *Ibid.*, III, 130.

13. *Ibid.*, III, 132.

14. *Ibid.*, III, 183; text of the letter *ibid.*

15. *Ibid.*, III, 196–7; texts of letters *ibid.*

16. *Ibid.*, III, 259; text of report 260; 266, 274. William Row, ed., *The Life of Robert Blair* (Edinburgh, 1848), 257–60.

17. *Records of Commissions*, III, 293.

18. *Ibid.*, III, 303–4, 339, 364–5.

19. *Ibid.*, III, 403, 420; report 429; 444, 459–60.

20. *Ibid.*, III, 295, 439, 446, 483, 490.

21. *Ibid.*, III, 559–60.

22. *APS, VI*, pt. 2, 609.

23. *Records of Commissions*, III, 133.

24. *Ibid.*, III, 138.

25. *Ibid.*, III, 283, 292, 436–7.

26. *APS*, VI, pt. 2, 615.

27. *Ibid.*, 618.

28. *Records of Commissions*, III, 158.

29. *Ibid.*, III, 159–60.

30. *Ibid.*, III, 161.

31. *Ibid.*, III, 268, 270, 336.

32. *APS*, VI, pt. 2, 647.

33. *Records of Commissions*, III, 356ff. and sederunts 345, 355, 356.

34. *Ibid.*, III, 361.

35. *Ibid.*, III, 362.

36. *Ibid.*, III, 367–9.

37. *Ibid.*, III, 388, 406.

38. *Ibid.*, III, 424–6.

39. *Ibid.*, III, 432, 433.

40. *Ibid.*, III, 443; see also 450–7.

41. *Ibid.*, III, 458.

42. *Ibid.*, III, 476–9.

43. *Ibid.*, III, 485.

44. *Ibid.*, III, 490.

45. *Ibid.*, III, 513; Stevenson, *Revolution and Counter-Revolution*, 203–8; Lamont, *Diary*, 34: the date is wrong, though; J. Nicholl, *A Diary of Public Transactions*, ed. David Laing (Edinburgh, 1836), 56–7.

46. *Life of Mr James Sharp*, 38; the same accusation is made by T. Kirkton, *Secret and True History*, ed. C. K. Sharpe (London, 1817), 76.

47. *CSPD*, Interregnum IV, 96 para 21.

48. GUL Ms Gen 210, Douglas to Sharp, 15 March, 1660.

49. CSPD, Interregnum IV, 213 para 10; *Life of Mr James Sharp*, 39.

50. Contacts between the prisoners and the English presbyterians are referred to in Robert Baillie, *Letters and Journals*, 3 vols, ed. D. Laing (Edinburgh, 1822), III, 204.

51. *Life of Mr James Sharp*, 37, 39.

52. Row, *Life of Blair*, 304.

53. *Minutes of the Presbyteries of St Andrews and Cupar*, 63, 64.

54. *Records of Commissions*, III, 549.

55. *CSPD*, Interregnum IV, 312 para 4; Crail Kirk Session Records: transcription in the possession of the Kirk Session.

56. *Records of Commissions*, III, 510.

57. The developments in the Resolutioner-Protester controversy are summarised in J. D. Ogilvie, 'A Bibliography of the Resolutioner-Protester controversy, 1650–1659' (*Edinburgh Bibliographical Society Publications* XIV, 1928–30), 59–74; *Records of Commissions*, III, 535, 536, 556.

58. For the background to what follows see Dow, 'Lilburne and the Scottish People, January 1653–April 1654', *Cromwellian Scotland*, Chapter 5.

59. Lamont, *Diary*, 69–71; Nicoll, *Diary*, 110; Baillie, III, 225–6.

60. For the background to what follows see Dow, 'Monck and the Scottish People, April 1654–September 1655', *Cromwellian Scotland*, Chapter 7.

61. Dow, *Cromwellian Scotland*, 105.

62. *Ibid.*, 198.

63. This was the endorsement on the minutes of their meetings.

64. For the background to what follows see Dow, 'Broghill and the Church Parties, 1655-1657', *Cromwellian Scotland*, Chapter 9.

65. *Ibid.*, 147.

66. Baillie, III, 279.

67. Dow, *Cromwellian Scotland*, 199-200; Baillie, III, 281.

68. Baillie, III, 315-7.

69. Dow, *Cromwellian Scotland*, 200.

70. *Ibid.*, 206.

71. John Thurloe, *A Collection of the State Papers of John Thurloe*, ed. Thomas Birch, 7 vols (London, 1742), V, 323.

72. *Register of Consultations* I, 203-14, 257. For a more general account of these negotiations see Dow, *Cromwellian Scotland*, 206-210. An older account is given in the introduction to Vol. II of the *Register of Consultations*.

73. *Register of Consultations*, I, 210-340.

74. *Ibid.*, I, 349-63.

75. *Ibid.*, I, 354.

76. *Ibid.*, I, 364-5.

77. The moment when Sharp was praised by Cromwell during the first debate, *Ibid.*, I, 351, sounds a possible origin for this story. Perhaps even more likely is the later occasion when Sharp was commended as a person of 'acute parts', *Ibid.*, II, 91.

78. *Ibid.*, I, 368.

79. *Ibid.*, II, 5-17 for the account of this meeting.

80. *Ibid.*, II, 20.

81. *Ibid.*, II, 20-27.

82. *Ibid.*, II, 34.

83. *Ibid.*, II, 36.

84. *Ibid.*, II, 40-41. ·

85. *Ibid.*, II, 41-4.

86. *Ibid.*, I, 264; II, 35, 63, 74, 88, 120, 125.

87. For these meetings, *Ibid.*, II, 49-126.

88. Baillie, III, 349. The letter here from Sharp gives a passing reference to Sharp's preferred way of negotiating behind the scenes.

89. *Register of Consultations*, II, 118, 121, 127, 128-9.

90. *Ibid.*, II, 130.

91. Baillie, III, 354; see also 362 for a comment with the same tone.

92. *Register of Consultations*, II, 123-4; see *Ibid.*, I, 241 for the expression of a very similar point of view by the Edinburgh ministers themselves.

93. Printed *Ibid.*, II, 131-6.

94. *Ibid.*, II, 146.

95. For the background to this section see Dow, 'Continuity and Change under Richard Cromwell and the Rump, September 1658-October 1659', *Cromwellian Scotland*, Chapter 11.

96. This was the perception of the English Presbyterians with whom Sharp had contacts, who responded far more warmly to Richard than ever they had done to his father, G. R. Abernathy, 'The English Presbyterians and the Stuart Restoration, 1648-1663', *Trans. of the American Philosophical Soc.*, 1965, n.s. 55, ii, 15-37.

97. For the instructions and his negotiations, *Register of Consultations*, II, 148-55.

98. Bodleian Rawlinson MS C 179 p. 24; Godfrey Davies, *Restoration of Charles II* (London, 1955), 127; Dow, *Cromwellian Scotland*, 241-2.

99. *Register of Consultations*, II, 174-6, 181-5, 187, 192.

Chapter 4

1. The evidence for this is contained in the letters which the ministers and Monck exchanged after he had left Scotland. These are in GUL Ms Gen 210 1-43 *passim*, and show the close relations that had existed between them in Scotland.

2. NLS Wodrow Folio XXXI no. 65.

3. This is asserted by T. Stephen, *The Life and Times of Archbishop Sharp* (London, 1839), 20-21, but I have been unable to discover where he got his information.

4. The major source for what follows is the last section of the *Consultations of the Ministers of Edinburgh*, which unfortunately has never been properly published. The original is in the Scottish Record Office. Wodrow made a transcription of the original which is now in the Library of the University of Glasgow, Ms Gen 210. I have checked his transcription against the original and found it to be almost perfectly accurate. However, in his introduction to the *History of the Sufferings of the Church of Scotland from the Restoration to the Revolution*, 4 vols. (Glasgow, 1829-30) Wodrow published extracts of these letters which have proved very misleading to students of Sharp ever since. By the omission of material in a way that it is very hard not to think was deliberate, he encouraged the perpetuation of allegations about Sharp which are simply untrue. The most familiar of these are that Sharp deliberately prevented anyone from joining or replacing him as Resolutioner agent in London, whereas the original reveals that he repeatedly asked to be returned to his parish and replaced; and further that he deliberately misled the Resolutioners about ecclesiastical negotiations, whereas he repeatedly voiced his fears that the Solemn League and Covenant would be completely ignored and that, at the very least, episcopacy would be restored in England. Both of these judgements are repeated in the latest book on the subject: I. B. Cowan, *The Scottish Covenanters 1660-1688* (London, 1976). In 1930 the Scottish History Society attempted to put matters straight but unfortunately did not think it was necessary to print the letters summarised by Wodrow but only to print 'a few passages supplementary to Wodrow' and apparently arbitrarily selected. The form of the publication in Volume II of the *Register of Consultations* makes it extremely awkward to use since the reader is referred also to other printed books for some of the texts. In consequence the significance of Wodrow's omissions has not been apparent to students of the period. In fact the correspondence reveals a good deal about the period which is not available from other sources and is consequently the major source for this chapter. As a matter of convenience I have used Wodrow's transcript corrected against the original. The letters are, however, in the same order and I have attempted to identify them in such a way that they can be easily found in either source. The letter headings are as they appear in the manuscript. Except where otherwise noted, references in this chapter are to GUL Ms Gen 210.

5. Monck from Dickson and Douglas, Edinburgh, 10 Jan. 1660; Instructions to Sharp, 6 Feb. 1660.

6. Auditor Thomson to Sharp, York, 15 Jan. 1659 [old style]; Monck to Dickson and Douglas, Ferrybridge, 16 Jan. 1659 [old style]; Pass to Sharp from Monck.

7. Sharp to Douglas, London, 14 Feb. 1660. This point is also made in G. R. Abernathy, 'The English Presbyterians and the Stuart Restoration, 1648-1663', *Transactions of the American Philosophical Society*, n.s. 55, pt. 2, 1965, 38. Abernathy is yet another historian who is eager to condemn Sharp as a traitor to his presbyterian brethren. Part of the reason for his inclination to do so is that he used Robert Wodrow's version of the letters between Sharp and the Edinburgh ministers. This, however, does not deny that fact that Abernathy asks some very searching questions about Sharp's activities, which will be discussed in the appropriate place in the text.

8. Sharp to Douglas, London, 21 Feb. 1660; Sharp from Douglas, Edinburgh, 1 March 1660.

9. Sharp to Douglas, London, 6 March 1660; Sharp from Douglas, Edinburgh, 13 March 1660.

10. Douglas to Sharp, Edinburgh, 23 Feb. 1660; Sharp to Douglas, London, 21 Feb. 1660; Sharp to Douglas, London, 1 March, 1660; Sharp to Smith, London 4 March 1660;

Sharp to Douglas, London, 6 March 1660; Sharp to Douglas, London, 10 March 1660.

11. Sharp to Douglas, London, 21 Feb. 1660. For other occasions when he raised the issue see Sharp to Douglas, London, 1 March, 6 March, 15 March, 17 March, 24 March, 27 March, 31 March, 5 April, 12 April 1660.

12. Sharp from Douglas, Edinburgh, 13 March 1660.

13. Broghill to Dickson, Douglas, Hutcheson, Wood and Sharp, Dublin, 12 March 1660; Sharp from Dickson and Douglas, Edinburgh, 24 March 1660; Monck from Dickson and Douglas, Edinburgh, 24 March 1660; Broghill from Dickson and Douglas, Edinburgh, 27 March 1660; Broghill from Douglas, Edinburgh, 27 March 1660; Broghill from Dickson, Douglas and Hutcheson, Edinburgh, 28 March 1660; Sharp from Douglas, Edinburgh, 29 March 1660; Sharp to Douglas, London, 31 March 1660; NLI Ms 13223 f.8 Orrery Papers, Sharp to Broghill, London, 30 April 1660. I am indebted to Dr Tony Barnard of Hertford College, Oxford for bringing this document to my notice.

14. Sharp to Douglas, London, 6 March 1660.

15. Sharp from Douglas, Edinburgh, 3 April 1660.

16. Sharp to Douglas, London, 24 March 1660; Sharp to Douglas, London, 27 March 1660; Sharp from Douglas, Edinburgh, 3 April 1660; Sharp to Douglas, London, 5 April 1660.

17. Sharp to Douglas, London, 10 March 1660; Sharp from Douglas, Edinburgh, 15 March 1660; Sharp to Douglas, London, 15 March 1660; Earl of Crawford from Douglas, Edinburgh, 20 March 1660; Earls of Crawford and Lauderdale, Lord Sinclair, from Dickson, Douglas, Hamilton, Smith and Hutcheson, Edinburgh, March 1660; Sharp from Douglas, Edinburgh, 22 March 1660.

18. Sharp from Douglas, Edinburgh, 29 March 1660; Sharp from Douglas, Edinburgh, 31 March 1660; Sharp to Douglas, London, 31 March 1660; Sharp to Douglas, London, 5 April 1660; Sharp to Douglas, London, 7 April 1660; Sharp to Douglas, London, 12 April 1660; Sharp to Douglas, London, 13 April 1660; Sharp from Douglas, Edinburgh, 21 April 1660.

19. Sharp to Douglas, London, 15 March 1660; Sharp to Douglas, London, 24 March 1660; Sharp to Douglas, London, 31 March 1660.

20. Abernathy, 44.

21. Sharp to Douglas, London, 10 March 1660.

22. Sharp to Smith, London, 4 March 1660; Sharp from Douglas, Edinburgh, 15 March 1660.

23. Sharp to Douglas, London, 6 March 1660; Sharp to Douglas, London, 27 March 1660; Sharp to Douglas, London, 31 March 1660.

24. Sharp to Smith, London, 4 March 1660.

25. Abernathy, 41, 43.

26. *Thurloe Papers*, VII, 856.

27. Abernathy, 44.

28. Sharp to Douglas, London, 10 March 1660.

29. Sharp to Douglas, London, 27 March 1660.

30. Douglas to Sharp, Edinburgh, 12 April 1660.

31. Abernathy, 45. As far as the English presbyterians were concerned, this was an old song. Attempts at rapport between them and the moderate episcopalians had been made on the basis of their common royalism since the middle '50s. As R. S. Bosher shows, however, in *The Making of the Restoration Settlement* (London, 1951), 45–8, the Laudian wing of the episcopalians would have nothing to do with this development, and in 1660 became powerful enough to be able to impose their will. See also: Sharp to Douglas, London, 31 March 1660; Sharp to Douglas, London, 5 April 1660; Sharp to Douglas, London, 7 April 1660; Sharp to Douglas, London, 12 April 1660.

32. Sharp to Douglas, London, 7 April 1660.

33. Sharp to Douglas, London, 19 April 1660; Sharp had also reported an earlier rumour to this effect: Sharp to Douglas, London, 13 April 1660.

34. Douglas to Sharp, Edinburgh, 24 April 1660; Sharp from Douglas, Edinburgh, 26 April 1660.

35. See their paper on the subject: 'Some observations upon the post-haste of those who pretend commission from Scotland', 19 April 1660; see also: Sharp to Douglas, London, 12 April 1660; Sharp to Douglas, London, 13 April 1660; Sharp from Douglas, Edinburgh, 21 April 1660; Sharp to Douglas, London, 19 April 1660; Sharp from Douglas, Edinburgh, 24 April 1660; Sharp from Douglas, Edinburgh, 26 April 1660; Sharp to Douglas, London, undated April 1660; Sharp to Douglas, London, 28 April 1660.

36. Sharp to Douglas, London, 19 April 1660; Sharp from Douglas, Edinburgh, 24 April 1660; Sharp to Douglas, London, undated April 1660.

37. Sharp from Douglas, Edinburgh, 26 April 1660; Sharp from Douglas, Edinburgh, 8 May 1660.

38. Sharp from Douglas, Edinburgh, 8 May 1660; Sharp to Douglas, London, 1 May 1660; Sharp to Douglas [?], London, 4 May 1660.

39. *Lauderdale Papers* ed. Osmund Airy, 3 vols. (London, 1884–5) I, 26 note.

40. F. J. Powicke, 'Eleven letters of John, Second Earl of Lauderdale (and First Duke) 1616–1682, to the Rev. Richard Baxter, 1615–1691', *Bulletin of the John Rylands Library*, VII, 1922–3, 73–105; F. J. Powicke, *A Life of the Reverend Richard Baxter, 1615–1691* (London, 1924), 137; Abernathy, 'The English Presbyterians', 44.

41. *Lauderdale Papers*, I, 28–30; A. Robertson, *The Life of Sir Robert Murray* (London, 1922).

42. BL Add Ms 23113 ff. 18–23.

43. Abernathy, 44.

44. Baillie, III, 317.

45. Sharp from Douglas, Edinburgh, 3 April 1660.

46. Gilbert Burnet, *History of his own Times*, ed. Osmund Airy, 2 vols. (Oxford, 1897, 1900), I, 165.

47. This assumes that the unnamed bearer of Glencairn's letters was indeed Sharp: Bodleian, Clarendon Mss Vol. 72 ff. 134, 135. The interpretation I have put upon the letters is strengthened by a further two letters written at the same time by Sir John Greenville to the king and Hyde, which describe Sharp as a moderate: Clarendon Mss. vol. 72 ff. 141, 174.

48. Sharp to [the Edinburgh ministers], Breda, 11 May 1660.

49. Edward, Earl of Clarendon, *Calendar of the Clarendon State papers*, ed. W. D. Macray (Oxford, 1932), IV, 603. The original ms. is in cipher.

50. Accounts of the interviews and Sharp's movements are given in Sharp to the [Edinburgh ministers], Breda, 11 May 1660; Sharp to Douglas, London, 29 May 1660; *Lauderdale Papers*, I, 26–7.

51. Sharp to Douglas, London, 29 May 1660.

52. Ibid.

Chapter 5

General note: as in the preceding chapter, references are to GUL Ms Gen 210 except where otherwise stated.

1. Sharp from Douglas, 8 May 1660; Letter to the King's Majesty from Douglas, Dickson, Hamilton, Smith and Hutcheson, Edinburgh, 8 May 1660; Instructions for Mr James Sharp in reference to the King; Letter to the King's Majesty from Douglas, Dickson, and Hutcheson, Edinburgh, 10 May 1660; Sharp from Douglas, Edinburgh, 10 May 1660; Sharp from Douglas, Edinburgh 22 May 1660; Sharp to Douglas, London, 26 May 1660; Sharp to Douglas, London, 29 May 1660.

2. Calamy, Ash, Manton from Dickson, Douglas, Hamilton, Smith, Hutcheson, Edinburgh, 12 May 1660; Mr Robert Eddison of Newcastle from Douglas, Edinburgh, 22 May 1660.

3. Calamy, Ash and Manton from Dickson, Douglas, Hamilton, Smith and Hutcheson, Edinburgh, 12 May 1660.

4. Sharp to Douglas, London, 29 May 1660. The incident is described in Edward, Earl of Clarendon, *The History of the Rebellion and Civil Wars in England*, 6 vols., ed. W. Dunn Macray (Oxford, 1888), VI, 231–2; Bosher, *Restoration Settlement*, 129–30.

5. Sharp to Douglas, London, 12 June 1660; Sharp to Douglas, London, 16 June 1660.

6. Sharp to Douglas, London 9 June 1660; 16 June 1660; 3 July 1660; 10 July 1660.

7. Sharp from Douglas, Edinburgh, 12 June 1660; Sharp from Douglas, Edinburgh, 14 June 1660; Sharp from Dickson, Douglas, Wood, Hamilton, Smith and Ker, Edinburgh, 21 June 1660.

8. Sharp from Douglas and Smith, Edinburgh, [undated, c 31 May] 1660; Sharp to Douglas, London, 2 June 1660; Sharp from Dickson, Douglas, Hamilton, Smith and Hutcheson, Edinburgh, 9 June 1660; Sharp to Douglas, London, 5 June 1660; 12 June 1660; 16 June 1660; 3 July 1660; 7 July 1660.

9. Sharp to Douglas, London, 14 June 1660; Sharp to Douglas, London, 28 June 1660.

10. All letters Sharp to Douglas, 14 June to 14 July 1660.

11. Sharp to Douglas, London, 14 July 1660.

12. Sharp to Douglas, London, [undated c. 18 July] 1660; Sharp to Douglas, London, [undated c. 31 July] 1660.

13. Minute of [1 September] 1660.

14. Text most readily available in Wodrow, I, 80–1.

15. NLS Wodrow Ms Quarto LXIII, Robert Douglas, 'A brief narration of the coming in of prelacy again within this kirk'.

16. *APS* V, 276–7.

17. The Presbytery of Edinburgh, their humble return to his Majesty's letter, Edinburgh, 20 September 1660; Wodrow, I, 82–3.

18. *Lauderdale Papers*, II, App. lxx.

19. Burnet, *Own Time*, 197–9; G. Davies and P. Hardacre, 'The Restoration of the Scottish Episcopacy', *Journal of British Studies*, I, ii, 1960, 37.

20. Sharp to Douglas, London, 21 February 1660; Sharp to Smith, London, 4 March 1660; Sharp to Smith, London, 17 March 1660; Sharp to Douglas, London, 24 March 1660; Sharp to Douglas, London, 31 March 1660; Sharp to Douglas, London, 5 April 1660; Sharp to Douglas, London, 5 June 1660; Sharp to Douglas, London, 9 June 1660; Sharp to Douglas, London, 10 July 1660; NLS Ms 2512 f.1.

21. *Minutes of the Presbyteries of St Andrews and Cupar*, 75–7; NLS Ms 2512 f. 1, 3.

22. W. Row, *The Life of Robert Blair*, ed. Thos. M'Crie (Edinburgh, 1848), 360–3; NLS Ms 2512, f. 3.

23. The minutes of the Committee of Estates which as an interim government ran Scotland from August to December are in the SRO PA 11/12–13.

24. *Lauderdale Papers*, I, 36–7, 41, 42; Baillie, III, 459.

25. Sir George Mackenzie of Rosehaugh, *Memoirs of the Affairs of Scotland*, ed. T. Thomson (Edinburgh, 1821), 5–12.

26. Davies and Hardacre, 'Restoration', 32–51; *Lauderdale Papers*, I, 43ff.

27. *Lauderdale Papers*, I, 43–56, 67–8.

28. BL Add. Ms 23115 ff. 18–20; *Lauderdale Papers* I, 56.

29. *Lauderdale Papers*, I, 61, 62, 66, 291, 293.

30. *Minutes of the Presbyteries of St Andrews and Cupar*, 77; Scott, *Fasti*, V, 193; *Lauderdale Papers*, I, 75,76; Row, *Life of Blair*, 373.

31. *Lauderdale Papers*, I, 48–9, 61, 62, 65, 68; *APS* VII, 162; *Registers of the Privy Council of Scotland, third series*, I, 4; Baillie, III, 461.

32. *APS* VI, pt. i, 41–3, 132–3; VII, 16, 17–18.

33. *Lauderdale Papers*, I, 72.

34. Text Wodrow, I, 110–11; *Lauderdale Papers*, I, 70–1.

35. Text Wodrow, I, 111; *Lauderdale Papers*, i, 74.

36. *Lauderdale Papers*, I, 75, 77, 91.

37. *Ibid.*, I, 77, 85, 88.

38. Wodrow, I, 114-7. From the wording it seems certain that these communications were sent before the Rescissory Act was passed. The information about who sent the letter is given in NLS Ms 2512 f. 6.

39. *APS* VII, 86-8.

40. NLS Ms 2512 f. 6; *Lauderdale Papers*, I, 93-4.

41. *Lauderdale Papers*, I, 97; *APS* VII, 193; *Calendar of Clarendon State Papers*, V, 88; Baillie, III, 468; NLS Ms 2512 f. 8.

42. *Lauderdale Papers*, I, 89; see also Row, *Life of Blair*, 362.

43. NLS Ms 2512 f. 8

44. *Calendar of Clarendon State Papers*, V, 88, 90; NLS Ms 1512 f. 8.

45. *Lauderdale Papers*, I, 92, 95-6, 98.

46. *Ibid.*, II, App. C, lxxviii. Airy has an utterly different interpretation of this letter; *ibid.*, I, App. I, xxix, 'I found that which your Grace [Middleton] was pleased often to tell me was not without ground'.

47. *Ibid.*, II, App. C, lxxix; *APS* VII, 271-2.

48. BL Add Ms 23116 f. 76; SHS *Miscellany* I (Edinburgh, 1893), 250; NLS Ms 3922 f. 17.

49. NLS Ms 2512 f. 10; Row, *Life of Blair*, 395; NLS Wodrow Ms Quarto LXIII, Douglas, 'Prelacy'; Kirkton, *History*, 134-5.

50. Nicol, *Diary*, 347, 354; Kirkton, *History*, 137; Burnet, *Own Times*, I, 247-8.

51. NLS Adv. Ms 5.2.8.

Chapter 6

1. *RPC*, 3rd. ser., I, 28-9, 31-2.

2. *APS*, VII, 367. It actually met in May.

3. BL Add. Ms 23117.f.11.

4. *RPC*, 3rd. ser., I, 119-20, 122-3; NLS Ms 597.f.73 for Charles's specific grant of this power to Sharp.

5. *RPC*, 3rd. ser., I, 125-6, 130-1.

6. *Lauderdale Papers* I, 88-9.

7. Kirkton, *History*, 141.

8. *RPC*, 3rd. ser., I, 126.

9. Nicholl, *Diary*, 364.

10. Lamont, *Diary*, 145; Burnet, *History* I, 252.

11. Row, *Life of Blair*, 404.

12. Lamont, *Diary*, 146; Row, *Life of Blair*, 405.

13. Lamont, *Diary*, 164; Row, *Life of Blair*, 405.

14. NLS Ms 597.f.75.

15. *Lauderdale Papers*, I, 56.

16. I am indebted to Dr Walter Makey former Edinburgh City Archivist, for discussions on this issue.

17. Donaldson, *James V-VII*, 365.

18. Lamont, *Diary*, 146-7; Nicholl, *Diary*, 365-6; Row, *Life of Blair*, 406-7.

19. St Andrews, Glasgow, Edinburgh, Aberdeen, Orkney, Dunkeld, Dunblane, Galloway, Moray, Ross, Caithness, Brechin, Argyll, the Isles.

20. Lamont, *Diary*, 148; Nicoll, *Diary*, 366-7; Mackenzie, *Memoirs*, 63.

21. Nicoll, *Diary*, 366.

22. *Ibid.*, 367.

23. *APS*, VII, 376.

24. *Ibid.*, VII, 377-8.

25. *Ibid.*, VII, 12, 18.

26. Nicoll, *Diary*, 382.

27. *RPC*, 3rd. ser., I, 269–70.

28. Mackenzie, *Memoirs*, 77–8; Row, *Life of Blair*, 424.

29. For this subject see W. R. Foster, *Bishop and Presbytery* (London 1958).

30. NLS Ms 2512.f.11.

31. NLS Ms 2512.f.11, 15.

32. Kirkton, *History*, 150; Burnet, *History*, I, 269.

33. Lamont, *Diary*, 156; Row, *Life of Blair*, 426: both very hostile reports.

34. *RPC*, 3rd. ser., I, 273–4, 279, 312–5; *Lauderdale Papers* I, 120.

35. *Lauderdale Papers*, I, 108, 109, 112–3, 115; NLS Ms 2512.f.11; NLS Ms 546.f.7.

36. *Lauderdale Papers*, I, 129.

37. The correspondence between Sharp and Lauderdale contained in SHS *Miscellany* I, 251–3 and NLS Ms 2512.f.13 seems to explain the episode described in Row, *Life of Blair*, 436–7 when Sharp's loyalty to Lauderdale is doubted. See also Burnet, *History*, I, 360–1.

38. NLS Ms 2512.f.17; *Lauderdale Papers*, I, 130.

39. Row, *Life of Blair*, 426; Mackenzie, *Memoirs*, 116–7; NLS Ms 2512.f.13.

40. Kirkton, *History*, 163–4.

41. Row, *Life of Blair*, 439; Kirkton, *History*, 160–2; Burnet, *History* I, 271, 275, 376.

42. Donaldson, *James V–James VII*.

43. *RPC*, 3rd. ser., I, 354, 357, 372–7; Kirkton, *History*, 162–3.

44. *RPC*, 3rd. ser., I, 350. James Turner, *Memoirs of His own Life and Times* (Edinburgh, 1829), 139. NLS Ms 597.f.129 for instructions to Turner to quarter on conventiclers and arrest disorderly ministers. BL Add. Ms 23119.f.26.

45. NLS Ms 2512.f.15.

46. *APS*, VII, 449 for the exact form of the election; also see *Lauderdale Papers*, I, 134.

47. *APS*, VII, 455; *Lauderdale Papers*, I, 154–5.

48. NLS Ms 573.f.77 for evidence that it was the king's resolve.

49. NLS Ms 2512.f.11.

50. BL Add. Ms 23119.f.86; *Lauderdale Papers*, I, 162.

51. *RPC*, 3rd. ser., I, 393.

52. *Ibid.*, I, 403–4; *Lauderdale Papers*, I, 176; Row, *Life of Blair*, 446–7.

53. See also *Lauderdale Papers*, II, Appendix A, i.

54. *APS*, VII, 465.

55. *Lauderdale Papers*, I, 183 for the king's satisfaction with it.

56. NLS Ms 7024.f.4; Burnet, *History*, I, 367.

57. NLS Ms 7023.f.4.

58. NLS Ms 597.f.116.

59. NLS Ms 2512.f.68.

60. Nicoll, *Diary*, 408–11 for the text; Kirkton, *History*, 201.

61. For the history of these powers see P. G. B. McNeill, The Jurisdiction of the Scottish Privy Council 1532–1708, Glasgow Ph.D. 1961, 33–6, 61.

62. NLS Ms 2512.f.27, 33, 52; Row, *Life of Blair*, 456, 462, 469–70; Kirkton, *History*, 205; *Lauderdale Papers*, I, 194, II, Appendix iii.

63. NLS Ms 2512.f.27, 31, 38.

64. Ibid.

65. NLS Ms 2512.f.31, 37, 38, 40, 56, 60.

66. Ibid., f.44, 46; Row, *Life of Blair*, 473; *Lauderdale Papers*, II, Appendix v, vii, ix.

67. Row, *Life of Blair*, 472; *Lauderdale Papers*, II, Appendix ix; Burnet, *History*, I, 373–4.

68. Burnet, *History*, I, 369; Row, *Life of Blair*, 456; NLS Ms 2512.f.52, 54.

69. NLS Ms 7023.f.4; Lamont, *Diary*, 172.

70. *Lauderdale Papers*, I, 224, II, Appendix xxvii.

71. NLS Ms 7023.f.16 for the necessity in Lauderdale's view of summoning the Convention; *APS*, VII, 529; Kirkton, *History*, 216; *Lauderdale Papers*, I, 211, 215.

72. NLS Ms 2512.f.74.

73. Ibid. f.76.

74. In January 1666. SHS *Miscellany* I, 260; NLS Ms 2512.f.235.

75. NLS Ms 2512.f.78.

76. Burnet, *History*, I, 366.

77. *Lauderdale Papers*, I, 228–33; Stephen, *Sharp*, 307; Row, *Life of Blair*, 477–8.

78. NLS Ms 5050.f.144; *Lauderdale Papers*, II, Appendix xxv.

79. *Lauderdale Papers*, II, Appendix xxvii. See also the correspondence in NLS Ms 5049, 5050 for Sir Robert Moray's intimacy with Lauderdale.

80. NLS Ms 5050.f.146.

81. NLS Ms 2512.f.87, 147.

82. NLS Ms 2512.f.80.

83. *Lauderdale Papers*, I, 226.

84. *Lauderdale Papers*, I, 228.

85. *APS*, VII, 420. See *RPC*, 3rd. ser. I, 329. This was the proclamation which Middleton omitted to publish, which delay finally ensured his fall. See Burnet, *History* I, 361–2.

86. Burnet, *History*, I, 579.

87. *Ibid.*, I, 613.

88. *Ibid.*, II, 92.

89. Burnet, *History*, I, 258–9.

90. NLS Ms 2512.f.68.

91. The immense number of begging letters in the unpublished Lauderdale Papers in the British Library is a testimony to the acute financial straits of many Scots nobles.

92. *Lauderdale Papers*, I, Appendix xiv.

93. Probably much exaggerated by Burnet in *Lauderdale Papers*, Appendix xii, xvi.

94. Row, *Life of Blair*, 489; Nicoll, *Diary*, 448.

95. NLS Ms 3136.f.18.

96. *Lauderdale Papers*, I, 237n and Burnet, *History*, I, 383–4.

97. *Lauderdale Papers*, I, 240.

98. Burnet, *History*, I, 380–1 probably conflates this incident with what follows in 1666 as NLS Ms 7023.f.1 shows.

99. *Lauderdale Papers*, I, 241.

100. *Lauderdale Papers*, I, 242.

101. *Ibid.*, I, 244.

102. Nicoll, *Diary*, 451.

103. From 15 November 1666. *RPC*, 3rd. ser., II, 208.

104. *Ibid.*, II, 210.

105. *Ibid.*, II, 229.

106. *Lauderdale Papers*, I, 247–8, 253, 259–60.

107. *Ibid.*, II, Appendix xlii.

108. It was perfectly clear to Sharp that his disgrace was political. See *Lauderdale Papers*, I, 269.

109. *Ibid.*, II, Appendix xliv; Burnet, *History*, I, 428.

110. *RPC*, 3rd. ser., II, 253, 305.

Chapter 7

1. *Lauderdale Papers*, I, 282.

2. *Ibid.*, II, Appendix C, lvi; Burnet, *History*, I, 428; Row, *Life of Blair*, 508.

3. *Lauderdale Papers*, II, 17.

4. *Ibid.*, II, 28–30, 93–5; NLS Ms 2512.ff. 106, 108, 110, 114.

5. *Lauderdale Papers*, II, 31, 34, 41, 70–71.

6. *Ibid.*, II, 84, 87, 90–1.

7. *HMC* 3rd Report, 423.

8. *Lauderdale Papers*, II, 93.

9. *RPC*, 3rd ser., II, 294, 305, 343; NLS Ms 7003.f.566; Kirkton, *History*, 261; *Lauderdale Papers*, II, 71.

10. *Lauderdale Papers*, II, 1–6, 47–8, 78; Burnet, *History*, I, 433.

11. The series of Tweeddale's and Moray's letters to Lauderdale begins spring 1667. Burnet *History*, I, 431.

12. The biographical details for Leighton to 1662 are taken from D. Butler, *The Life and Letters of Robert Leighton* (London, 1903) and E. A. Knox, *Robert Leighton, Archbishop of Glasgow* (London, 1930).

13. Alexander Leighton, *An Appeal to Parliament or Zion's Plea against Prelacy* (Holland, 1628).

14. Baillie, *Letters and Journals*, III, 258–9.

15. *Ibid.*, III, 244.

16. Burnet, *History*, I, 244.

17. See the extracts from his Diary in Butler, *Leighton*, Chapter x; also Burnet, *History*, I, 335–8.

18. Butler, *Leighton*, 333.

19. Burnet, *History*, I, 248–9.

20. *Ibid.*, I, 251–2; Row, *Life of Blair*, 404.

21. Row, *Life of Blair*, 407.

22. *Ibid.*, 407; Burnet, *History*, I, 253.

23. Row, *Life of Blair*, 453.

24. Burnet, *History*, I, 256; Row, *Life of Blair*, 408–9.

25. Burnet, *History*, I, 382–3.

26. Clarendon, *Continuation of the life of Edward Earl of Clarendon*, 3rd. ed., 3 vols. (Oxford, 1761), II, 300.

27. Burnet, *History*, I, 455, 465, 496.

28. *Ibid.*, I, 433, 497–9.

29. *Lauderdale Papers*, II, 8, 13–14, 45, 65–6; Burnet, *History*, I, 443.

30. *Lauderdale Papers*, II, 49–50, 52; Burnet, *History*, I, 499–500.

31. *Lauderdale Papers*, II, Appendix lv–lvi.

32. *Ibid.*, II, 15, 16, 23; NLS Ms 2512.f.104, 106.

33. NLS Ms 2512.f.104.

34. NLS Ms 2512.f.110. ·

35. *Lauderdale Papers*, II, 32, 34, 51.

36. *Ibid.*, II, 105, 107–8, 109.

37. NLS Ms 2512.f.114, 116.

38. *Lauderdale Papers*, II, 105, 107.

39. *Ibid.*, II, 109; Burnet, *History*, I, 501. Burnet's assertion that he was deliberately allowed to escape is hardly credible: Kirkton, *History*, 278–9.

40. *RPC*, 3rd. ser., II, 486–9; *Lauderdale Papers*, II, 109–11.

41. For Mitchell's appearances before the Council in connection with the Rising see *RPC*, 3rd. ser., II, 231, 345, 349.

42. *Lauderdale Papers*, II, 111, 116; *RPC*, 3rd. ser., II, 495, 500–1, 502–3. The sentences of banishment were not carried out: *RPC*, 3rd. ser., III, 46; Kirkton, *History*, 282–3.

43. *Lauderdale Papers*, II, 111.

44. SHS *Miscellany*, I, 263–4.

45. NLS Ms 2512.f.118.

46. *Lauderdale Papers*, II, 118.

47. The biographical information on Burnet is taken from J. A. Lamb, 'Archbishop Alexander Burnet, 1614–1684' (*RSCHS* XI, 1951–3), 133–48.

48. The Earl of Teviot's possibly: Mackenzie, *Memoirs*, 156.

49. BL Add. Ms 23127.f.152. See also *Lauderdale Papers*, II, 34.

50. *Lauderdale Papers*, II, 54, 57.

51. For more detail of this episode and what follows see J. M. Buckroyd, 'The Dismissal of Archbishop Alexander Burnet, 1669' (*RSCHS*, XVIII, 1973), 149–55.

52. *Lauderdale Papers*, II, 1, 59, Appendix xlix; NLS Ms 2512.f.122, 124.

53. *Lauderdale Papers*, II, 86, Appendix lviii.
54. *Lauderdale Papers*, II, 118.
55. *Ibid.*, II, 122.
56. Burnet, *History*, I, 502; *Lauderdale Papers*, II, 120; NLS Ms 3136.f.44.
57. NLS Ms 2512.f.122, 124.
58. *Lauderdale papers*, II, 121.
59. *Ibid.*, II, 146, 190.
60. NLS Ms 3136.f.100, 107.
61. Ibid., f.107.
62. NLS Ms 2512.f.126.
63. Ibid., f.129; *Lauderdale Papers*, II, 136.
64. *RPC*, 3rd. ser., III, 38.
65. *Ibid.*, III, 40.
66. NLS Ms 2512.f.130; see also BL Add. Ms 35125.f.214.
67. *Lauderdale Papers*, II, 189.
68. *Ibid.*, II, 130; NLS Ms 2512.f.130.
69. *RPC*, 3rd. ser., III, 47; *Lauderdale Papers*, II, 192.
70. *Lauderdale Papers*, II, 191.
71. Mackenzie, *Memoirs*, 159.
72. Printed in *Lauderdale Papers*, II, Appendix lxiv.
73. NLS Ms 7003.f.166.
74. *Lauderdale Papers*, II, 137-9, 141.
75. *RPC*, 3rd. ser., III, 84.
76. *Lauderdale Papers*, II, 166-7, 172, 175.
77. *Ibid.*, II, 172.
78. *APS*, VII, 551-2.
79. NLS Ms 3136.f.116.
80. Baillie, *Letters and Journals*, III, 461.
81. *APS*, VII, 372.
82. *Ibid.*, VII, 554.
83. *Lauderdale Papers*, II, 152.
84. Burnet, *History*, I, 512; *Lauderdale Papers*, II, 164, 168.
85. *RPC*, 3rd ser., I, 130.
86. In his letter to Kincardine printed Stephen, *Sharp*, 307-18.
87. See Lauderdale's clear view that they were alternative theories: *Lauderdale Papers*, II, 172.
88. *Ibid.*, II, 152.
89. *APS*, VII, 465.
90. Mackenzie, *Memoirs*, 159-60; Row, *Life of Blair*, 527-9; Burnet, *History*, I, 512; *Lauderdale Papers*, II, 153, 163.

Chapter 8

1. For this chapter I have profited from kindly being permitted to read an unpublished paper, 'Lauderdale's Ecclesiastical Policy 1669-79', by Rev. M. Yould.
2. Introduction, *RPC*, 3rd. ser., III & IV. It must be borne in mind for comparison with earlier period that Sharp was in Scotland constantly from 1669 to late 1674.
3. *Lauderdale Papers*, II, 165-6, 169, 171, 176.
4. *Ibid.*, II, 181-3.
5. NLS Ms 2512.f.134.
6. Despite Sharp's boast: *Lauderdale Papers*, II, 214.
7. *Lauderdale Papers*, II, 170.
8. *Ibid.*, II, 179.
9. *Ibid.*, II, 187; Burnet, *History*, I, 517.
10. Burnet, *History*, I, 524.

11. *Ibid.*, I, 370.
12. Printed SHS *Miscellany*, II (Edinburgh, 1904), 340–58.
13. See *ibid.*, 332 for one account of this event and Burnet, *History*, I, 388 for his own.
14. Burnet, *History*, I, 389.
15. *Ibid.*, I, 520.
16. *Lauderdale Papers*, II, 216.
17. *Lauderdale Papers*, II, 204–7; Kirkton, *History*, 296–7.
18. *Lauderdale Papers*, II, 213–4, 215; Burnet, *History*, I, 520, 522.
19. *Lauderdale Papers*, II, 218–9, 220. This despite Lauderdale's letter of August: SHS *Miscellany*, I, 267; Burnet, *History*, I, 531, 536.
20. NLS Ms 2512.f.148; Burnet, *History*, I, 552–3.
21. *RPC*, 3rd. ser., III, 586–91.
22. Burnet, *History*, I, 606.
23. For this and the following paragraph see Donaldson, *James V-James VII* and the lists of ecclesiastical legislation in the introduction to *RPC*, 3rd. ser., III and IV.
24. Kirkton, *History*, 336.
25. NLS Ms 597.f.248.
26. *Lauderdale Papers*, II, 236.
27. For example *ibid.*
28. NLS Ms 2512.f.157.
29. *RPC*, 3rd. ser., IV, 190–2.
30. Butler, *Leighton*, 476–7.
31. *Lauderdale Papers*, II, 231–2.
32. *Lauderdale Papers*, III, 46–7.
33. *Ibid.*, III, 42–4. See also Lauderdale's account of the various motions made: *ibid.*, III, 52–4.
34. *Ibid.*, II, 241ff; Mackenzie, *Memoirs*, 251–65; Kirkton, *History*, 339–41.
35. *Lauderdale Papers*, III, 23.
36. *Ibid.*, III, 33–4; Burnet, *History*, II, 43–4.
37. *Lauderdale Papers*, III, 70; *RPC*, 3rd. ser., IV, 195–7.
38. *Lauderdale Papers*, III, 26–8, 73–4. See Hamilton's continuation of opposition in the Council in March: *RPC*, 3rd. ser., IV, 38–40.
39. For indications of Hamilton's links with them see R. K. Marshall, The House of Hamilton, Ph.D. Edinburgh, 1970, Section 2: 'A Calendar of the Correspondence', Vol. II, 441–6; SHS *Miscellany*, I, 271.
40. *RPC*, 3rd. ser., IV, 220.
41. NLS Ms 2512.f.159.
42. *Lauderdale Papers*, III, 64, 75.
43. Mackenzie, *Memoirs*, 273; Kirkton, *History*, 344–5.
44. Burnet, *History*, II, 73–4, 78.
45. *True and Impartial Account*, 69; Burnet, *History*, II, 63.
46. Edinburgh Episcopal Theological College Ms 1789.
47. NLS Ms 2512.f.181, 187, 189.
48. Ibid., f. 187.
49. *RPC*, 3rd. ser., IV, 285–6.
50. *Lauderdale Papers*, III, 62–3, 75–6.
51. *True and Impartial Account*, 69.
52. NLS Ms 2512.f.181.
53. Ibid; RPC 3rd. ser., IV, 577–8.
54. NLS Ms 2512.f.187.
55. *Lauderdale Papers*, III, 154–9.
56. Kirkton, *History*, 376; *Lauderdale Papers*, III, 80; NLS Ms 2512.f.195; Mackenzie, *Memoirs*, 321–2.
57. Scott, *Fasti*, II, 159.

58. *RPC*, 3rd. ser., III, 586–8.

59. *RPC*, 3rd. ser., IV, 34.

60. *Ibid.*, IV, 108.

61. *Ibid.*, IV, 193, 203.

62. *Ibid.*, IV, 238–9.

63. *Ibid.*, IV, 399–402.

64. *Ibid.*, IV, 435–6.

65. Kirkton, *History*, 367–9; Burnet, *History*, II, 113–4.

66. *RPC*, 3rd. ser., V, 2, 10–11, 72.

67. *Ibid.*, V, 34.

68. *Ibid.*, V, 12, 18.

69. Burnet, *History*, II, 114; *Lauderdale Papers*, III, 83–5.

70. Burnet, *History*, II, 114; Kirkton, *History*, 370; Mackenzie, *Memoirs*, 317.

71. NLS Ms 2512.f.201.

72. Kirkton, *History*, 369; *Lauderdale Papers*, III, 84–5.

73. Burnet, *History*, II, 136.

74. *A Complete Collection of State Trials*, 2nd. ed., II (London, 1730), 620.

75. *RPC*, 3rd. ser., IV, 135.

76. *RPC*, 3rd. ser., IV, 152–3; Burnet, *History*, II, 136–7.

77. *RPC*, 3rd. ser., IV, 172.

78. *Ibid.*, IV, 494.

79. *Ibid.*, V, 198.

80. *RPC*, 3rd. ser., V, 198.

81. Burnet, *History*, II, 138.

82. The two cases were dealt with on the same day, 6 December 1677, which may suggest such a connection. *RPC*, 3rd. ser., V, 291–2. Mackenzie, *Memoirs*, 328 asserts that plans for another attempt on Sharp had been discovered and that this was the precipitating factor.

83. For what follows see *State Trials*, II, 623–37.

84. For this incident see John Lauder of Fountainhall, *Historical Notices*, 2 vols. (Edinburgh, 1848), I, 183–6.

85. For example *RPC*, 3rd. ser., V, 196.

86. *Ibid.*, V, 206–9.

87. *Ibid.*, V, 213–6.

88. NLS Ms 3420.f.188.

89. NLS Ms 597.f.270. For further details of these arrangements see J. R. Elder, *The Highland Host of 1678* (Glasgow, 1914), 17–37.

90. Elder, *Highland Host*, Chapter III.

91. Neither Elder nor Airy provides any evidence for his assertions that the idea came from the bishops.

92. Mackenzie, *Memoirs*, 322.

93. For more on this subject see Elder, *Highland Host*, Chapter I.

94. *Lauderdale Papers*, III, 95.

95. Letter quoted Elder, *Highland Host*, 81.

96. *Ibid.*, Chapter IV; *Lauderdale Papers*, III, 99–113.

97. Elder, *Highland Host*, 87.

98. *Lauderdale Papers*, II, 99ff.

Chapter 9

1. Russell, and deposition of James Anderson in Tewchetts.

2. Russell.

3. Russell; *Coppie of the Maner*.

4. According to Russell there were troops in Cupar, Linderney, Balkirsty, Largo and Auchtermuchty.

5. *Coppie of the Maner; Life of Mr James Sharp.*

6. Russell.

7. *Accompt of the Manner.*

8. *Ibid.*

9. Russell.

10. Reprinted in *True and Impartial Account.*

11. Russell; some details confirmed in *Accompt of the Manner* and *Coppie of the Maner*; T. Stephen, *Life and Times of Archbishop Sharp* (London, 1839), 583.

12. *Accompt of the Manner.*

13. Russell.

14. *Coppie of the Maner* has a 'boy'; *Accompt of the Manner* has 'a servant of ---- Black'; *Life of Mr James Sharp* has 'one of our number at a distance'; Russell has 'a boy from Baldinny'.

15. Russell ed. C. K. Sharpe, 413n.

16. Russell. *Accompt of the Manner* has in Ceres; *Coppie of the Maner* has 'coming towards Ceres'. One account, *Accompt of the Manner*, has it that Sharp had stopped in Ceres 'to smoke a pipe with the episcopal encumbent'. If that were so it would explain why the murderers had time to discuss the ethics of what they were about to do.

17. Russell.

18. See the paper dropped in Cupar, printed in *True and Impartial Account.*

19. Russell; *Accompt of the Manner; Coppie of the Maner; Life of Mr James Sharp.*

20. Sir James Stewart of Goodtrees, *Naphtali, or the Wrestlings of the Church of Scotland*, first published 1667; *Ius Populi Vindicatum* (Rotterdam [?], 1669).

21. Russell.

22. *True Relation.*

23. *Clear Discovery.*

24. *True Relation* and *Clear Discovery* say precisely opposite things.

25. Russell; deposition of John Pollock under torture.

26. *Life of Mr James Sharp; Coppie of the Maner*; Russell. *Accompt of the Manner* says 'he opposed it as a matter of blood'.

27. Russell ed. C. K. Sharpe, 410n.

28. *True and Impartial Account*; Stephen, *Sharp*, 591.

29. As the depositions of the people of Magus undoubtedly prove. See Stephen, *Sharp*, 591–2 for their confusion.

30. *Accompt of the Manner* says that is what happened, but that then they came back. One of the depositions of the people of Magus supports this.

31. The murderers may have realised this from an exclamation made by his daughter, according to *Accompt of the Manner.*

32. Unfortunately the depositions of the servants about what happened at the murder have not been found, with the exception of that of Carruthers the footman.

33. Deposition of one of the burgesses of Cupar. Stephen, *Sharp*, 592.

34. Deposition of Thomas Cow.

35. Russell.

36. Deposition of James Anderson.

37. Russell; depositions of Adam Smith and William Wallace; depositions taken at Cupar 26 May 1679.

38. Depositions of Andrew Aytoun and Henry Southall. There seems to be some confusion about the name of Aytoun's companion. The name on the depositions is Southall, but the privy council always refer to him as Henry Shaw. Stephen, *Sharp*, 591.

39. *RPC*, 3rd ser., VI, 180.

40. Depositions of Carruthers and Bowie.

41. Depositions of Wallace and Smith.

42. *RPC*, 3rd ser., VI, 356.

43. Depositions in Cupar 4, 7 and 8 May.

44. *RPC*, 3rd ser., VI, 186–94.

45. *Ibid.*, VI, 199–200.

46. *RPC*, 3rd ser., VI, 201–2.

47. Precedency Book, Court of the Lord Lyon, Edinburgh.

48. Stephen, *Sharp*, 625–6 gives the inscription.

49. Depositions of Anderson and Cow.

50. Depositions of the people of Magus.

51. *RPC*, 3rd ser., VI, 207–8.

52. *Ibid.*, VI, 322.

53. *Ibid.*, VI, 322–3.

54. *Ibid.*, VI, 256.

55. *Ibid.*, VI, 260.

56. *Ibid.*, VI, 294–5. Commemorative stones still mark the site.

57. *Ibid.*, VI, 304; however, this same order was made again on 20 September and so cannot have been put into effect the first time, *Ibid.*, VI, 323.

58. *Ibid.*, VI, 308.

59. *Ibid.*, VI, 313.

60. *Ibid.*, VI, 320.

61. *Ibid.*, VI, 322–3.

62. *Ibid.*

63. *Ibid.*, VI, 279.

64. Edinburgh University Library; collection of MSS on the murder of Archbishop Sharp. EUL Ms Dc. 1. 16.

65. Ibid.

66. Ibid.

67. Patrick Walker, *Life of Cargill* (Falkirk, 1782), appendix.

68. *Ibid.*, and in Edinburgh University Library MS collection on the murder.

69. Deposition of John Pollock under torture.

70. Depositions.

71. Trial of Hackstone of Rathillet 30 July 1680. SRO Justiciary Court Records, Books of Adjournal.

72. SRO Justiciary Court Records, Book of Adjournal, Trial of Andrew Guillan, 12 July 1683. There was no question that the trial would find him innocent.

73. SRO Justiciary Court Records, Book of Adjournal, Trial of Balfour of Kinloch, 2 April 1683.

74. Russell, ed. C. K. Sharpe, 423n.

Index